Mastering Analytics Lifecycle Management

Complete Guide to CAP Expert & Pro Certification

Dr. Ibrahim Said

Independence and non-affiliation
This is an independent publication. It is not affiliated with, authorized by, endorsed by, or sponsored by INFORMS or any certifying body. It contains no actual examination questions and no confidential examination content. Use of this book does not guarantee success on any certification examination.

Disclaimer
This book is an independent educational resource covering analytics concepts and professional certification preparation. The author has taken care to ensure accuracy at the time of publication but cannot guarantee that all content remains current. Examples and use cases are for learning purposes only and do not constitute professional advice. Readers are responsible for verifying all certification requirements, exam content, and program policies using current official sources. The author shall not be liable for any loss of profit or any other commercial or personal damages arising from the use of this book.

Trademarks
All trademarks and registered trademarks appearing in this book are the property of their respective owners and are used solely for identification and educational purposes. CAP®, CAP Expert, CAP Pro, and INFORMS® are trademarks or registered trademarks of the Institute for Operations Research and the Management Sciences.

Publisher Information
Published by Dr. Ibrahim Said
Toronto, Ontario, Canada

ISBN
Paperback: 978-1-0677995-1-9
eBook: 978-1-0677995-0-2

Edition
First Edition: 2026

Library and Archives Canada Cataloguing in Publication
Complete CIP data will be available upon publication deposit with Library and Archives Canada.

Editorial Note
This book was planned and developed by the author, with AI-based tools used throughout for research, drafting, editorial support, and cover design. The manuscript was reviewed by independent readers for accuracy and clarity. All content has been verified and approved by the author, who is responsible for the accuracy of the work.

Cover and Interior Design: Dr. Ibrahim Said

TABLE OF CONTENTS

LIST OF FIGURES

LIST OF TABLES

Preface

Welcome to *Mastering Analytics Lifecycle Management.*

This book starts with a simple observation. Professionals in analytics, whether they are data scientists, business analysts, project managers, or leaders, often find themselves in a fragmented landscape. They possess strong technical skills. The gap is in connecting those skills to a clear, end-to-end process that delivers measurable business value. Teams struggle not because they lack talent, but because they lack a shared framework and common language to move from problem to solution.

This book provides that framework.

The content covers the full analytics lifecycle, from identifying business problems to maintaining deployed solutions. You will learn to frame problems as analytical questions, assess and prepare data, select appropriate methods, build and validate models, deploy solutions, and manage them over time. Each chapter builds on the previous one, creating a connected understanding you can apply across industries, organization sizes, and technical environments.

This book supports those preparing for analytics certifications by aligning with exam domains and professional job tasks. Its structured approach, real-world examples, and lifecycle framing help connect concepts to practice and build applied knowledge. It is also designed for anyone involved in analytics projects who wants to work more effectively, communicate with clarity, and deliver solutions that produce measurable business results.

Throughout these pages, you will find a consistent lesson structure designed for learning and retention. Each chapter begins with clear objectives, offers detailed explanations of core concepts, defines essential terminology, provides step-by-step methods you can apply right away, illustrates ideas with real-world examples, and warns of common pitfalls to avoid. This format allows you to build knowledge gradually while always understanding how each part fits into the bigger picture.

The journey through the analytics lifecycle is rarely straightforward in practice. Projects often loop back, assumptions are tested, and new insights emerge. The framework outlined here offers a dependable map, a way to stay oriented regardless of where you are in the process, understand what steps come next, and communicate clearly with everyone involved.

I hope this book proves useful whether you're preparing for certification, leading analytics projects, or building foundational knowledge for your career. The methods and frameworks here are developed through years of experience and the collective wisdom of many analytics professionals who have learned what works and what doesn't.

Welcome to the journey. Let us begin.

Who This Book Is For

This book is for anyone who works with analytics or relies on analytical insights to make decisions. Whether you build models, oversee projects, lead teams, or act on the outputs, the frameworks in these pages will help you contribute more effectively.

Analytics professionals, data scientists, and business analysts will learn to turn vague business concerns into precise analytical questions, choose appropriate methods under real-world constraints, validate models against business goals, and maintain solutions over time. These techniques apply regardless of industry, organization size, or technical stack.

Those working toward professional certification will find content aligned with the CAP Expert and CAP Pro exams. In-depth coverage of problem framing, methodology, data needs, model building, deployment, and lifecycle management helps connect concepts to real-world situations.

Project managers, team leads, and functional managers receive a roadmap for guiding analytics initiatives. You will learn what questions to ask at each phase, what deliverables to anticipate, and how to spot risks early. Stakeholder alignment and governance are highlighted throughout.

Business leaders and decision-makers will learn how to collaborate effectively with technical teams, identify problems that lead to actionable solutions, assess investment value, and recognize warning signs of struggling projects.

Regardless of your role, a working understanding of the full analytics lifecycle, from problem framing to long-term solution management, will strengthen your contributions to any analytics initiative and help your organization get consistent value from its data investments.

How This Book Is Organized

The book follows the seven domains of the industry-standard analytics framework: problem framing, analytics problem framing, data, methodology selection, model development, deployment, and lifecycle management. Each lesson guides you through a critical stage of the analytics lifecycle. **Chapters 1 through 7 map directly to these domains in order**, providing a structured journey from initial business understanding to ongoing solution maintenance.

Chapter 1: Business Problem Framing. You will learn to translate vague organizational challenges into clear, actionable problem statements with defined scope and stakeholder alignment.

Chapter 2: Framing the Analytics Problem. You will learn to convert business goals into structured analytical questions with defined inputs, outputs, success measures, and documented assumptions.

Chapter 3: The Data. You will learn to assess data quality, identify inconsistencies, handle missing values and outliers, and apply necessary transformations to prepare clean, reliable data for analysis.

Chapter 4: Methodology Selection. You will learn to classify analytical needs, evaluate methods against practical constraints, and select appropriate technologies and approaches.

Chapter 5: Model Development and Implementation. You will learn to design, build, and validate analytical models while managing bias, ethical risk, and stakeholder expectations.

Chapter 6: Deployment of Solutions and Operational Integration. You will learn to validate business value, align stakeholders, define production requirements, and monitor live deployments.

Chapter 7: Overseeing and Managing the Analytics Lifecycle. You will learn to monitor performance, maintain and recalibrate models, and sustain the long-term value of solutions.

Chapter 8: Analytics Concepts Reference. A structured reference chapter covering foundational analytics terminology and concepts, organized by category for quick review.

Each lesson follows a consistent structure: Objective, Detailed Explanation, Key Definitions, Step-by-Step Method, Examples, and Common Pitfalls. This format lets you build knowledge gradually while understanding how each piece fits into the larger analytics cycle.

Special Features

Appendix - Practice question answers for Chapters 1-7.

Glossary - Definitions of all key terms for quick reference.

References - APA-formatted bibliography of sources that informed this book, for further exploration.

Index - Quick location of topics, concepts, methods, and names across the entire book.

Introduction

Mastering the analytics lifecycle requires more than technical skill. It requires a structured approach that connects business problems to analytical solutions and sustains their value over time. Whether you are preparing for professional certification or building a stronger analytics practice within your organization, the frameworks in this book provide a common language that helps teams work together and deliver results.

Analytics projects rarely fail solely because of technical shortcomings. They fail when business leaders and data professionals do not share a common language, when project scope expands without control, when data quality problems surface too late, or when models that perform well in development break down in production. This book addresses each of these failure points by walking you through the complete analytics lifecycle, from framing business problems to managing deployed solutions.

The analytics lifecycle is the end-to-end sequence of activities that transforms a business problem into a deployed, maintained solution. Several established lifecycle frameworks exist. In this book, the framework spans seven domains, from initial problem framing to long-term solution management. It includes not only technical work but also the decisions, stakeholder interactions, and governance activities that determine whether the solution delivers lasting business value.

Defining the Business Problem

Every successful analytics project starts with a well-defined problem. Chapter 1 teaches you to move past surface-level symptoms to identify root causes, define clear objectives, map stakeholder influence, and build a business case that justifies the investment. By the end of this chapter, you will know how to frame a problem in a way that aligns technical work with business intent from the start.

Translating Business Goals into Analytical Questions

Chapter 2 takes a defined business problem and converts it into a structured analytical question. You will learn to specify what the analysis needs to produce, what data and methods are required, and what success looks like. This translation step is where many projects lose alignment. This chapter shows you how to maintain it.

Working with Data

Chapter 3 moves from planning to execution. You will assess data sources, prepare and clean datasets, evaluate quality, and validate your problem framing against what the data actually shows. Data work is where most project effort is spent. This chapter gives you a repeatable process for doing it well.

Choosing the Right Analytical Methods

Chapter 4 connects your problem framing to a practical solution design. You will classify the type of analytical need, evaluate candidate methods against real-world constraints, and select the tools and technologies that fit your context. The goal is not the most sophisticated method but the most appropriate one.

Building and Validating Models

Chapter 5 covers the construction and evaluation of analytical models. You will design model structures, build and test them against business-aligned metrics, and refine them through stakeholder feedback. You will also learn to recognize the most common errors that cause models to fail before they reach production.

Putting Solutions into Production

Chapter 6 covers deployment. You will learn to validate business value in a controlled environment, align stakeholders on deployment plans, define production requirements, and monitor live systems. A model that cannot survive production has not delivered value. This chapter prepares you to bridge that gap.

Sustaining Long-Term Value

Chapter 7 addresses what happens after deployment. Solutions degrade without active management. You will learn to monitor performance, detect and respond to model drift, maintain documentation, and ensure your solution continues to serve its original business purpose over time.

These seven chapters guide you through the entire analytics lifecycle in order. Each chapter builds on the previous one, setting the stage for the next. The analytics lifecycle is iterative, not strictly linear, and does not follow a simple start-to-finish flow. Whether you're aiming for professional certification, managing an analytics team, or enhancing your skills, the frameworks provided are meant to be applied, not just understood. The journey starts with Chapter 1.

Chapter 1: Business Problem Framing

Introduction

Business Problem Framing transforms unclear organizational challenges into well-defined, actionable initiatives ready for investigation, analysis, and resolution. It connects executive strategy with technical execution, ensuring analytical efforts stay focused, resource-efficient, and aligned with core business value.

The process involves clarifying stakeholder roles, defining objectives with precision, assessing analytical suitability, and building a credible investment case. Developing this skill means shifting from a solution-focused mindset to a problem-oriented one, a defining trait of strategic analytics professionals. The techniques in this chapter apply across industries and organization sizes, from targeted operational improvements to enterprise-wide initiatives.

Figure 1 The Problem Framing & Scoping Process

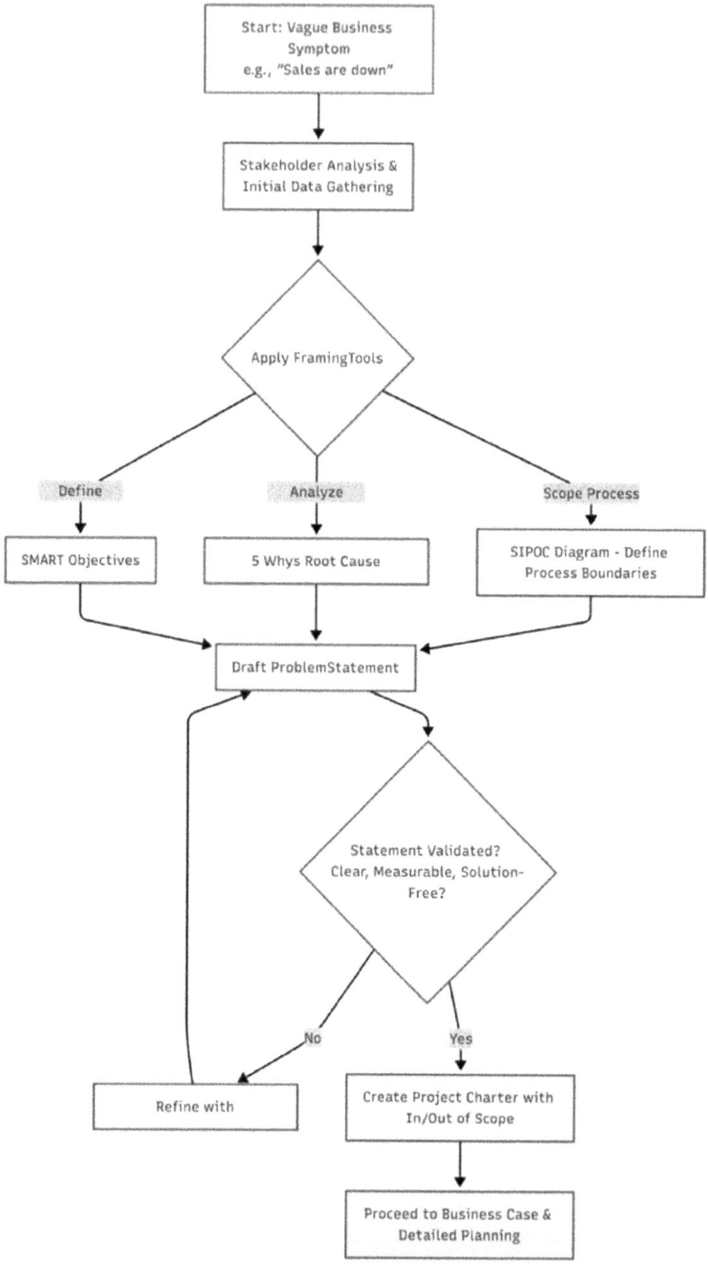

Lesson 1.1: Crafting Precise Problem Statements and Objectives

Objective:
Learn to turn vague business concerns into precise, actionable problem statements and establish specific, measurable goals that guide the entire analytics project.

Detailed Explanation:
The success of any analytics project depends on a clear, precise problem definition. A well-formulated problem statement identifies the gap between the current state and the desired future state, emphasizing the 'what' and 'why' while deliberately avoiding premature solutions. Structured frameworks make the problem specific, measurable, and aligned with business impact. Project objectives must also be explicitly defined to set clear success criteria. This combined focus on defining the problem and specifying what success looks like builds the foundation for every analytical step that follows, from data collection to model deployment.

Key Definitions:

- **Problem statement:** A concise description of an issue that identifies its root cause, highlights the specific negative impacts, and outlines measurable business effects, without proposing solutions.
- **SMART criteria:** A framework that ensures objectives are **Specific, Measurable, Achievable, Relevant, and Time-bound**.
- **Symptom:** A visible sign of a problem, such as declining sales.
- **Root cause:** The underlying reason for the symptom. When the root cause is resolved, the symptom does not recur.
- **Analytics question:** A well-defined, data-driven restatement of a business problem, suggesting an analytical approach such as prediction (including classification and regression) and optimization, and outlining the steps for technical implementation.

Table 1 SMART framework for problem statements

Criteria	What It Means	Vague Statement	SMART Improvement
Specific	Focuses on a particular area, process, or population.	"Improve our website."	"Improve the checkout process on our mobile app."
Measurable	Quantifies the problem and success with clear metrics.	"Make it faster."	"Reduce mobile checkout abandonment rate from 80% to 50%."
Achievable	Can be accomplished with available resources, data, and time.	"Predict the stock market perfectly."	"Predict customer churn with 85% accuracy using our 2-year transaction history."
Relevant	Aligns with key business goals and strategic objectives.	"Increase social media likes."	"Increase conversion rate to directly impact Q4 revenue targets."
Time-bound	Specifies a clear timeframe for achievement.	"Eventually."	"Achieve this reduction within the next 6 months."

Step-by-Step Method:

1. **Document the observed symptom:** Start with the initial, broad concern voiced by stakeholders, such as "Customer satisfaction is dropping."
2. **Perform a root cause analysis:** Use the "**5 Whys**" technique to trace the problem from its visible symptom to its underlying root cause. Ask 'why' repeatedly until you reach the factor that, if addressed, would prevent the problem from recurring. See Figure 1.2 for a step-by-step illustration of this process.

Figure 2 The 5 Whys Process

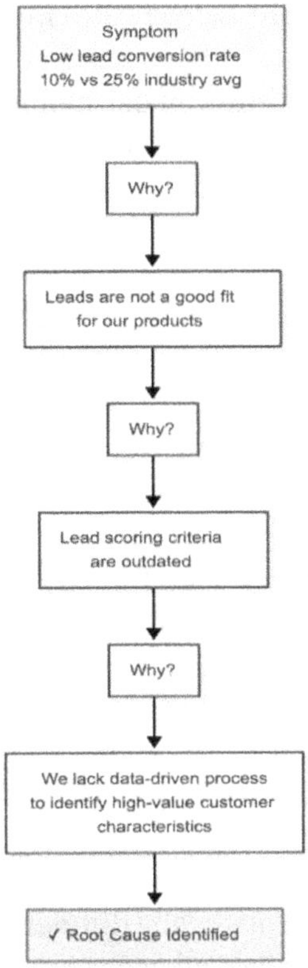

3. **Quantify the current state:** Gather preliminary data and attach metrics to the problem's impact, such as "The net promoter score has decreased from 42 to 35 over two quarters."
4. **Draft the primary problem statement:** Use a standard format: "Due to [**root cause**], we face [**negative effect**], leading **to [business impact**]."
5. **Create a SMART objective:** Define the target outcome. For example: "To [**specific action**] resulting in [**measurable improvement**] by [**timeframe**], considering [**relevant constraints**]."
6. **Translate into an analytics question:** Convert the objective into a question that can be answered with data, for example, "What are the top three factors predicting customer churn?" or "Which production parameters optimize yield while minimizing cost?"

Examples:

- **Example 1: E-Commerce Checkout Optimization:**
    - **Symptom:** "A large number of customers leave their carts unfinished on our mobile site."
    - **Root Cause (5 Whys):** The checkout process includes more than 12 form fields and spans 5 pages.
    - **Problem statement:** "Due to an excessively lengthy and complex checkout process, our mobile site abandonment rate is 80%. This results in approximately $2 million in lost revenue each year."
    - **SMART objective:** "Decrease the mobile checkout abandonment rate from 80% to 50% over six months by redesigning the user flow, while ensuring payment security."
    - **Analytics question:** "Which steps in the current checkout process are most strongly linked to session abandonment?"

- **Example 2: Marketing Lead Quality:**
    - **Business question:** "Why are our marketing leads not converting?"
    - **Analytics question:** "Are customers who make a purchase statistically different in their profile, such as firmographics and engagement history, compared to leads that do not convert?"

Common Pitfalls:

- **Solutioneering:** Embedding a specific solution into the problem statement, such as "We need a new CRM to manage our leads."
- **Vague language:** Using ambiguous terms such as "optimize," "improve," or "leverage" without providing specific numbers or clear metrics to define their meaning.
- **Confusing model success with project success:** Assuming that a model with high statistical accuracy (model success) will automatically lead to business impact (project success) is a mistake. Define both types of success separately from the start.
- **Ignoring the "Achievable" and "Relevant" elements in the SMART framework:** Setting goals that are either unrealistic based on available data or do not align with a key business KPI.

Lesson 1.2: Conducting Stakeholder Analysis and Defining Roles

Objective:

Systematically identify, categorize, and plan engagement with all individuals and groups affected by an analytics project, while clarifying decision rights and responsibilities using the RACI matrix and related frameworks.

Detailed Explanation:

Analytics projects operate within a complex network of organizational relationships. Even the most technically sound solution fails when key individuals feel excluded, misinformed, or threatened. Stakeholder analysis is a proactive approach to mapping these relationships, managing expectations, securing support, and reducing political risks before they affect the project. It involves identifying not only who is involved but also their levels of influence, interests, and specific roles. The RACI matrix, Responsible, Accountable, Consulted, Informed, is a key tool from this analysis, providing a clear, consensus-based responsibility map that prevents confusion and ensures accountability.

Key Definitions:

- **Stakeholder:** Any individual, group, or organization that influences or is affected by a project's decisions or outcomes.
- **Power/Interest grid:** A two-dimensional matrix used to categorize stakeholders by their authority (power) and concern (interest) about the project, helping to shape engagement strategies.
- **RACI matrix:** A chart that assigns roles such as **Responsible** (carries out the work), **Accountable** (has final decision authority), **Consulted** (offers input), and **Informed** (kept updated) for each major task or deliverable.
- **Project sponsor:** The senior executive who backs the project, secures resources, and owns the business case.
- **Business process owner:** The manager in charge of the operational area where the issue occurs and where the solution will be put into place.

Step-by-Step Method:

1. **Create a complete Stakeholder list:** Brainstorm all possible individuals and groups affected by the project, including primary (directly affected), secondary (indirectly affected), and often-overlooked groups such as legal, compliance, and related departments.
2. **Analyze and categorize:** Place each stakeholder on a **Power/Interest grid**:
    - **High Power, High Interest (Manage closely):** Engage frequently and in-depth communication, such as serving as a Project Sponsor and Process Owner.
    - **High Power, Low Interest (Keep satisfied):** Ensure they stay informed about key decisions to sustain their support.
    - **Low Power, High Interest (Keep informed):** Communicate regularly to collect useful feedback and encourage adoption.
    - **Low Power, Low Interest (Monitor):** Offer only basic, broad updates.
3. **Define project roles:** Assign formal responsibilities such as Sponsor, Process Owner, Lead Analyst, and IT Lead, based on the analysis.
4. **Create a RACI matrix:** List main project tasks or workstreams as rows and key stakeholders or roles as columns. For each task, assign one '**A**' (Accountable), one or more '**R**s' (Responsible), and identify who needs to be '**C**onsulted' and '**I**nformed'.
5. **Validate and socialize:** Review the grid and matrix with the project sponsor and core team to confirm alignment and shared understanding.

Table 2 Stakeholder Power/Interest Analysis Grid

	High Interest	Low Interest
High Power	**Manage Closely** • Engage deeply & frequently • Key decision-makers & sponsors • Example: Project Sponsor, Business Process Owner	**Keep Satisfied** • Keep informed of major decisions • Ensure continued support • Example: Senior Executive, CFO
Low Power	**Keep Informed** • Communicate regularly • Seek feedback for adoption • Example: End Users, Subject Matter Experts	**Monitor** • Minimal effort required • General updates suffice • Example: Adjacent departments, External regulators

Examples:

- **Project:** Developing a predictive maintenance system for manufacturing equipment.
- **Stakeholder analysis:**
    - **High power/High interest:** VP of Operations (Sponsor), Plant Manager (Process Owner).
    - **High power/Low interest:** CFO (needs to approve budget).
    - **Low power/High interest:** Maintenance Technicians (End Users), Union Representative (Influencer).
    - **Low power/Low interest:** HR Department.
- **RACI Matrix Entry:**
    - **Task:** "Verify the accuracy of sensor data from Line A."
    - **R:** Data Engineer (conducts the validation).
    - **A:** Lead Data Scientist overseeing quality approval.
    - **C:** Maintenance Supervisor provides context on typical versus abnormal readings.
    - **I:** Plant Manager (receives weekly quality report).

Common Pitfalls:

- **Having multiple 'A's (accountable) for a task:** This creates ambiguity in decision-making and weakens the clarity of accountability.
- **Focusing only on organizational charts:** Missing influential individuals who lack formal authority, such as respected senior analysts and key user representatives.
- **Ignoring "informed" stakeholders:** Failing to update secondary groups can cause surprises, resistance, or overlooked dependencies later.
- **Developing the RACI matrix without stakeholder input:** The matrix must be created collaboratively. A matrix built solely by the project team and then presented to stakeholders will often be ignored or contested, undermining the clarity it was designed to provide.

Lesson 1.3: Framing Problems with SIPOC and DMAIC

Objective:
Use structured process frameworks, especially SIPOC and the Define phase of DMAIC, to effectively scope a business problem, set clear boundaries, and lay the groundwork for a thorough, data-driven project approach.

Detailed Explanation:
Before analyzing data, define the boundaries of the process or system under review. **SIPOC** (Suppliers, Inputs, Process, Outputs, Customers) is a high-level mapping tool used during the Define phase of the **DMAIC** (Define, Measure, Analyze, Improve, Control) methodology. Its purpose is to establish a shared, clear understanding of the process, including its start and end points, as well as who provides inputs and who receives outputs. This prevents scope creep and ensures all stakeholders are aligned on what will be examined. During DMAIC's Define phase, this SIPOC is then used to develop a formal **project charter**, which involves quantifying the problem and setting success metrics.

Key Definitions:

- **SIPOC** is an acronym that stands for a high-level process map: **Suppliers** (those who provide inputs), **Inputs** (materials, data, triggers), **Process** (the four to seven key high-level steps), **Outputs** (the results produced by the process), and **Customers** (those who receive the outputs).
- **DMAIC:** A data-driven cycle used for process improvement in Six Sigma. The **Define** phase focuses on identifying the problem, project goals, and scope.
- **Process boundaries:** The clearly defined start and end points of the process being analyzed.
- **Project charter:** A formal document created during the Define phase that authorizes the project, presents the business case, and outlines its scope, objectives, and main stakeholders.

Step-by-Step Method:

1. **Draft the initial problem statement:** Begin with the business concern (e.g., "Order fulfillment is too slow").
2. **Create the SIPOC diagram:**
   - **Process:** Determine the initial action (e.g., "Customer clicks 'Purchase'") and the outcome (e.g., "Customer receives shipping confirmation email"), then outline 4-7 main steps that occur in between.
   - **Outputs:** What does this process produce? (e.g., "Fulfilled order," "Shipping label")
   - **Customers:** Who is the target audience for these outputs? (e.g., "Customer," "Shipping Carrier")
   - **Inputs:** What information is required to carry out the process? (e.g., "Order details," "Inventory data," "Payment")
   - **Suppliers:** Who provides the inputs? (e.g., "E-commerce Platform," "Warehouse Inventory System," "Payment Processor").
3. **Refine the problem statement using SIPOC:** SIPOC helps clarify the scope. The issue could be stated as: "The 'Pick and Pack' sub-process within order fulfillment is too slow."
4. **Apply the DMAIC 'Define phase' rigor:** Quantify the problem from the vague statement. Establish a baseline: "The 95th percentile cycle time for the Pick and Pack process is 8 hours, exceeding the target of 4 hours, and contributing to 20% of late shipments."
5. **Develop the project charter:** Include the quantified problem, the goal (e.g., "Reduce Pick and Pack 95th percentile cycle time to 5 hours"), the scope (as described by SIPOC), and the key milestones.

Examples:

- **Problem:** "Long wait times for patients in the emergency room."
- **SIPOC scope:**
  - *Process initiation:* The patient completes triage.
  - *Process end:* The patient is discharged or admitted to a hospital bed.
  - *Key high-level steps:* Triage Assessment, Registration, Physician Evaluation, Diagnostics, Treatment, and Disposition.

- **Defined and quantified the problem using DMAIC 'Define':** Patients classified as 'Urgent' experience an average of 45 minutes from triage to physician evaluation, surpassing the standard of 30 minutes. This delay is associated with decreased patient satisfaction and increased clinical risk.

Common Pitfalls:

- **Overloading the SIPOC with details:** The SIPOC should serve as a high-level, one-page overview and avoid detailed process steps.
- **Defining overly broad process boundaries:** Starting too early or ending too late makes the project unmanageable. Using SIPOC helps maintain the necessary focus.
- **Skipping quantification in Define:** Relying solely on a qualitative problem statement results in vague success criteria and complicates measurement.
- **Using SIPOC/DMAIC for purely exploratory projects:** These frameworks are best suited to defined process improvement problems with measurable baselines. For open-ended research or discovery initiatives where the problem itself is unclear, a more flexible scoping approach is more appropriate. Applying SIPOC/DMAIC in those contexts imposes premature structure on a problem that is not yet well enough understood to be bounded.

Lesson 1.4: Refining and Validating the Problem Scope

Objective:
Iteratively refine and validate the initial problem definition by removing ambiguity, bias, and vague language, producing a statement that is clear, actionable, and agreed upon by all key stakeholders.

Detailed Explanation:
The initial draft of a problem statement is rarely the final version. Refinement is an iterative, collaborative effort that sharpens focus, questions assumptions, and translates technical or business language into clear, understandable terms. The aim is to produce a statement that is rigorous enough for the analytics and clear enough for an executive sponsor. This process involves actively identifying and removing "**solutioneering,**" the early inclusion of a technical fix within the problem definition. Validation entails sharing the refined statement with a diverse group of stakeholders to confirm it accurately captures their shared understanding of the main issue before resources are committed.

Key Definitions:

- **Solutioneering:** The mistake of framing a problem based on a presumed solution, such as saying "We need a dashboard to..." instead of clearly stating "We lack visibility into...".
- **Jargon:** The specialized language used by particular professions or groups, which can hinder understanding for those outside of them.
- **Ambiguity:** Refers to having multiple interpretations, which can hinder clear problem statements.
- **Stakeholder validation:** The process of formally reviewing and obtaining agreement on the problem statement from key individuals identified during stakeholder analysis.

Step-by-Step Method:

1. **Conduct a "solutioneering" review:** Carefully examine the draft statement, eliminating phrases that mention specific tools, technologies, or methods such as "build a model," "create a dashboard," or "implement new software", and replacing them with the desired capability or result of those solutions.

2. **Replace vague language:** Substitute subjective terms such as "optimize," "improve," "streamline," or "leverage" with specific, measurable actions or clear objectives.
3. **Quantify all claims:** Whenever possible, use specific numbers, percentages, timeframes, or financial impacts. For example, replace "high cost" with "costs exceeding the budget by 15%."
4. **Simplify and clarify:** Write the statement as if explaining it to a knowledgeable but non-technical business leader. Use plain English instead of abbreviations and technical jargon.
5. **Verify the logical flow:** Ensure the statement clearly links the root cause to the observed effect and then connects that effect to a key business outcome.
6. **Conduct validation workshops:** Present the refined statement to various groups of stakeholders, including sponsors, users, and subject matter experts (SMEs). Ask: "Does this accurately capture the problem? Is anything major missing?"

Examples:

- **Initial Draft (Poor):** "We should leverage Machine Learning (ML) to enhance our conversion process and optimize the Marketing Qualified Leads-to-Sales Qualified Leads (MQL-to-SQL) process, as the current method is inefficient."
    - **Issues:** Overuse of solutioneering ("leverage ML"), jargon ("MQL," "SQL"), and vague terms ("optimize," "inefficient").
- **Refined Statement:** Our current lead-ranking approach consistently fails to identify leads ready for sales conversations. As a result, sales reps may spend around 30% of their time on unsuitable leads, and approximately 15% of highly qualified leads go uncontacted quickly, resulting in missed revenue opportunities.
- **Validation Question:** To the Sales Director: "Does the 30% time-waste estimate seem accurate? Is the loss of ready-to-buy leads a more significant issue than spending time on unqualified leads?"

Common Pitfalls:

- **Adding length, not clarity:** Making the statement wordier without enhancing its precision.
- **Settling for polite agreement:** A room full of nodding stakeholders does not mean the problem statement is accurate. It

often means no one wants to raise a concern in a group setting. Healthy validation involves direct questions, structured debate, and explicit sign-off, not passive acceptance.

- **Over-narrowing the scope:** Trying to be too specific about the problem, potentially overlooking relevant issues, and reducing the solution's effectiveness.
- **Failing to convey the "so what?":** Not clearly explaining why it affects the company's bottom line or strategic goals.

Lesson 1.5: Creating a Persuasive Business Case

Objective:
Developing a thorough justification for an analytics project by systematically analyzing and documenting its expected benefits, associated costs, primary risks, and essential trade-offs.

Detailed Explanation:
A business case converts a defined problem into a financial and strategic justification for investment. Its strength depends on detailed analysis rather than intuition, and it must account for both tangible and intangible factors. Decision-makers need a balanced view that covers expected benefits, total costs, realistic risks, and key trade-offs. Key components include a clear **Return on Investment** (**ROI**), an evaluation of the **Total Cost of Ownership** (**TCO**), and a realistic assessment of project risks, including non-technical issues such as stakeholder resistance or challenges arising from process changes.

Key Definitions:

- **Return on Investment (ROI):** A performance metric that evaluates how efficiently an investment performs. It is calculated using the formula: *(Net Benefits / Total Costs) * 100%, where* Net Benefits equal Total Benefits minus Total Costs.
- **Total Cost of Ownership (TCO):** The full calculation of all direct and indirect expenses associated with a project across its entire lifecycle, from acquisition and implementation to operation, maintenance, and retirement.
- **Net Present Value (NPV):** A financial metric that assesses the current value of future cash flows (benefits minus costs) by discounting them to today's dollars, helping to determine the project's long-term worth.
- **Payback period:** The time required for an investment to recover its initial cost through the net cash inflows it generates.
- **Tangible versus intangible benefits:** Tangible benefits are measurable and can be assigned a dollar value, such as cost savings or increased revenue. Conversely, *intangible benefits* are real but harder to quantify, including enhanced brand reputation, improved employee morale, or increased decision-making flexibility.

Step-by-Step Method:

1. **Quantify project benefits:**
   - **Revenue increase:** Estimate new revenue from upselling, cross-selling, or market expansion enabled by the analytics solution.
   - **Cost reduction/avoidance:** Determine savings from enhanced efficiency, reduced waste, lower fraud losses, or reduced manual effort.
   - **Strategic/Intangible benefits:** List these benefits and, if feasible, include a well-supported estimate for areas like risk mitigation, compliance, or enhancements in customer satisfaction.
2. **Calculate total costs:**
   - **Direct project costs:** Software, hardware, external consultants, and one-time development labor.
   - **Ongoing operational costs:** Annual license fees, cloud hosting, and internal maintenance and support labor.
   - **Indirect/Hidden costs:** Training, change management, and productivity drops during implementation.
3. **Perform financial analysis:**
   - Calculate **net benefits** (Total Benefits minus Total Costs).
   - Calculate **ROI** and **payback period**.
   - For multi-year projects, build a simple discounted cash flow model to calculate **NPV**. This gives decision-makers a more accurate picture of long-term value than a single-year **ROI** calculation.

4. **Identify and assess risks & trade-offs:**
   - Identify key risks such as data quality issues, departure of key stakeholders, or integration challenges. Evaluate their likelihood and potential impact.
   - Highlight key trade-offs, such as choosing a quick, simple, low-cost solution versus a more comprehensive approach that offers greater potential value but entails higher risk and longer timelines.
5. **Document the business case:** Compile the analysis into a clear report for decision-makers, beginning with the executive

summary, followed by the problem statement, recommended solution, financials, risks, and conclusion.

Examples:
Analytical Type: Predictive (forecasting future equipment failures to enable proactive intervention)
Scenario: A delivery fleet aims to shift from reactive repairs to predictive maintenance using IoT sensor data and machine learning models.

- **Benefits:**
  - *Cost Reduction:* Reduce unplanned breakdowns by 40%, saving $200,000 annually in towing and repair expenses and $150,000 in lost delivery revenue.
  - *Efficiency:* Boost vehicle utilization by 10%, postponing the purchase of two new trucks, saving $250,000 in capital expenditure.
- **Costs:**
  - *Project (Year 1):* $180,000 for sensors, integration, and model development.
  - *Operational (Recurring):* $30,000 per year for data plans and platform subscription.
- **Financials (Year 1):**
  - Net Benefit = ($200K + $150K + $250K) – ($180K + $30K) = **$390,000**
  - ROI = ($390K / $210K) × 100 = **186%**
  - Payback Period ≈ **4 months** ($180K initial investment / $50K average monthly benefits)
- **Key Risk:** Union opposition to vehicle monitoring sensors.
  - *Mitigation:* Engage union representatives early to highlight driver safety benefits and emphasize that data is used solely for vehicle health, not performance or behavior tracking.

Common Pitfalls:

- **Over-optimistic benefit projections:** Overestimating expected savings or revenue without applying conservative assumptions.
- **Underestimating the total cost of ownership:** Neglecting ongoing expenses for maintenance, support, and scaling after deployment.

- **Ignoring intangible benefits entirely:** While difficult to quantify, they should still be considered and discussed qualitatively, as they often serve as the strategic justification.
- **Focusing solely on technical risks:** The biggest risks often arise from people and processes, such as adoption and change management.

Lesson 1.6: Project Planning and Securing Stakeholder Support

Objective:
Apply project scheduling techniques such as PERT and CPM to build a feasible project timeline, and formally secure stakeholder approval of the scope, objectives, and plan through a signed Project Charter.

Detailed Explanation:
Once a problem is defined and a business case is approved, the project moves into formal planning. This means scheduling work, identifying dependencies, managing uncertainty, and securing official organizational sign-off before execution begins. Scheduling techniques such as **Program Evaluation and Review Technique** (**PERT**) and **the Critical Path Method** (**CPM**) offer a structured way to estimate project timelines, identify the tasks that affect the project's completion date (the critical path), and manage uncertainty. The results of this planning phase, combined with the updated problem statement, stakeholder analysis, and business case, are incorporated into a **Project Charter**. This document serves as the official agreement between the project team and sponsors, clearly outlining the scope and serving as the primary tool to secure the necessary sign-off to transition from planning to execution.

Key Definitions:

- **PERT:** A project management technique used to plan, organize, and coordinate tasks. It calculates the expected duration of each task by averaging three estimates, Optimistic, Most Likely, and Pessimistic, with weights to reflect uncertainty. The formula is: (O + 4M + P) / 6.
- **CPM:** A scheduling method that maps project activities based on estimated task durations. It identifies the **critical path**, which is the longest sequence of dependent tasks and determines the minimum possible project duration. Tasks on the critical path have zero slack time, meaning any delay in one task delays the entire project.
- **Project charter:** A concise, formal document that officially authorizes the project, grants authority to the project manager, and records key details like objectives, scope, stakeholders, and major risks.

- **Scope creep:** The uncontrolled expansion of a project's scope after it has started, often resulting in budget and schedule overruns.

Step-by-Step Method:

1. **Define the work breakdown structure (WBS):** Divide the project into manageable tasks and subtasks.
2. **Estimate task durations:** For uncertain tasks, which are common in analytics and R&D phases, use **PERT** with three estimates. For well-understood tasks, such as data extraction, use a single point estimate for **CPM**.
3. **Determine task dependencies:** Identify which tasks need to be completed before others can start (Finish-to-Start is the most common).
4. **Create a network diagram and identify the critical path (CPM):** Map out the dependencies. The longest path through this network is the critical path. Any delay in a critical path task will delay the entire project.
5. **Create the project charter:** Include the problem statement, S.M.A.R.T. objectives, key stakeholders (using RACI), a high-level timeline (from CPM), the budget (based on the business case), and, most importantly, the **in-scope** and **out-of-scope** deliverables.
6. **Review and sign-off:** Present the charter to the project sponsor and key stakeholders. Their formal signature indicates agreement on the project's foundation and authorizes the allocation of resources.

Examples:

- **Analytics project:** Customer Segmentation Model.
- **Critical path task:** "Acquire and clean 12 months of historical transaction data." If this task is delayed by 3 days, the model development, validation, and deployment will all be delayed by at least 3 days.
- **Non-critical path task:** "Design final report layout." This task may have 10 days of slack. A delay here might not affect the final delivery date.
- **Project charter excerpt:**
    - **In scope:** Analyzing transaction and demographic data for retail customers, creating a segmentation model, and providing a report that outlines 4-6 customer segments.

    - **Out-of-scope:** Integration of segment labels into the email marketing platform and creation of automated campaign workflows, which are planned for Phase 2.

Common Pitfalls:

- **Not identifying the true critical path:** Failing to consider all dependencies or misjudging durations results in unrealistic timeline schedules.
- **Vague scope definitions in the charter:** Using broad phrases like "anything related to customer insight" rather than clearly defining specific deliverables.
- **Omitting out-of-scope items:** This is the most common cause of scope creep. Clearly stating what the project will *not* do is more important than listing what it will do.
- **Treating charter sign-off as a formality:** Rushing through approval without genuine stakeholder review removes the charter's value as a governance tool. When scope disputes arise later, a hastily signed charter provides no real protection.

Lesson 1.7: Structured Decision Analysis for Business Problems

Objective:
Apply formal decision analysis frameworks, including payoff matrices, decision criteria, and multi-objective methods, to structure complex business decisions, clarify trade-offs, and identify the best course of action under uncertainty.

Detailed Explanation:
Many business challenges require choosing from several competing options. Structured decision analysis provides a quantitative, defensible method for making those choices when outcomes are uncertain and the stakes are high. It begins with clearly defining available options and possible outcomes. Tools like payoff matrices organize these results, while decision rules such as Maximax, maximin, and minimax regret provide rationales aligned with different risk tolerances. When decisions involve multiple conflicting goals, frameworks such as **Multiple Objective Decision Analysis** (**MODA**) and the **Analytic Hierarchy Process** (**AHP**) help evaluate and score options across various criteria. This approach enhances the rigor and transparency of often subjective executive decision-making.

Key Definitions:

- **Payoff matrix:** A chart showing decision options in rows, possible scenarios or states of nature in columns, and the resulting payoffs for each combination.
- **Decision criteria under uncertainty:** Guidelines for selecting an alternative when future outcome probabilities are unknown.
    - **Optimistic (Maximax):** Select the option with the highest possible payoff.
    - **Pessimistic (Maximin):** Select the option that offers the highest among the worst-case payoffs (risk-averse strategy).
    - **Minimax regret:** Choose the option that minimizes the maximum potential "regret" or opportunity cost.
    - **Equal likelihood (Laplace):** Assume that all states have the same probability and select the option with the highest expected payoff.

Table 3 Decision Criteria Under Uncertainty

Criterion	Philosophy	Method (from Payoff Matrix)	Best For...
Optimistic (Maximax)	"Go for the gold!" Focus on the best possible outcome.	For each alternative, find the maximum payoff. Choose the alternative with the maximum of these maximums.	Risk-seeking decision-makers willing to accept potential losses for a chance at the highest gain.
Pessimistic (Maximin or Wald)	"Avoid disaster." Focus on the worst-case scenario.	For each alternative, find the minimum payoff. Choose the alternative with the maximum of these minimums (the best worst-case).	Risk-averse decision-makers who prioritize security and avoiding significant losses.
Minimax Regret (Savage)	"Minimize missed opportunities." Focus on reducing future "what if" regret.	1. Create a Regret Matrix (subtract each payoff from the best payoff in its column). 2. For each alternative, find the maximum regret. 3. Choose the alternative with the minimum of these maximum regrets.	Decision-makers concerned about post-decision justification and opportunity cost.
Equally Likely (Laplace)	"Assume a level playing field." No reason to believe one state is more likely.	Assume all states of nature are equally probable. Calculate the average payoff for each alternative and choose the highest average.	Situations with truly unknown probabilities and a desire for a balanced approach.

- **Expected Monetary Value (EMV):** The average of possible payoffs for an option, calculated by weighting each with its probability. Applied when probabilities *are* known.
- **Analytic Hierarchy Process (AHP):** A structured approach to organize and analyze complex decisions involving multiple criteria, using pairwise comparisons to establish weights and scores.
- **Multiple Objective Decision Analysis (MODA):** Helps navigate complex choices by organizing conflicting goals, weighing subjective trade-offs, and finding the best compromise when preferences are uncertain. It's a powerful tool that guides us toward informed and balanced decisions.

Step-by-Step Method:

1. **Identify options and uncertainties:** List all potential actions along with the main uncertainties that may affect their results.
2. **Create a payoff matrix:** Estimate the payoff, such as profit, cost, or utility, for each combination of alternative and state.
3. **Apply relevant decision criterion:**
    - If probabilities are **unknown**, consider using criteria like Maximin for caution or Maximax for aggressiveness.
    - If probabilities are **known**, determine the **EMV** for each option and choose the one with the highest EMV.
    - To compute **Minimax Regret**, first construct a regret matrix. This involves subtracting each payoff from the highest payoff in its column. Then, for each alternative, find its maximum regret and choose the alternative with the smallest of these maximums (the minimax rule applied to regrets).
4. **For multi-objective decisions (MODA/AHP):**
    - List all relevant objectives such as Cost, Quality, and Speed.
    - Use pairwise comparisons in AHP to determine the weight of each objective.
    - Rate each alternative against each objective, then compute a weighted sum to determine the overall ranking.

Examples:

- **Decision:** Choose a cloud infrastructure strategy.
- **Alternatives:** Adopt All-in on Cloud A or Cloud B or opt for a Hybrid Multi-Cloud approach.
- **States of nature:** Vendor A experiences a major outage, Vendor B experiences a major outage, or there are no major outages.
- **Payoff matrix:** Shows the costs and performance outcomes for each scenario.
- **Analysis:** A risk-averse (Maximin) company may choose Hybrid to avoid the worst-case risk of relying on a failing single vendor.
- **AHP example:** Selecting a new analytics software vendor by evaluating Cost (40%), Features (35%), and Support (25%). Vendors receive scores, and a weighted total identifies the best option.

Common Pitfalls:

- **Omitting key alternatives or scenarios:** The analysis is only as good as the options and scenarios it considers, including the "do nothing" baseline
- **Incorrect application of decision criteria:** Using Maximin when probabilities are known (should use EMV) or assigning equal weights in MODA without justification.
- **Ignoring qualitative factors:** Focusing solely on numerical analysis risks overlooking strategic fit, partner relationships, and ethical considerations. These factors often determine whether a technically sound decision succeeds in practice. Quantitative analysis supports the decision, it does not replace judgment.
- **Inconsistent pairwise comparisons in AHP**: Might result in an unreliable judgment matrix, therefore, it is crucial to verify the consistency ratio.

Lesson 1.8: Defining Detailed Functional and Non-Functional Requirements

Objective:
Identify all the capabilities, performance criteria, and limitations that an analytics solution needs to fulfill, distinguishing between its core functions (functional requirements) and its quality or efficiency standards (non-functional requirements).

Detailed Explanation:
Before development begins, translate all stakeholder needs into a clear, precise, and testable specification. **Functional requirements** specify what the system does, including its behaviors and capabilities, and are often documented as user stories or use cases. **Non-functional requirements** (NFRs), also known as quality attributes or **'ilities'**, describe how well the system performs those functions, covering performance, scalability, security, usability, and reliability. NFRs are critical to user adoption and long-term success, as a functional system that is slow, insecure, or hard to use can lead to project failure. Documenting both types of requirements ensures that the final product fulfills business needs while meeting operational and user experience standards.

Key Definitions:

- **Functional requirement:** A description of a system's required functions or capabilities, typically expressed as "The system shall..." (for example, "The system shall generate a daily list of the top 100 customers by churn risk score").
- **Non-Functional Requirement (NFR):** A criterion that describes how effectively the system performs a function. It specifies system qualities such as performance under load, usability, and security standards (e.g., "The prediction API shall respond within 200 milliseconds for the 95th percentile of requests under normal load").
- **User story:** An informal, user-centered description of a functional requirement, typically formatted as: "As a [user role], I want [goal] so that [benefit]."
- **Service Level Agreement (SLA):** A formal commitment between a service provider and a user that specifies measurable

NFRs, like uptime percentage (e.g., 99.9% availability) and response times.

Table 4 Functional vs. Non-Functional Requirements

Aspect	Functional Requirements (The "What")	Non-Functional Requirements (The "How Well")
Definition	Describe what the system must do, its features, capabilities, and behaviors.	Describe the qualities or constraints of the system, its performance, security, usability, etc.
Focus	System functionality and user interactions.	System properties, performance, and operational characteristics.
Example	"The system shall generate a daily report of top 10 at-risk customers."	"The report must load in under 5 seconds for 100 concurrent users."
Key Categories	• Data inputs/outputs • User interactions • Business rules • Administrative functions	• Performance: Speed, throughput, latency • Scalability: User/data growth capacity • Reliability: Uptime, accuracy • Security: Access control, encryption • Usability: Learnability, efficiency • Maintainability: Ease of update & repair
Testability	Verified through functional testing (Does it work?).	Verified through performance testing, load testing, security audits, etc. (How well does it work under stress?).

Step-by-Step Method:

1. **Gather requirements:** Conduct interviews, workshops, and observations with all stakeholder groups, including users, sponsors, IT, and compliance.
2. **Categorize requirements:**

    - **Functional:** List all actions the system is required to perform, the data it needs to process, and the outputs it should produce.
    - **Non-Functional:** Identify qualities across categories:
        - *Performance:* Evaluating speed, throughput, and latency.
        - *Scalability:* The ability to manage increasing data volume or user numbers.
        - *Reliability and Availability:* Measures of uptime and average time between failures.
        - *Security:* Implement data encryption, access controls, and maintain audit logs.
        - *Usability*: Ease of learning, efficiency, and user satisfaction.
        - *Maintainability:* How easily the system can be updated, debugged, and expanded.
3. **Make requirements SMART:** Ensure each requirement is Specific, Measurable, Achievable, Relevant, and Time-bound. For NFRs, this means attaching a clear metric (e.g., not "fast," but "< 2 sec load time").
4. **Document and prioritize:** Use a requirements management tool or a framework such as MoSCoW (Must-have, Should-have, Could-have, Won't-have) to document and prioritize features.
5. **Confirm with stakeholders:** Review the requirements document to ensure it fully reflects all needs before beginning design and development.

Examples:

- **Project:** Real-time fraud detection system.
- **Functional requirements:**
    - The system assigns a fraud risk score from 0 to 100 to each incoming transaction.
    - Transactions with a score above 85 will be marked for manual inspection by the fraud team.
- **Non-functional requirements:**
    - *Performance:* The system should process and score at least 95% of transactions within 100 milliseconds after receipt.
    - *Availability:* The scoring engine must sustain 99.95% uptime during core business hours (9 AM - 9 PM GMT).

- *Security:* "All transaction data, whether in transit or at rest, shall be encrypted using AES-256."
- *Scalability:* "The architecture must accommodate a fivefold (5x) increase in transaction volume without needing a re-architecture."

Common Pitfalls:

- **Vague NFRs:** Stating "the system must be user-friendly" without clarifying what that entails or how to measure it.
- **Ignoring "Ilities":** Focusing solely on functional requirements and neglecting key NFRs like maintainability or scalability can lead to substantial technical debt.
- **Confusing NFRs with design or architecture:** NFRs describe *the required* quality (e.g., "respond in <1 second"), not the met*hods* to achieve it (e.g., "use a Redis cache").
- **Excluding stakeholders from NFR definition:** Different stakeholder groups own different categories of NFRs. IT defines performance and security requirements. End users define usability standards. Business teams specify availability and reliability targets. Leaving any group out creates gaps that surface as failures after deployment.

Summary

Business problem framing turns vague organizational issues into clear, actionable projects ready for analysis. Accurate problem statements are developed through root cause analysis techniques such as the "5 Whys," by assessing the current situation, and by applying the SMART criteria to set clear, measurable goals. These statements are then refined with stakeholders to remove ambiguity and prevent solutioneering before resources are allocated.

Stakeholder analysis using the Power/Interest grid helps create targeted engagement strategies for each group, while the RACI matrix clearly assigns responsibilities for project tasks. Process frameworks, including SIPOC and the Define phase of DMAIC, set clear project boundaries, measure problems against baselines, and develop formal project charters that specify in-scope and out-of-scope items to prevent scope creep.

The business case transforms problem definitions into investment justifications by estimating tangible benefits and total costs, and by using financial metrics such as Return on Investment, net present value, and payback period. Project planning methods such as PERT and CPM help create realistic timelines, while risk assessment considers both technical challenges and non-technical factors, such as stakeholder resistance.

Structured decision analysis frameworks simplify complex choices by combining data and judgment. Payoff matrices compare options across scenarios, while criteria like Maximax, Maximin, Minimax Regret, and Equal Likelihood evaluate risk based on preferences. Probabilities enable Expected Monetary Value calculations, and the Analytic Hierarchy Process helps compare multiple goals. Core functions are outlined by functional requirements, while non-functional requirements specify attributes like speed, scalability, security, usability, and reliability, ensuring systems meet expectations.

Chapter 1: Practice Questions

Q1. The primary goal of using the "5 Whys" technique during problem framing is to:
A) Assign blame for the problem to a specific individual or team.
B) Identify multiple potential solutions to explore at the same time.
C) Investigate from a surface-level symptom to uncover the fundamental, underlying root cause.
D) Immediately quantify the financial impact of the business problem.

Q2. A key characteristic that sets a **well-written** problem statement apart from a poor one is:
A) Proposes a specific technical solution to implement.
B) Is free of solution bias and focuses on describing the gap between current and desired states.
C) Uses complex technical jargon to demonstrate analytical rigor.
D) Is approved solely by the data science team without business input.

Q3. When setting SMART objectives for an analytics project, the 'A' (Achievable) mainly means:
A) The objective aligns with the company's overall strategy.
B) The objective has a clear, numerical target.
C) The objective can be accomplished given available data, time, and resources.
D) The objective is assigned to a specific person for accountability.

Q4. In a **RACI matrix**, the critical rule for the 'A' (Accountable) role is that there should be:
A) At least two people are accountable for every major task to ensure oversight.
B) Exactly one and only one person is ultimately accountable for each task or deliverable.
C) No one is accountable for exploratory or research-oriented tasks.
D) The project manager is listed as Accountable for all tasks.

Q5. The **SIPOC framework** is most effectively used during problem framing to:
A) Design the detailed architecture of the technical solution.
B) Create a high-level, shared understanding of the process boundaries, inputs, outputs, and involved parties.

C) Calculate the precise return on investment (ROI) for the project.
D) Develop the machine learning model's training and testing protocol.

Q6. Solutioneering in a problem statement is a major pitfall because it:
A) Makes the statement too long and detailed.
B) Unnecessarily restricts exploration and leads to accepting an answer before fully understanding the problem.
C) Uses too much data-driven terminology.
D) Focuses too heavily on the financial cost of the problem.

Q7. When building a **business case**, the **Total Cost of Ownership (TCO)** should include:
A) Only the initial software and hardware purchase costs.
B) All costs associated with the project over its full lifecycle, including initial development, ongoing operation, maintenance, and support.
C) Only the costs that can be directly billed to the client or business unit.
D) The projected revenue increases, but not the cost savings.

Q8. In project scheduling, the Critical Path is defined as:
A) The path with the most tasks.
B) The sequence of dependent tasks with the longest total duration that determines the shortest possible project timeline.
C) The most expensive sequence of tasks.
D) The tasks that involve the highest level of technical risk.

Q9. The main purpose of a formally signed **Project Charter** is to:
A) Serve as detailed technical documentation for the development team.
B) Provide a legally binding contract with external vendors.
C) Obtain official authorization for the project and establish a shared agreement on scope, objectives, and resources among stakeholders.
D) Replace the need for a business case or stakeholder analysis.

Q10. A project team uses a Payoff Matrix to select one of three marketing strategies under two different economic scenarios. If the team leader is very risk-averse and aims to prevent the worst possible outcome, they should choose the:
A) Maximax (Optimistic) criterion.
B) Maximin (Pessimistic) criterion.
C) Equally Likely (Laplace) criterion.
D) Expected Monetary Value (EMV) criterion.

Q11. The Analytic Hierarchy Process **(AHP)** is particularly useful for decisions that involve:
A) A single, clear objective with many similar alternatives.
B) High uncertainty with completely unknown probabilities.
C) Multiple, conflicting objectives that require subjective judgments about their importance.
D) Urgent, time-sensitive choices with limited data.

Q12. A requirement stating, "The system must allow users to filter the customer report by region and date range," is an example of a:
A) Non-Functional Requirement.
B) Functional Requirement.
C) Project constraint.
D) Business case assumption.

Q13. A requirement stating "The dashboard must load in less than 3 seconds for 99% of users" is an example of a:
A) Non-Functional Requirement related to performance.
B) Functional Requirement related to user interaction.
C) Strategic objective.
D) User story acceptance criteria.

Q14. In stakeholder analysis, where should a department head with high authority over budget allocation but limited interest in daily project details be positioned on the Power/Interest Grid?
A) High Power, High Interest (Manage Closely)
B) High Power, Low Interest (Keep Satisfied)
C) Low Power, High Interest (Keep Informed)
D) Low Power, Low Interest (Monitor)

Q15. The **Minimax Regret** decision criterion aims to:
A) Maximize total potential profit.
B) Choose the alternative with the best possible best-case scenario.
C) Minimize the maximum possible "opportunity loss" or the sense of having made the wrong choice.
D) Assume all future states are equally likely.

Q16. When defining benefits for a business case, which option signifies an intangible benefit?
A) A 15% reduction in raw material waste.
B) A projected $500,000 increase in annual sales.

C) An improvement in brand perception and customer loyalty.
D) Savings from automating manual processes, calculated as labor hours saved.

Q17. The primary defense against **scope creep** in an analytics project is:
A) Having a very large project budget contingency.
B) A detailed, stakeholder-approved Project Charter that explicitly lists out-of-scope items.
C) Using agile development methods exclusively.
D) Frequently changing project managers.

Q18. In the context of the **DMAIC** methodology, the creation of a **SIPOC** diagram is a key activity in which phase?
A) Define
B) Measure
C) Analyze
D) Improve

Q19. Value-Focused Thinking in decision-making stresses that the process should begin with:
A) Comparing the costs of obvious alternatives.
B) Clearly articulating fundamental objectives and values, which then guide the development of better alternatives.
C) Performing a detailed risk analysis of the current situation.
D) Gathering all available data before beginning any discussion.

Q20. The most significant risk to an analytics project is often:
A) Choosing a programming language that is not the most popular.
B) Technical issues, such as data quality problems or model accuracy.
C) People- and process-related, such as stakeholder resistance or poor change management.
D) The cost of cloud computing resources.

Chapter 2: Framing the Analytics Problem

Introduction

Framing the analytics problem is a structured process that converts a business challenge into a clear, actionable, and technically sound analytical project. It bridges the gap between a business leader's goals and the models a data scientist builds. This phase determines whether analytical effort creates real value or becomes an expensive, unused deliverable. Success depends on asking the right analytical questions, making sound methodology decisions, setting measurable success criteria, and managing risks and constraints from the start. A well-defined problem keeps all subsequent technical work focused, measurable, and aligned with stakeholder expectations.

Figure 3 The Translation Bridge

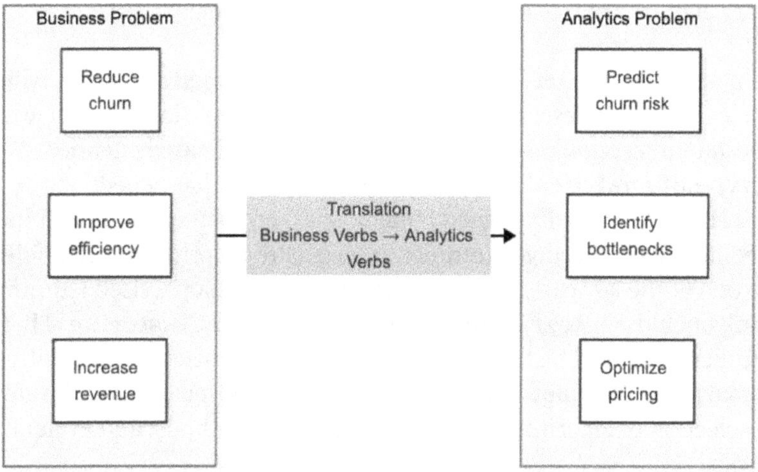

Lesson 2.1: Translating Business Goals into Analytical Questions

Objective:
Transform a broad business goal into a clear analytics problem statement by identifying the desired output (such as prediction, classification, or optimization), outlining the inputs, assumptions, and success criteria, and aligning it with the suitable task category (like regression, clustering, or forecasting) to direct methodology and evaluation.

Detailed Explanation:
This initial translation is a defining step in the analytics lifecycle. A business problem describes the 'what' and 'why,' such as 'we are losing customers.' An analytics problem reframes that concern by specifying both what needs to be achieved (for example, predicting which customers are at risk) and how to approach it analytically (for example, through binary classification using transaction and engagement data).

The main task is to develop an **analytics problem statement,** which is a clear, concise description of the data-driven question to be answered. This statement should be precise, measurable, and clearly define the **type of analytical task**: understanding what happened (Descriptive), why it happened (Diagnostic), predicting future results (Predictive), or offering recommendations (Prescriptive). It often falls into one of the key categories of supervised and unsupervised learning, mainly including **Regression**, **Classification**, or **Clustering**. There are other analytical tasks such as forecasting, optimization, simulation, anomaly detection, and recommendation. The chosen category influences the selection of algorithms, data preprocessing methods, and evaluation metrics.

Figure 4 Process - Translating Business Goals to Analytics Questions

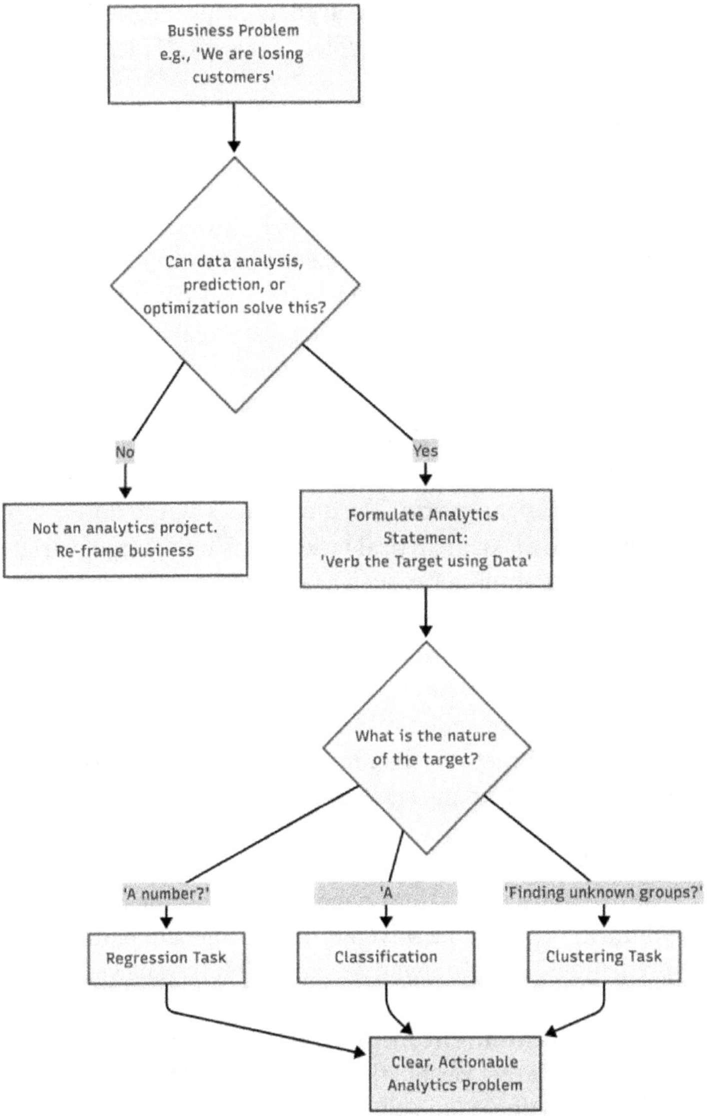

Key Definitions:

- **Analytics problem statement:** A brief description of the data-driven question to be solved, typically beginning with analytical verbs such as "predict," "classify," "identify," "optimize," or "forecast."
- **Descriptive analytics:** Summarizing historical data through reports and dashboards to understand past events, "what happened".
- **Diagnostic analytics:** Examining historical data through drilldowns, segmentation, and correlation analysis to uncover root causes and explain past events, "why did it happen".
- **Predictive analytics:** Applying statistical models and machine learning techniques to forecast future results, "what will happen".
- **Prescriptive analytics:** Using models to recommend actions that improve future results through techniques like optimization or simulation, answering the question "what to do".
- **Regression:** An analytical task in which the target variable is continuous or numeric, such as estimating sales figures or temperature.
- **Classification:** An analytical task involving a categorical target variable, such as fraud versus non-fraud or risk categories.
- **Clustering:** An analytical technique that does not rely on a predefined target variable. Instead, it aims to identify natural groupings in the data, such as customer segments.

Step-by-Step Method:

1. **Identify the analytical core:** For the business problem, ask yourself: "Can this be solved by analyzing data patterns, making predictions, or optimizing decisions?" If the answer is yes, proceed.
2. **Create a statement following this structure:** '[Analytical verb] the [Target variable] using [Input data/Features] to achieve [Business objective].'
3. **Identify the problem's nature:** Assess the expected output. Is it a numerical value (regression)? A category from a predefined set (classification)? Or are you tasked with uncovering unknown groups (clustering)?
4. **Assess prior research:** Review previous analyses to understand their methodology, findings, and limitations. Identify

the logical next steps, such as validation, extension, or implementation.

Examples:

- **Example 1: Customer Churn**
  - *Business problem:* The lack of a proactive retention strategy causes a 15% monthly churn rate among premium customers, leading to substantial revenue loss.
  - *Analytics problem statement:* "Predict the likelihood of churn for each premium customer in the next 30 days using their usage history, support tickets, and payment data to achieve a targeted retention response before revenue is lost."
  - *Problem classification:* **Binary Classification** (churn versus not churn).

- **Example 2: Inventory Management**
  - *Business problem:* "Frequent stockouts of high-demand products cause lost sales and customer dissatisfaction."
  - *Analytics problem statement:* "Predict weekly demand for each SKU using historical sales, seasonality, and promotional calendars to set optimal reorder points."
  - *Problem classification:* **Regression** (demand is a continuous variable).

Common Pitfalls:

- **Confusing business and analytics issues:** "reduce churn" is a business objective, while "predict churn" is an analytics challenge.
- **Creating an overly broad statement:** "Understand our customers" is vague. "Segment customers based on purchasing behavior" is actionable.
- **Misclassifying the problem:** Treating an ordinal categorical target, such as a 1 to 5 star rating, as a standard regression problem without first assessing whether that choice is appropriate. Regression can be used for ordinal targets when the intervals between categories are treated as approximately equal, but the default starting point should be ordinal classification.
- **Ignoring previous work:** Duplicating analysis rather than building on it to advance the project.

Lesson 2.2: The Build vs. Buy Decision

Objective:
Evaluate the strategic and operational factors that determine whether to build a custom analytics solution in-house or purchase an existing product and apply a structured decision framework to make and document that choice.

Detailed Explanation:
Before allocating resources to develop a model, a crucial strategic decision must be made: **Build** or **Buy**. This involves comparing developing a custom in-house solution with licensing an existing product or service. The choice depends on whether the capability provides a competitive advantage, the specificity of the requirements, the urgency of deployment, the total cost of ownership over time, and the availability of in-house skills to build and maintain the solution. Choose to "build" when the capability provides a unique competitive edge or when requirements are highly specific. In contrast, the "buy" approach is generally better for common needs that do not offer differentiation, where quick deployment and proven reliability are necessary.

Table 5 Build vs. Buy Decision Framework

Decision Factor	Favors BUILD	Favors BUY
Strategic Importance	Core differentiator, source of competitive advantage	Commodity function, not a source of differentiation
Solution Specificity	Requirements are highly unique, no off-the-shelf fit	Needs are standard, well-solved by vendor products
Time-to-Market	Time is available, long-term control valued over speed	Speed is critical, rapid deployment is primary need
In-House Expertise	Team possesses necessary skills and can maintain solution	Lacks skills, difficult or costly to recruit/train
Total Cost of Ownership	Lower long-term cost expected and justified	Lower upfront and ongoing cost expected

Key Definitions:

- **Build decision:** The choice to develop an analytics solution using in-house or contracted resources.
- **Buy decision:** The choice to select and adopt a pre-built analytics solution from an external vendor.
- **Total Cost of Ownership (TCO):** The overall expense of a solution over its entire lifetime, including development, licensing, implementation, maintenance, and support.

Step-by-Step Method:

1. **Identify the key criteria:** Determine the main evaluation factors, including strategic importance, requirement specificity, time-to-market, total cost of ownership (TCO), and in-house skills.
2. **Gather information:** Research vendor solutions for Buy and estimate internal development and maintenance costs for Build.
3. **Evaluate using a decision matrix:** Score each option (Build and Buy) against key criteria and assign weights based on business priorities.
4. **Make a recommendation:** The option with the highest weighted score represents the most strategically aligned choice. Document the reasoning behind the decision so stakeholders can understand the rationale and revisit it if conditions change.

Examples:

- **Buy:** A regional bank selecting an anti-money laundering (AML) system. Buying is the right choice because robust, regulatory-compliant vendor solutions already exist, building one internally carries high cost and risk, and compliance deadlines require rapid deployment.
- **Build:** A large e-commerce company developing a real-time 'next-best-offer' engine for customers. Building is the right choice because proprietary customer behavior data is a competitive asset, and the recommendation system requires deep integration with internal platforms that no vendor product can replicate.

Common Pitfalls:

- **Underestimating the TCO for development:** Only accounting for initial costs while ignoring long-term maintenance, updates, and technical debt.

- **Overestimating the ease of integration:** Assuming a vendor's product will seamlessly connect to complex, legacy data systems without substantial customization.
- **Treating the decision as purely technical:** The build vs. buy choice is fundamentally a business strategy decision. It determines where the organization invests its resources and what it considers a core capability worth owning and maintaining internally.

Lesson 2.3: Defining Inputs, Outputs, and Data Needs

Objective:
Identify the main variables for analysis, hypothesize their relationships, and systematically assess the data needed to evaluate project feasibility.

Detailed Explanation:
This lesson focuses on establishing both the conceptual and practical foundations for your analysis. First, define the **conceptual model** by identifying the output, also called the dependent variable or target, and the inputs, also called independent variables or features, believed to influence it. Some variables may serve as outputs in one context and inputs in another, such as customer satisfaction. Simultaneously, **conduct a data needs assessment**, systematically evaluating the data necessary to support these conceptual variables, including an examination of data sources, granularity, quality, volume, and accessibility. This combined approach effectively connects the theoretical problem with data realities, enabling early detection of critical feasibility issues.

Key Definitions:

- **Input/Driver/Independent variable:** A variable that is manipulated or measured to see if it influences the output.
- **Output/Target/Dependent variable:** The variable that represents the outcome that is intended to be explained, predicted, or optimized.
- **Data needs assessment:** The process of evaluating the data required for an analytics project, including its availability, accessibility, and suitability for use.
- **GIGO (Garbage In, Garbage Out):** The principle that a model's output quality is determined by the quality of its input data. No amount of algorithmic sophistication compensates for poor, biased, or incomplete inputs.

Step-by-Step Method:

1. **Define the output:** Start with the primary result of your analytics problem statement.

2. **Brainstorm conceptual inputs:** List all possible factors that might affect the output using domain expertise and stakeholder insights.
3. **Classify variables:** Identify each as **output, input, both** (input to this model but output elsewhere), or **neither** (not relevant to this context).
4. **Formulate hypotheses:** Clearly define a testable hypothesis for main factors, for example, "Longer service wait times increase the likelihood of churn."
5. **Map to data sources:** For each conceptual variable, identify potential data sources (e.g., "customer loyalty" -> CRM tenure data, repeat purchase logs).
6. **Evaluate data appropriateness:** For each source, verify that it exists, is accessible to the project team, provides the right level of granularity for the target variable, and meets acceptable standards for quality and timeliness.

Examples:

- **Predictive Maintenance**
  - *Analytics problem:* "Predict the chances of a machine failing within the next 7 days."
  - *Variable classification:*
    1. **Output:** Machine failure (Yes/No).
    2. **Inputs:** Vibration levels, operating temperature, and hours since last maintenance.
    3. **Both:** None in this context.
    4. **Neither:** Machine color, operator's name.
  - *Data Needs Assessment:*
    1. *Vibration data:* Comes from sensors connected through an IoT platform, offering high frequency and high quality. **Gap:** Historical data is only stored for 30 days, so an archive is necessary for model training.
    2. *Maintenance logs:* Stored in the CMMS system and accessible as text notes (unstructured). **Gap:** Requires extensive extraction and transformation.

Table 6 Variable Classification Framework

Classification	Definition	Customer Churn	Predictive Maintenance
Output (Target)	Primary variable to be explained, predicted, or optimized	churn_status (Yes/No)	machine_failure (Yes/No)
Input (Feature)	Factor believed to influence or drive changes in output	usage_frequency, support_tickets	vibration_level, hours_since_maintenance
Both	Variable that is output of one process and input to another in project scope	customer_satisfaction_score	repair_cost_estimate
Neither	Data with no plausible link to output in current analytical context	employee_ID_of_sales_rep	machine_serial_number

Common Pitfalls:

- **Confusing correlation with causation:** Two variables changing together does not mean one causes the other. Building a model on a spurious correlation produces predictions that break down when conditions change. Always apply domain knowledge and logical reasoning to assess whether a relationship is plausible before treating it as analytically meaningful.
- **Omitting key latent variables:** Failing to include important but difficult-to-measure factors like "employee morale".
- **Assuming data exists and is clean:** Proceeding with modeling without verifying data availability and quality (the GIGO trap).
- **Not involving data engineering teams early:** Failing to consult those responsible for data infrastructure during the assessment.

Lesson 2.4: Documenting Critical Assumptions and Constraints

Objective:

Explicitly document the core beliefs (assumptions) and fixed limitations (constraints) that underpin the analytics project, so that hidden risks are visible and manageable before they affect project outcomes.

Detailed Explanation:

Every analytics project rests on certain **assumptions**, the unverified beliefs that must hold true for the solution to remain valid and useful. **Implicit assumptions** can be especially risky since they are often left unspoken. This lesson highlights the importance of explicitly defining **constraints**, including real-world business, technical, and ethical limits, which shape the scope of possible solutions. Clearly documenting these assumptions makes hidden risks easier to manage, helps set realistic expectations, and reduces the likelihood of costly rework or project failure.

Key Definitions:

- **Assumption:** A factor believed to be true but not yet verified at the beginning of the project. It functions as an educated guess that supports the project plan.
- **Implicit assumption:** A hidden, core belief (e.g., "the past predicts the future," "data is recorded accurately").
- **Constraint:** A fixed limitation or restriction the project must work within, such as budget caps, regulatory requirements, or a mandated technology stack. Unlike risks, constraints are known from the start and are non-negotiable.
- **Business environment limitation:** Constraints arising from the organizational context, such as culture, timelines, or data governance policies.

Step-by-Step Method:

1. **Identify underlying assumptions:** Consistently examine and challenge how the problem is framed.
    - *Data:* What must be true about the data? (e.g., it is representative and unbiased).

    - *Process:* What conditions must be true about the real-world processes? (e.g., historical relationships will remain valid)
    - *Context:* What conditions must be present in the business environment? (For instance, decision-makers will act based on insights).
2. **Identify explicit constraints:** Brainstorm limitations.
    - *Technical:* " Model must return a prediction score in under 100 milliseconds."
    - *Business:* "Budget cannot exceed $50,000."
    - *Regulatory:* "Model must be explainable to meet audit requirements."
3. **Verification plan:** For each critical assumption, outline how it will be tested, such as data profiling for data assumptions or stakeholder interviews for business assumptions.
4. **Document explicitly:** Record assumptions and constraints within the project charter, explicitly stating each and noting verification plans or implications.

Table 7 Assumptions & Constraints Log

ID	Type	Statement	Verification Plan - Implication
A1	Assumption	Underlying relationships in training data remain stable for 12 months post-deployment	Monitor for model/concept drift monthly, plan retraining if drift exceeds X%
A2	Assumption	Key input data available in production with <5% missing values	Implement data quality checks in production pipeline, alert on violation
C1	Constraint	Model must produce prediction in <100 milliseconds	Limits algorithm complexity, requires load testing
C2	Constraint	All model decisions must be explainable for regulatory requirements	Excludes "black box" models, explained through SHAP/LIME techniques

Examples:

- **Credit Scoring Model**
  - *Analytics problem:* "Predict the likelihood of loan default for new applicants."
  - *Critical assumptions:*
    1. Economic conditions at the time of model training will reflect those during deployment. *(Verification: Compare economic indicators.)*
    2. The information provided by the applicant is accurate. *(Verification involves logic checks and cross-referencing with external data.)*
  - *Key constraints:*
    1. The model must comply with fair lending laws, which include avoiding the use of ZIP codes as direct inputs.
    2. The scoring process must complete in under 15 seconds on the online portal.
    3. The solution must use the current cloud analytics platform.

Common Pitfalls:

- **Assumptions are not documented**: Assumptions remain implied and unverified.
- **Relying on unverifiable assumptions:** Building the project on assumptions that cannot be objectively tested.
- **Treating a constraint as an assumption:** These are distinct concepts. 'We assume the software license will be approved' is a risk that needs a mitigation plan. 'The software must be open source' is a constraint that shapes the solution from the start. Confusing the two leads to poor risk planning and scope surprises late in the project.
- **Ignoring regulatory and ethical constraints:** Failing to consider them until late in the project.

Lesson 2.5: Defining Success Measures and Performance Targets

Objective:
Establish clear, measurable criteria that cover both business results and technical model performance to definitively evaluate project success.

Detailed Explanation:
Success in analytics requires more than model accuracy. It requires a measurable business impact. A dual-layered system of metrics captures both dimensions effectively. The p**rimary measure** of success is typically a **key performance indicator (KPI)** directly aligned with the initial goal, such as "reduce fraud losses by 40%", while supporting **model performance metrics** (such as Precision, Recall, RMSE) are set up to reinforce this primary measure. **Performance targets** define numerical goals for these metrics, ensuring the project stays both meaningful and achievable. This approach turns vague goals into clear, measurable objectives.

Key Definitions:

- **Primary measure of success / Business KPI:** The specific, measurable business metric that indicates whether the project achieved its intended impact, such as a 15% reduction in monthly churn rate, a 10% increase in on-time delivery, or a 20% decrease in annual fraud losses.
- **Model performance metric:** A statistical measure of a model's predictive or explanatory ability (e.g., Precision, Recall, RMSE).
- **Performance target:** The quantitative threshold a model must meet to be considered ready for deployment, defined in advance and verified against an independent test set.
- **Baseline performance:** The current state performance of an existing process or system, used to measure improvement.
- **Guardrail metric:** A secondary performance boundary that must not be crossed even when optimizing for the primary metric. Guardrail metrics protect against unintended consequences, such as a fraud model that achieves high recall but generates a volume of false alarms that overwhelms the review team.

Step-by-Step Method:

1. **Align with business objectives:** Identify the key business metric from the original problem statement. This serves as the primary success measure.
2. **Select supporting model metrics:** Choose technical metrics aligned with the business goal and analytical task (see Table 8).
3. **Set performance targets:**
    - Identify the **minimum useful improvement** over the baseline that justifies the project's expense.
    - Establish targets for primary metrics, such as AUC > 0.80, and **guardrail metrics,** such as False Positive Rate < 10% and inference latency < 1 second.
4. **Define the verification process:** Specify *how* success will be measured.
    - *Model metrics:* Use a rigorous train/validation/test split or cross-validation.
    - *Business metrics:* Design an A/B test or pilot study to measure impact against the baseline.

Table 8 Model Metric Selection Guide

Analytic Task	Primary Metrics	Key Consideration
Binary Classification	Precision, Recall, F1-Score, AUC-ROC	Use Precision when false positives costly, Recall when false negatives costly
Forecasting	RMSE, MAPE	RMSE punishes large errors, MAPE intuitive but problematic near zero
Optimization	% Improvement in Objective, Cost Savings	Always measure against baseline (current state) performance
Clustering	Silhouette Score, Domain-based Validation	Internal metrics are guides, ultimate validation is business utility

Examples:

- **Fraud Detection System**
    - *Business problem:* "We are losing an estimated $2 million each year due to fraudulent transactions."
    - *Primary success metric:* Decrease annual fraud losses by 40% within one year of deployment.

- *Model performance targets:* Aim for a **recall** of 95% to detect 95% of actual fraud cases. Maintain **precision** at or above 85%, meaning no more than 15% of transactions flagged as fraudulent are actually legitimate. This balance limits unnecessary customer disruption while keeping fraud detection effective.

Common Pitfalls:

- **Choosing vanity metrics:** Optimizing for a metric that appears impressive but does not represent business value. Overall accuracy on a highly imbalanced dataset is a common example. A model that always predicts the majority class can achieve high accuracy while completely failing its actual purpose.
- **Failing to establish a baseline**: Hindering the measurement of actual improvements derived from the new model.
- **Setting unrealistic targets:** Aiming for "99.9% accuracy" without accounting for inherent noise and uncertainty present in the data.
- **Neglecting guardrail metrics:** Failing to establish targets for key secondary factors such as fairness, explainability, or operational costs.

Lesson 2.6: Establishing Baseline Performance

Objective:
Assess the current process or system's performance against the primary success metric and establish a clear benchmark to evaluate the new solution's improvement.

Detailed Explanation:
You cannot demonstrate the value of a new solution without understanding your starting point. The **baseline performance** is the "before" snapshot, measured using the same primary success metric outlined in Lesson 2.5. It acts as the reference against which all lift, ROI, and success claims will be measured. A well-documented baseline transforms qualitative statements ("it's better") into quantitative facts ("it improved the metric by 18%").

Key Definitions:

- **Baseline Performance:** A documented measure of how the current process or system performs against the primary success metric, calculated over a representative historical period. It serves as the reference point against which all improvements from the new solution are measured.

Step-by-Step Method:

1. **Choose the metric:** Use the primary measure of business success identified earlier.
2. **Gather historical data:** Collect information on this metric from a recent, representative, and stable period. Ensure the period is long enough to capture typical business fluctuations.
3. **Establish the baseline:** Calculate the average or typical performance and identify any trends or seasonal patterns.
4. **Document the baseline:** Record the value, time period, calculation method, and any conditions that affected it. Example: "The baseline conversion rate is 3.2%, calculated as the average daily rate across all website traffic from Q1 of this year, excluding promotional campaign periods."

Examples:

- **Example 1: Marketing Campaign**
    - *Primary metric:* Conversion Rate of Online Leads.

- *Baseline performance:* The average conversion rate for leads generated through the standard website contact form over the past 180 days is 3.2%.

- **Example 2: Supply Chain**
  - *Primary metric:* On-time delivery rate.
  - *Baseline performance:* Over the previous fiscal year, 87% of all orders were delivered on or before the promised date.

Figure 5 Relationship - Baseline, Target, and Business Goal

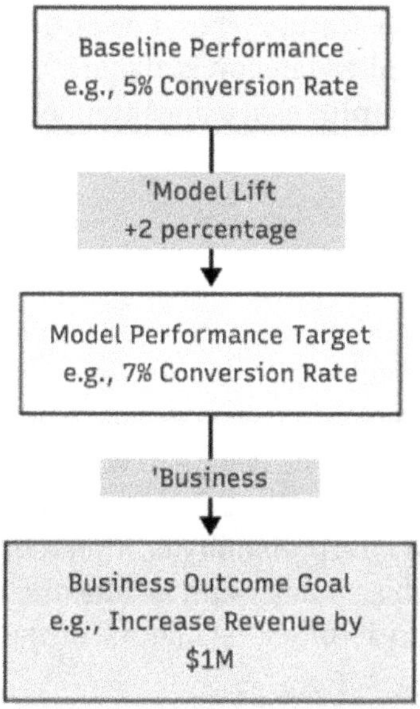

Common Pitfalls:

- **Using an inappropriate time period:** A baseline drawn from an atypical period, such as holiday sales data used as an annual baseline, produces a distorted starting point. The baseline period must reflect normal operating conditions for the comparison to be meaningful.
- **Insufficient data:** Selecting a time period that is too short, which fails to capture typical business cycles or variations.
- **Not documenting the methodology:** Failing to record *how* the baseline was determined can cause disagreements later.

Lesson 2.7: High-Level Method Selection

Objective:
Select the appropriate category of analytical techniques for the problem by narrowing options based on features, data, and constraints.

Detailed Explanation:
Following the classification of problems, this stage involves selecting methods for prototyping. The objective is not to determine the final algorithm but to identify a promising, manageable subset of approaches for initial evaluation. This decision is guided by a mental decision tree that considers the problem type (regression, classification, clustering), data characteristics (size, feature types, noise), and key project constraints (interpretability, latency, scalability). The recommended approach is to **start simple** (e.g., a linear model) before exploring more complex methodologies.

Key Definitions:

- **High-level method selection:** The process of narrowing down algorithmic approaches to relevant categories, such as tree-based ensembles, linear models, or neural networks, for initial prototyping.
- **Interpretability:** The degree to which a human can understand and explain the reasoning behind a model's prediction or decision. High interpretability is often required in regulated industries such as finance and healthcare, where decisions must be justifiable to auditors, regulators, or the individuals affected.

Figure 6 Guide - High-Level Method Selection

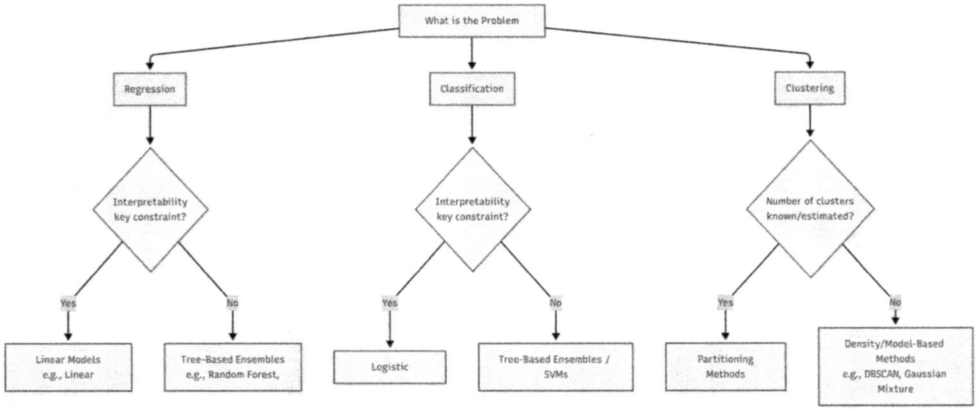

Step-by-Step Method:

1. **Verify the problem type:** Confirm whether it is Regression, Classification, or Clustering.
2. **Profile the data:** Evaluate key features such as sample size, feature types (numeric, categorical, text), missing data, and suspected nonlinearity.
3. **Apply constraints:** Consider non-negotiable requirements: Is interpretability of the model essential? Is real-time latency needed? Are there any computational limits?
4. **Select candidate families:** Use the profile and constraints to choose 2-3 method families for initial testing.
   - *Need interpretability and linear relationships?* Consider using Linear/Logistic Regression.
   - *Have mixed data types and likely non-linear patterns?* Consider tree-based methods (e.g., Decision Trees and Random Forests).
   - *Have large volumes of data and require high accuracy for perception tasks such as image recognition or text analysis?* Consider deep learning methods.
   - *Have no labels and need to find groups?* Consider using clustering algorithms such as K-Means and hierarchical clustering.

Examples:

- **Problem:** Predict equipment failure (binary classification).
- **Data:** 10,000 instances, 50 mixed features, with some missing data.
- **Constraints:** Require moderate interpretability and high precision.
- **High-level selection:** Begin with **logistic regression** as an interpretable baseline and **random forest** as a stronger candidate given its ability to handle mixed data types and provide feature importance scores. Address missing values through imputation before finalizing the method selection, as algorithms handle missing data differently.

Common Pitfalls:

- **Defaulting to complexity:** Choosing the most advanced method, such as a neural network, when data characteristics and project constraints do not justify it. Complex models require more data, more computational resources, and more validation effort. Starting with a simpler model and adding complexity only when the data demands it is a more disciplined and defensible approach.

- **Ignoring business constraints:** Selecting a "black box" model even when explainability is required by regulations or operational needs.
- **Not establishing a baseline:** Failing to test a simple model first makes it difficult to justify using a more complex method.

Lesson 2.8: Identifying Risks and Mitigation Strategies

Objective:
Proactively identify potential failure points across technical, operational, and business areas and to develop specific plans to prevent or mitigate their impact.

Detailed Explanation:
Risk management is fundamental to ensuring the success of any project. A risk is any uncertain event or condition that could affect the project's value, schedule, or feasibility, whether positively (an opportunity) or negatively (a threat). The most critical analytical risks are frequently non-technical, involving user adoption, ethical considerations, and stakeholder support. A principal technical risk involves **data bias**, which occurs when training data lacks representativeness, leading to unfair or inaccurate predictions. For each identified risk, a customized **mitigation strategy** should be developed to shift the project from reactive to proactive management.

Key Definitions:

- **Risk:** An uncertain event or condition that can impact project goals, either positively or negatively.
- **Mitigation strategy:** A proactive step taken to reduce the likelihood or impact of a negative risk.
- **Data bias:** Systematic errors that occur during data collection or preparation, leading to inaccurate representations of the true population and resulting in skewed or unfair model results.
- **Model drift:** The degradation of a model's predictive performance over time. It takes two forms. **Data drift** occurs when the statistical distribution of input variables shifts while the relationship between inputs and output remains stable. **Concept drift** occurs when the underlying relationship between inputs and outputs changes, rendering the model's learned patterns invalid. Both require active monitoring and trigger retraining.

Figure 7 Risk Prioritization Matrix

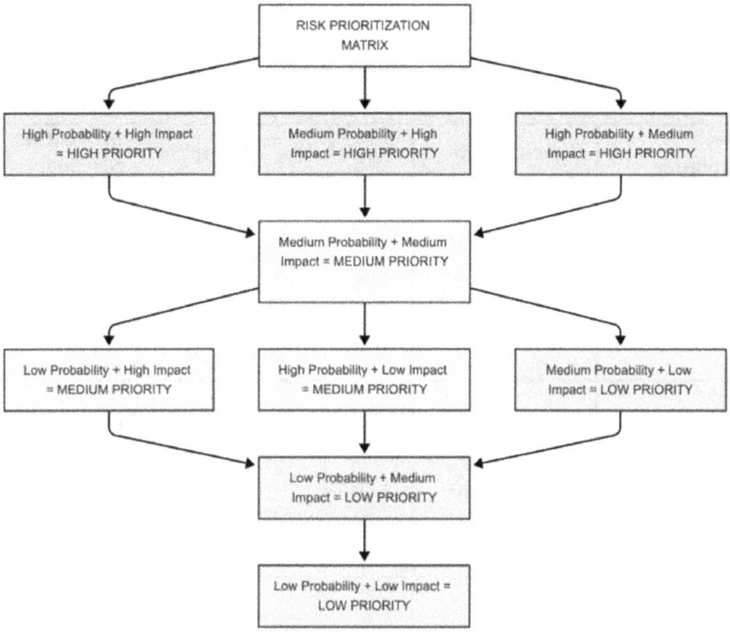

Step-by-Step Method:

1. **Brainstorm risks:** Consider all categories:
    - *Data risks:* Poor quality, sampling bias, incomplete coverage, and unavailability of required data sources.
    - *Model risks:* Poor performance on unseen data, overfitting to training data, lack of interpretability, and model drift over time as data distributions or underlying relationships change.
    - *Implementation risks:* Integration challenges and computational costs.
    - *Business risks:* Stakeholder resistance, inability to act, ethical concerns, and regulatory non-compliance.
2. **Prioritize risks:** Assess each risk's probability and impact. Focus on **high-probability, high-impact** risks.
3. **Define mitigation strategies:** For each key risk, assign a specific, proactive action.
4. **Special focus on data bias:**
    - *Risk:* Biased training data leads the model to continue historical inequalities.

- *Mitigation:* Audit datasets to confirm they are representative, using fairness-aware algorithms, and ongoing monitoring for any unfair disparities.

Table 9 Risk Assessment & Mitigation Matrix

Risk Category	**Specific Risk**	**Probability**	**Impact**	**Mitigation Strategy**
Data	Training data not representative of live environment	High	High	Conduct data provenance audit, use stratified sampling based on live data profiles
Business	End-users reject model due to lack of trust or understanding	Medium	High	Co-design output format with users, build explainability into interface, run training workshops
Ethical	Model perpetuates/amplifies historical bias against protected group	Medium	Critical	Implement fairness constraints during training, conduct pre-deployment disparity testing
Operational	Model performance degrades over time due to data drift or concept drift	High	Medium	Create an automated dashboard for key metrics. Use performance triggers, not just fixed schedules, for retraining, and validate new models before deployment.

Examples:

- **Automated Resume Screening**
  - **Risk:** Hiring managers might ignore the tool's suggestions due to a lack of trust.
    - **Mitigation:** Involve managers in the design process, use an explainable model, and organize training workshops.
  - **Risk:** Model performance declines over time (model drift).
    - **Mitigation:** Conduct quarterly performance reviews and annual retraining.
  - **Biased data risk:** Past hiring data shows gender and racial bias.
    - **Mitigation:** Proactively gather balanced data, eliminate proxy variables for protected attributes, test for fair outcomes before deployment.

Common Pitfalls:

- **Only focusing on technical risks:** Ignoring the people, process, and ethical risks that are the main causes of failure.
- **Vague mitigation plans:** Stating 'we will monitor data quality' is not a mitigation strategy. A valid plan specifies which metric will be monitored, how often, what threshold will trigger action, and who is responsible for responding. Without those details, the plan exists only on paper.
- **Failing to plan for model drift:** Assuming a deployed model will perform perfectly forever without a maintenance plan.
- **Treating bias as an afterthought:** Addressing fairness only after modeling, not as a fundamental part from the beginning.

Lesson 2.9: Securing Sponsor Agreement on the Analytics Scope

Objective:
Officially secure stakeholder approval for a consolidated Analytics Project Charter, which outlines the technical scope, deliverables, and boundaries, and approve progressing to the development phase.

Detailed Explanation:
This lesson concludes the problem-framing phase. The main objective is to obtain approval for a document summarizing all prior work. A central requirement is clearly defining the **technical scope**, which is the precise description of what the analytics team will create, rather than the broader business scope that other teams will manage. This covers the final dataset and model specifications, output formats, and explicitly states **out-of-scope** items. Such clarity helps prevent "analytics **scope creep**" during development and promotes a shared understanding between technical teams and business sponsors.

Key Definitions:

- **Analytics project charter:** A formal document that authorizes the project and grants the analytics team authority to allocate resources. It consolidates the outputs of the problem-framing phase, including the analytics problem statement, variable definitions, data needs assessment, assumptions and constraints log, success measures, baseline performance, identified risks, and technical scope boundaries.
- **Technical scope:** The detailed definition of specific technical deliverables, tasks, data sources, and the boundaries of the analytics work.
- **Scope creep:** The uncontrolled expansion of a project's scope without corresponding adjustments to time, budget, or resources. It typically begins with small, seemingly reasonable additions that accumulate into significant changes in workload and deliverables, often without formal review or approval.

Step-by-Step Method:

1. **Consolidate the findings:** Compile outputs from Lessons 2.1-2.8 into a single Analytics Charter.
2. **Define the technical scope:** Be clear about deliverables.

    - **In-scope:** Specific models, exact data sources, output format and frequency, and performance targets.
    - **Out-of-scope:** Analytical approaches not being evaluated in this phase, data sources deferred to later phases, and downstream tasks such as system integration, change management, and campaign execution, which are owned by other teams.
3. **Review and obtain sign-off:** Present the charter to the sponsor and key stakeholders, explaining the problem, scope, success measures, baseline, and key risks. Formal approval confirms everyone understands and authorizes the project to proceed.

Examples:

- **Customer Lifetime Value (CLV) Project**
    - **In-scope for Analytics scope:**
        1. Development of a predictive CLV model utilizing 3 years of transactional and demographic data.
        2. Monthly delivery of a segmented customer list (High/Medium/Low CLV).
        3. A diagnostic report on the main drivers of high CLV.
    - **Out-of-scope for analytics phase:**
        1. Integrating CLV scores into the email marketing platform.
        2. Design and execute marketing campaigns.
        3. Developing a real-time CLV API for the website.

Common Pitfalls:

- **Rushing the sign-off:** Not giving stakeholders enough time to review and understand the technical details.
- **Ambiguous scope definitions:** Using vague language such as 'explore advanced models' instead of 'test Random Forest and Gradient Boosting' gives the project team no clear deliverable and gives sponsors no basis for evaluating progress. Scope definitions must name specific models, data sources, and output formats to be actionable.
- **Confusing analytics with business scope:** Failing to differentiate between what the analytics team creates (a model) and how the business uses it (conducting a campaign).

Summary

Transforming business goals into analytical questions sets the foundation for all subsequent analysis. A clear analytics problem statement follows this format: '[Analytical verb] the [Target variable] using [Input data/Features] to achieve [Business objective].' The type of problem determines whether to use regression for continuous outcomes, classification for categorical outcomes, or clustering to find natural groupings. When deciding whether to build or buy, considerations include strategic importance, specific requirements, time-to-market, and total cost of ownership, which help determine whether to develop a custom solution or opt for an existing vendor product.

After defining the analytical question, the conceptual model is created by systematically categorizing variables. Outputs are the main targets for prediction or optimization, while inputs are the factors thought to influence them. A data needs assessment links each conceptual variable to actual data sources and evaluates the availability, accessibility, granularity, quality, and timeliness of those sources. Assumptions, which are unverified beliefs about data, processes, or the business environment, must be confirmed through verification plans. Constraints such as technical requirements, budgets, and regulatory mandates directly shape the boundaries of acceptable solutions and must be documented before method selection begins.

Success measures operate on two connected levels. Primary business KPIs align with the initial objectives, while supporting model performance metrics match the analytical task. Performance targets set quantitative standards for both levels, and baseline performance establishes the current state against which improvements are measured. High-level method selection then proceeds, narrowing down algorithmic approaches based on problem type, data features, and project constraints: linear models for interpretability, tree-based methods for mixed data and nonlinear patterns, deep learning for large datasets and perception tasks, and clustering for discovering natural groupings.

Risk identification covers technical, operational, and business aspects, including issues like poor quality, bias, model drift, integration problems, and computational costs. It also involves stakeholder resistance, ethical issues, and regulatory adherence. Each key risk demands targeted mitigation strategies rather than vague monitoring methods. The

Analytics Project Charter consolidates all prior work into a formal document, clearly defining the technical scope, deliverables, data sources, output formats, and performance targets, while also listing out-of-scope items. Sponsor approval ensures shared understanding and officially moves the project from problem identification to development.

Chapter 2: Practice Questions

Q1. The main goal of translating a business problem into an analytics problem statement is to:
A) Obtain a larger project budget.
B) Define a clear, data-driven question that can be answered with analytical methods.
C) Impress stakeholders with technical jargon.
D) Meet a procedural requirement.

Q2. Which of the following is the BEST example of a well-defined analytics problem statement?
A) "Make our marketing better."
B) "Use a clustering algorithm to group our customers."
C) "Reduce manufacturing waste by 10%."
D) "Identify which product features are most strongly correlated with customer renewal rates using usage log data."

Q3. In an analytics project, the variable you are trying to predict or explain is called the:
A) Input variable
B) Independent variable
C) Output variable
D) Driver variable

Q4. When analyzing relationships between drivers and an output, it is most important to:
A) Prove causation definitively before proceeding.
B) State a clear, testable expectation based on logic or domain knowledge.
C) Use complex statistical terminology.
D) Ensure all relationships are assumed to be linear.

Q5. The implicit assumption that "historical patterns will continue into the future" is most critical for which type of analytics?
A) Descriptive Analytics
B) Diagnostic Analytics
C) Predictive Analytics
D) Prescriptive Analytics

Q6. To verify the assumption that "our customer data is representative of our entire customer base," you should:
A) Assume it is true if the dataset is large.
B) Compare the distributions of key demographics in your data to the known demographics of the full population.
C) Ask the Sales Director for their opinion.
D) Build a model and see if it works well.

Q7. A business environment limitation to consider when framing an analytics problem to "optimize delivery routes" is:
A) The mathematical elegance of the solution.
B) Driver union rules governing maximum shift length.
C) The brand color of the delivery vehicles.
D) The version of Python used for development.

Q8. For a model designed to filter spam emails, prioritizing the reduction of false positives (legitimate emails marked as spam) means the main model metric should be:
A) High Recall
B) High Accuracy
C) High Precision
D) Low Latency

Q9. The correct process to verify if a model meets its target accuracy of 90% is to:
A) Check its accuracy on the training data.
B) Deploy it and monitor for complaints.
C) Evaluate its accuracy on a held-out test set that wasn't used during model development.
D) Have the data science team vote on whether it seems accurate enough.

Q10. The main reason for establishing a baseline performance is to:
A) Document the current team's underperformance.
B) Provide an objective benchmark to measure the improvement of the new solution.
C) Meet a requirement in the project management methodology.
D) Determine the project's initial budget.

Q11. A common non-technical risk in an analytics project is often:
A) The choice of programming language.
B) Resistance from end-users who are asked to change their workflow.

C) The selection of a random seed.
D) The number of CPU cores available.

Q12. The primary risk of deploying a model trained on biased data is that it:
A) Will require more memory.
B) May produce systematically unfair or inaccurate outcomes for certain population groups.
C) Will be too slow for real-time use.
D) Will be difficult to explain to managers.

Q13. When defining the scope of work for the analytics team, stating that "building the production API is out-of-scope" aims to:
A) Hide the true project cost.
B) Clearly define responsibilities between the analytics and engineering teams.
C) Make the project appear simpler than it actually is.
D) Allow the analytics team to use less robust code.

Q14. Which success measure most directly connects an analytics project to business value?
A) Model accuracy on validation data.
B) Reduction in monthly customer churn rate.
C) The F1-score of the classification model.
D) The RMSE of the forecasting model.

Q15. If a pilot study shows your new model achieves a 12% conversion rate compared to the old system's 10%, what is the relative percentage increase in performance?
A) 2%
B) 20%
C) 83%
D) 120%

Q16. A mitigation strategy for the risk of "model drift" is to:
A) Use the most complex model available.
B) Schedule periodic model retraining with fresh data.
C) Lock the model code, so no one can change it.
D) Use data from only a single, stable time-period.

Q17. An analytics problem statement that starts with "Optimize..." best matches which type of analytics?
A) Descriptive
B) Diagnostic
C) Predictive
D) Prescriptive

Q18. During stakeholder alignment for the analytics scope, the main goal is to:
A) Get approval to use any data source desired.
B) Ensure a shared understanding of what the analytics team will deliver, preventing later disagreements.
C) Assign blame if the project fails.
D) Negotiate for the highest possible budget.

Q19. In a model predicting employee turnover, "employee salary" would typically be considered a:
A) Output Variable
B) Input Variable
C) Variable that is both an input and an output
D) Irrelevant variable (Neither)

Q20. Which of these is a verifiable assumption for a credit risk model?
A) "Applicants are inherently truthful."
B) "The economic environment will remain stable."
C) "The distribution of applicant incomes in our training data is the same as that of current applicants."
D) "Bank managers will always adhere to the model's recommendation."

Chapter 3: The Data

Introduction

The Data chapter covers the core execution stage of the analytics lifecycle, where ideas turn into actions. It emphasizes practical skills such as sourcing, acquiring, preparing, and analyzing data. This phase transforms the theoretical concepts from the framing phase into analysis-ready datasets. Mastering this area ensures that data is relevant, high-quality, ethically sourced, and well understood, all of which are key factors for successful analytics. This chapter provides structured methods for data scoping, governance, preparation, and exploration, connecting problem definition directly to model development.

Lesson 3.1: Scoping and Prioritizing Data Requirements

Objective:

Carefully determine the data you need to address the analytical problem, and then create a practical, value-driven data collection plan that makes the process more efficient and meaningful.

Detailed Explanation:

This first step turns the conceptual model from problem framing into detailed data requirements. It involves identifying specific data elements, exploring sourcing options, and carefully setting priorities. Proper prioritization ensures key data needs are met while considering practical constraints such as cost, accessibility, and integration efforts. A structured approach helps teams focus on essential data and avoid distractions from non-critical information that could divert resources from the main goals.

Key Definitions:

- **Data requirements:** The necessary data fields and their types needed to populate each input variable in the analytical model.
- **Prioritization matrix:** A tool to rank data sources based on factors such as business value, cost, and availability.
- **Data acquisition process:** The logical sequence for collecting data, typically beginning with key internal sources.
- **Usage constraints:** Legal, contractual, or technical limits on data storage, processing, or usage.

- **Data sources:** The origins of data, categorized as internal (company databases, logs) or external (APIs, public datasets, third-party vendors). Source selection affects cost, quality, and timeliness.

Step-by-Step Method:

1. **Map variables to data elements:** For each input variable identified during problem framing, specify the exact data fields required. For example, "Customer Engagement" might need data such as "login frequency," "feature usage logs," and "support ticket count."
2. **Identify potential sources:** For each data element, evaluate both internal and external sources that may provide it. Review each source for relevance, accuracy, timeliness, and cost considerations.
3. **Prioritize using a value-feasibility framework:** Evaluate each source against two criteria. First, business value: how much does this data contribute to the model's success? Second, feasibility: how easy or cost-effective is it to acquire and incorporate?

Figure 8 The 2x2 Value-Feasibility Prioritization Matrix

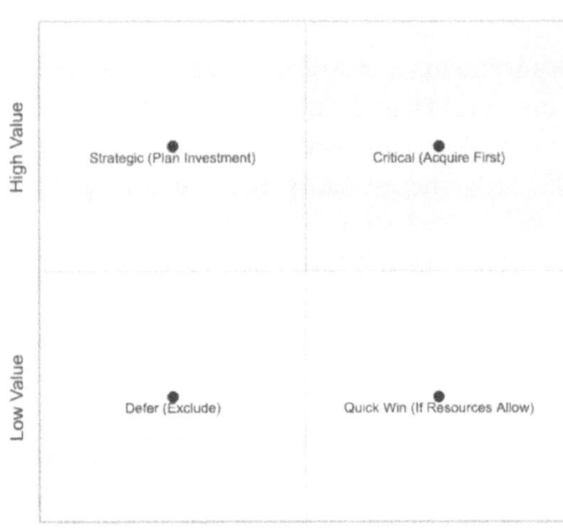

4. **Categorize and sequence:** Classify sources as:
   - *Critical (High Value, High Feasibility):* Must be acquired first.

    - High-Value, Low-Feasibility: Strategic investment.
    - *Low-Value, High-Feasibility:* "Quick wins", pursue if resources permit.
    - *Low-Value, Low-Feasibility:* Defer or exclude.
5. **Document costs and constraints:** For high-priority sources, formally document acquisition expenses, estimated preparation time, and any legal or technical restrictions on usage.

Examples:

- **Predictive Maintenance Project**
    - *Conceptual variable:* Machine Health Indicator.
    - *Data elements and sources:*
        - Vibration Sensor Readings (Source: Internal IoT Platform)
        - Internal Temperature (Source: Machine logs)
        - Ambient Factory Temperature (Source: External Weather API)
    - *Prioritization and rationale:*
        - *Critical:* Vibration and internal temperature data. They are high in value (direct signals) and high in feasibility (internal).
        - *High-Value, Low-Feasibility:* Ambient Temperature. Offers high value for accuracy but has low feasibility due to API integration costs. Approved as a strategic addition.
        - *Excluded:* Audio recordings from microphones. Considered low value for this model and low feasibility due to complex processing.

Common Pitfalls:

- **"What we have" vs. "What we need":** Developing the model solely on easily accessible data rather than seeking data that genuinely addresses the business problem.
- **Underestimating integration complexity:** Assuming connecting to a new data source is simple, without considering API limitations, format mismatches, or the need for data cleansing.
- **Ignoring constraints early:** Neglecting data licensing, privacy laws, or retention policies until late in the project, leading to rework or cancellation.

Lesson 3.2: Evaluating Data Sources and Architecture

Objective:
Assess data sources carefully and select an appropriate data architecture that effectively balances performance, flexibility, and governance.

Detailed Explanation:
Not all data is equal. This lesson highlights the importance of due diligence for every data source by analyzing its structure, limitations, and governance framework. At the same time, select a technical architecture that aligns with the data's characteristics, specifically its **Volume**, **Velocity**, **Variety**, **Veracity**, and **Value** (the **5 Vs**), and the project's analytical needs. This approach ensures the data foundation is both reliable and suited to the technical requirements of the project.

Table 10 The 5 Vs of Data

"V"	Definition	Analytical Implication
Volume	The sheer scale of data.	Drives storage solution choice (e.g., data lake, cloud).
Velocity	The speed of data generation and processing needs.	Determines processing paradigm (batch vs. streaming).
Variety	The diversity of data types and sources.	Influences architecture and preparation tools (e.g., handling unstructured text).
Veracity	The trustworthiness, quality, and accuracy of data.	Mandates rigorous quality assessment and provenance tracking.
Value	The business worth derived from analysis.	Justifies the project and guides the focus of modeling efforts.

Key Definitions:

- **Data provenance:** The origin, lineage, and history of data, which are essential for evaluating its trustworthiness.
- **Data governance:** The structured management of data's availability, usability, integrity, and security, supported by defined roles, responsibilities, and processes.
- **Data architecture:** The overall design of how an organization collects, stores, transforms, and accesses data.

- **Data warehouse:** A centralized repository for structured, filtered data optimized for analysis and reporting (Schema-on-Write).
- **Data lake:** A storage repository that holds large amounts of raw data in its original format until required (Schema-on-Read).
- **Structured vs. unstructured data:** Structured data is organized in a predefined, tabular format with rows and columns. Unstructured data does not follow a specific model, such as text or video.
- **Semi-structured data**: Data in formats such as JSON or XML, which represents a significant hybrid data category.

Table 11 Data Architecture Comparison: Warehouse vs. Lake

Characteristic	Data Warehouse	Data Lake
Schema	Schema-on-Write (Rigid)	Schema-on-Read (Flexible)
Data Type	Structured, processed data	Raw data (structured, semi-structured, unstructured)
Primary Users	Business analysts, for reporting	Data scientists, engineers, for exploration & ML
Processing	Highly optimized for complex queries	Optimized for large-scale batch/stream processing
Cost Structure	Higher cost per TB (processed data)	Lower cost per TB (raw storage)
Key Strength	Performance, consistency, security	Agility, scalability, cost for raw data
Key Risk	Inflexibility, "silos"	Becoming a "data swamp" without governance

Step-by-Step Method:

1. **Profile the source:** Review a sample of the data. Record its structure, data types, value ranges, and completeness. Classify it as structured, semi-structured, or unstructured.
2. **Assess limitations:** Identify known issues like missing data, sampling bias, accuracy problems, or latency (how recent is the data?). Evaluate its veracity (trustworthiness).
3. **Understand governance:** Identify the data owner, steward, and any access controls or usage policies. Look for overlaps or gaps in responsibilities.

4. **Choose architecture:** Match data characteristics (**Volume, Velocity, Variety**) to an architectural pattern.
    - Use a **Data Warehouse** for consistent, structured, and repetitive reporting on clearly defined metrics.
    - Use a **Data Lake** to store raw, unstructured, or high-volume data for exploratory analytics or machine learning.
    - Use a **hybrid Lakehouse** architecture when workloads combine structured reporting and exploratory or machine learning tasks on the same data.
5. **Evaluate the trade-offs:** Clearly identify the advantages of the chosen architecture, including performance and security, and its disadvantages, such as rigidity and complexity, in relation to your project's **Value** requirements.

Examples:

- **Customer 360-Degree View Project**
    - **Source assessment:**
        - *CRM Data:* Well-structured, high-quality, owned by Sales. Limitation: Lacks real-time updates.
        - *Social Media Feed:* Unstructured, fast-paced, owned by Marketing. Limitation: Noisy, needs sentiment analysis.
    - **Governance gap:** No individual owner is accountable for managing the unified customer ID across both systems.
    - **Architecture choice:** A **Data Lake** is selected. The reason is to ingest raw data from both sources (structured CRM and unstructured social) to enable flexible processing and model training. A data warehouse would be too inflexible for social media data.

Common Pitfalls:

- **Provenance blindness:** Using data without understanding how it was created or modified, resulting in mistaken interpretations.
- **Governance as an afterthought:** Assuming data access is automatic, only to be restricted later by compliance or security policies.
- **Architecture Misalignment:** Selecting a complex data lake for straightforward reporting or a rigid warehouse for exploratory data science.

Lesson 3.3: Developing a Data Management Strategy

Objective:
Develop a strategy for managing data across its entire lifecycle, maintaining quality, security, and responsible use while reducing risks to the organization and its stakeholders.

Detailed Explanation:
A Data Management Strategy (DMS) serves as a blueprint that transforms disorganized data into a reliable resource. It extends beyond a single project to define how an organization consistently manages data from collection to disposal. An inadequate or missing strategy leads to inconsistent data, security breaches, compliance issues, and a loss of trust, all of which carry serious consequences for both the business and society. A well-executed strategy also implements **metadata management**, which is data about data, to support discovery, consistency, and lineage tracking across the organization.

Key Definitions:

- **Data lifecycle:** The stages through which data progresses, including Acquisition, Storage, Processing, Usage, Archival, and Destruction, with governance policies enforced at each stage.
- **Data quality standard:** Established thresholds for dimensions such as completeness, accuracy, and timeliness that data must meet.
- **Data stewardship:** The operational responsibility for maintaining data quality and ensuring policy enforcement is assigned to specific roles.
- **Societal impact:** The wider consequences of data misuse, such as privacy breaches, algorithmic bias, and discrimination.
- **Metadata management:** The administration of data that describes other data, including technical (such as data type and source), business (definitions), and operational (lineage and refresh schedule) metadata.

Figure 9 The Data Lifecycle

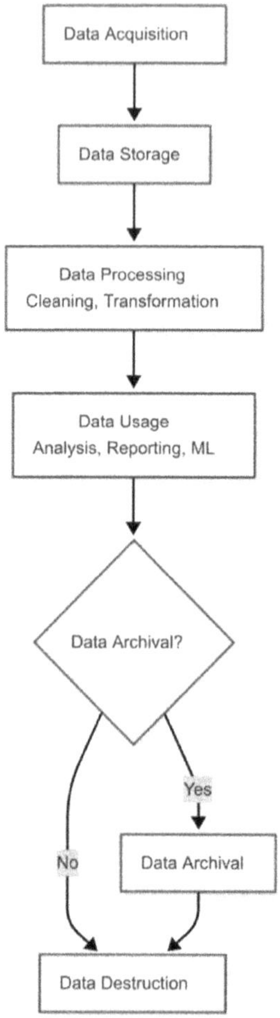

Step-by-Step Method:

1. **Define the data lifecycle:** Outline each stage for your key data assets. What are the entry and exit criteria for each stage?
2. **Establish quality standards:** For high-priority data elements, set measurable targets for dimensions such as **accuracy**, **completeness**, and **timeliness**. Example: "Customer email field must be 95% complete and valid."
3. **Implement security and access controls:** Define protocols that specify who can access which data, under what conditions, and how data is encrypted (both at rest and in transit).

Classify **Personally Identifiable Information (PII)** and other sensitive data for special handling.

4. **Assign stewardship roles:** Clearly designate data owners (accountable) and stewards (responsible for quality).
5. **Assess broader impact:** Proactively evaluate risks related to privacy, fairness, transparency, and potential misuse. Document mitigation plans.
6. **Implement a metadata repository:** Use a centralized data catalog to document source systems, business definitions, calculation logic, and data lineage, supporting governance and collaboration.

Examples:

- **Healthcare Analytics Initiative**
  - **Data lifecycle stage (Storage):** "All Patient Health Information (PHI) must be encrypted using AES-256. Data at rest must be encrypted, and access logs must be immutable."
  - **Quality standard:** "Diagnosis codes must be validated against the current clinical coding standard within 24 hours of entry."
  - **Stewardship:** "The Chief Medical Officer is the Data Owner for clinical trial results. The Head of Data Engineering is the Data Steward for pipeline integrity."
  - **Societal impact assessment:** "Risk: Anomaly detection model for insurance claims could disproportionately flag clinics in low-income areas. Mitigation: Regular fairness audits on model outputs and training data."
  - **Metadata example:** For a "Patient Readmission Risk" column, metadata details its source (EHR.Discharge table), calculation logic (a specific predictive algorithm), business owner (Clinical Operations), and refresh schedule (weekly).

Common Pitfalls:

- **Paper strategy:** Designing an attractive document that remains unimplemented or unenforced.
- **Ignoring data disposal:** Failing to plan for secure data deletion increases the risk of retaining data unnecessarily.
- **Treating data as purely technical:** Ignoring the human, ethical, and legal aspects of data management.

Lesson 3.4: Ethical Data Acquisition and Lineage

Objective:
Collect necessary data using appropriate methods, thoroughly evaluate bias, follow ethical guidelines, and establish clear lineage for reproducibility and auditability.

Detailed Explanation:
Gathering data is a technical process with equally important ethical and practical dimensions. This lesson explains how to select the appropriate acquisition method, identify data-collection biases, manage ethical risks associated with sensitive data, and establish a solid data lineage. **Lineage**, which is the origin and transformation history of data, is central to troubleshooting, compliance, and ensuring that analytical results are accurate and reproducible. An important aspect of data acquisition is choosing the right **sampling method** when collecting new data.

Table 12 Ethical Risks & Mitigations in Data Acquisition

Ethical Risk	Description	Example Mitigation Strategy
Sampling Bias	Data collection systematically excludes or over-represents parts of the population.	Use stratified sampling, apply post-collection weighting, document bias for transparency.
Privacy Violation	Inappropriate handling of Personally Identifiable Information (PII) or sensitive data.	Anonymize or aggregate data, implement strict access controls, follow regulations (e.g., GDPR principles).
Lack of Informed Consent	Using data for purposes beyond what the subject agreed to.	Review data licenses and terms of service, establish clear use protocols.
Provenance Opacity	Using data without understanding its origin, creation process, or prior transformations.	Implement and document data lineage tracking from source.
Re-identification	Combining anonymized datasets or using quasi-identifiers to re-identify individuals.	Apply k-anonymity or differential privacy techniques, risk-assess datasets before release.

Key Definitions:

- **Acquisition method:** The technique used to collect data (e.g., API call, database query, web scraping, sensor stream).

- **Sampling bias:** A flaw in data collection where certain members of the intended population are systematically more likely to be included than others.
- **Sensitive data categories:** Data that needs special protection, such as Personally Identifiable Information (PII), health data, financial records, or biometric data.
- **Data lineage:** A record of the data's origins, movements, characteristics, and transformations throughout its lifecycle.
- **Sampling methods:** Techniques for selecting a study subset include **simple random sampling** (every individual has an equal probability of selection), **stratified sampling** (the population is divided into homogeneous subgroups, and a random sample is drawn from each), and **cluster sampling** (naturally occurring groups are randomly selected, then individuals within those groups are sampled, either fully or partially).

Step-by-Step Method:

1. **Select an acquisition method:** Choose one that balances data needs with source constraints (for example, use an official API instead of scraping a website). If gathering new data, pick a sampling method that supports inference (e.g., stratified sampling to ensure subgroup representation).
2. **Audit for bias:** Critically examine how the data was collected. Ask: "Who or what is systematically missing or overrepresented?" Document these **sampling biases**. Distinguish between **statistical uncertainty** (reducible with more data) and **systemic uncertainty or bias** (a flaw in design not fixed by more data).
3. **Flag ethical risks:** Identify sensitive data, implement protocols like anonymization (irreversible removal) or pseudonymization (reversible with a key).
4. **Implement lineage tracking:** From the moment of acquisition, record the source, extraction time, sampling method used, and any initial transformations. Use tools or metadata tagging to preserve this trail.
5. **Implement version control:** Treat important datasets with the same discipline applied to code. Use versioning tools to track changes, enable rollback to prior versions, and support comparison between dataset iterations.

Examples:

Example 1: Training a Resume-Screening Model

- *Acquisition method:* Anonymized resume data exported from the internal HR system.
- *Bias assessment:* The historical data over-represents applicants from three specific universities, creating an educational institution bias (a **systemic uncertainty**).
- *Ethical risk flag:* Although anonymized, the data may still include proxy variables for gender or ethnicity.
- *Lineage record:* Dataset v1.0: Source: HR_System_Export_2023_Q4. Sampling: N/A (full historical extract). Anonymization: Employee_ID removed. Date: 2024-01-15.

Example 2: Customer Satisfaction Survey

- *Acquisition method:* New survey sent to a sample of customers.
- *Sampling method*: Stratified random sample of active customers, segmented by tenure and product usage to ensure representation across key customer profiles.
- *Bias consideration*: The sample may still underrepresent customers who have already churned and are no longer contactable.

Common Pitfalls:

- **Terms of service violation:** Scraping or using data in ways that breach the source's legal agreements.
- **Bias blindness:** Assuming all collected data is unbiased and representative without questioning it.
- **Lineage as an afterthought:** Attempting to reconstruct data history weeks later, resulting in inaccurate or incomplete records.
- **Confusing anonymization with pseudonymization:** Assuming replacing only direct identifiers offers enough privacy. Pseudonymization is reversible and doesn't meet the legal standards of full anonymization under most privacy laws.

Lesson 3.5: Data Preparation and Feature Engineering

Objective:
Build a reliable and easy-to-repeat pipeline that cleans, harmonizes, and merges raw data using ETL processes. Then, apply creative feature engineering to uncover hidden patterns, giving you a high-quality, analysis-ready dataset that preserves data integrity and supports dependable future modeling.

Detailed Explanation:
Data preparation is the most time-consuming part of analytics, often accounting for 60-80% of the project effort. It involves cleaning errors, managing missing values, harmonizing inconsistent data, merging datasets, and creating new features. This process, known as **data wrangling**, is not just janitorial work, it directly affects the quality of insights. **Feature engineering**, which is the process of creating new variables from existing ones, is a creative and high-value step that reveals patterns hidden in raw data. This process is often formalized in **ETL (Extract, Transform, Load)** pipelines.

Key Definitions:

- **Data cleaning:** Addressing errors, handling missing data, and removing duplicates.
- **Data harmonization:** Standardizing values to a common format, such as dates, currency, and categorical labels.
- **Data transformation:** Modifying the structure or values of data, such as normalization, aggregation, or encoding.
- **Feature engineering:** The process of developing new input variables (features) from raw data to enhance model performance.
- **Join/Merge:** Combine datasets by linking entries through a common identifier, such as Customer_ID.
- **ETL (Extract, Transform, Load):** The core data integration process. It extracts data from source systems, transforms it through cleaning, aggregation, and business rule application, then loads it into a data warehouse or data mart for analysis.
- **Data schemas:** The structured framework for organizing data within a data warehouse.

- **Star schema:** A central fact table linked to denormalized dimension tables.
- **Snowflake schema:** A normalized variant in which dimensions are decomposed into sub-dimensions.

Figure 10 The ETL High-Level Process

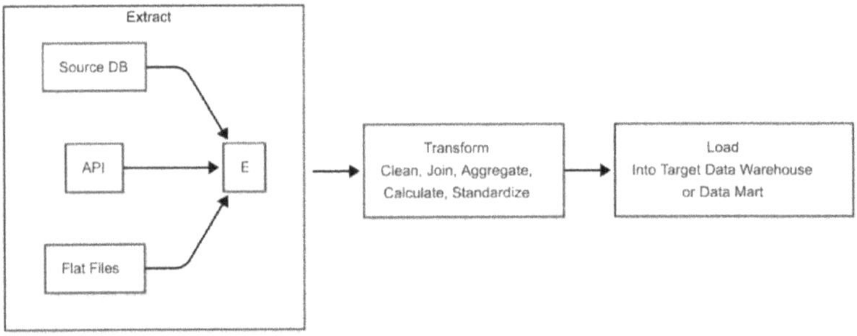

Figure 11 Star Schema vs. Snowflake Schema

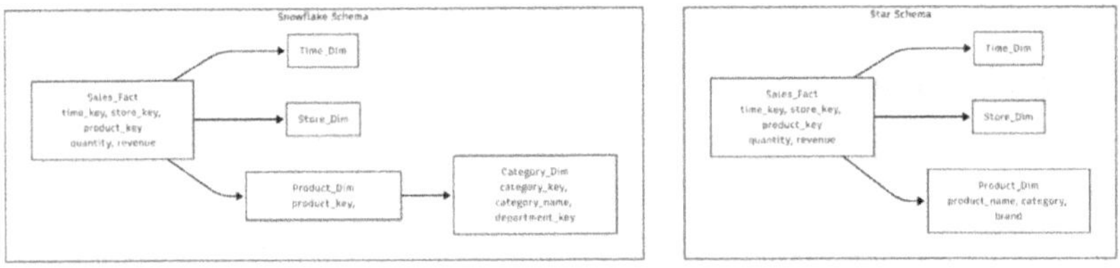

Step-by-Step Method:

1. **Clean:** Address **missing values** by imputing, flagging, or removing them using methods like **K-Nearest Neighbors imputation**. Correct obvious errors and investigate **outliers** before deciding how to handle them, such as **trimming** or **winsorizing.**
2. **Harmonize:** Standardize formats such as dates to YYYY-MM-DD, units, and categorical values like mapping "NY," "New York," and "N.Y." to "New York".
3. **Transform and Engineer Features:** Create new, informative variables. Apply transformations, such as **logarithmic or Box-Cox**, to address **skewness**. Apply **standardization (z-score)** or **normalization (min-max)** techniques to scale features appropriately for the chosen algorithm. Examples include:

    - From Dates: Calculate 'Customer Tenure'.
    - From Transactions: Create 'Average Transaction Value'.
    - **Composite Feature:** Create payment_to_income _ratio = monthly_payment / monthly_income.
4. **Merge/Join datasets:** Carefully combine datasets using appropriate join types (inner, left, right) to retain necessary records without duplicating or losing data. This step is essential to creating a **star schema** for analysis.
5. **Validate output:** After each major step, perform checks to confirm data integrity, such as verifying row counts and maintaining key relationships.

Table 13 Data Transformation Methods & Purpose

Transformation Method	Primary Purpose	Common Use Case
Log / Square Root	Correct positive skewness, stabilize variance.	Monetary amounts, size metrics, time intervals.
Standardization (Z-score)	Center data around zero with unit variance.	Preprocessing for distance-based algorithms (k-means, PCA).
Normalization (Min-Max)	Scale data to a fixed range (e.g., [0,1]).	Preparing data for neural networks.
One-Hot Encoding	Convert categorical (nominal) variables to numeric format.	Including categorical predictors in regression/ML models.
Binning / Discretization	Group continuous values into categories.	Simplifying complex relationships, creating ordinal features.

Examples:

- **E-Commerce Customer Segmentation**
    - **Raw data:** Separate tables for Orders, Customers, and Product_Catalog.
    - **Cleaning:** Remove test orders from Orders where customer_id is null.
    - **Harmonization:** Standardize state abbreviations to two-letter codes in Customers.
    - **Feature engineering & transformation:**
        - avg_order_value: Total revenue divided by the number of orders.
        - days_since_last_purchase: The current date minus the date of the most recent order date.

        - Apply **log transformation** to avg_order_value to decrease positive skew.
    - **Merge & schema:** Perform joins to build a **star schema** with a central Customer_Fact table connected to Product_Dim and Time_Dim tables.

Common Pitfalls:

- **Over-Cleaning:** Eliminating significant outliers that indicate important business cases (e.g., fraud).
- **Join Errors:** Using an inner join instead of a left join, accidentally excluding an entire customer segment.
- **Feature Frenzy:** Creating hundreds of new features without a solid hypothesis, resulting in overfitting and models that are difficult to interpret.
- **Defaulting to mean imputation:** using straightforward imputation that disregards relationships in the data.
- **Choosing the wrong schema:** Designing a complex **snowflake schema** when a simple **star schema** would suffice, which harms query performance.

Lesson 3.6: Data Quality Assessment and Exploration

Objective:
Assess data against established quality standards and conduct exploratory analysis to uncover patterns, relationships, and features that guide modeling.

Detailed Explanation:
Before building models, evaluate the data's health and understand its characteristics. This lesson combines quantitative data quality assessment with **Exploratory Data Analysis** (EDA). It assesses data against standard quality dimensions, using statistical summaries and visualizations to reveal distributions, correlations, and potential anomalies. This approach ensures the data is fit for purpose and aids in forming key hypotheses for modeling. Understanding the **Levels of Measurement**, specifically Nominal, Ordinal, Interval, and Ratio, is required to select appropriate statistical methods and visual tools.

Table 14 Levels of Measurement

Level	Properties	Central Tendency	Example
Nominal	Categories, no order.	Mode	Country, Product Type
Ordinal	Categories with meaningful order.	Median, Mode	Satisfaction Rating (Poor...Excellent)
Interval	Numeric, ordered, no true zero.	Mean, Median, Mode	Temperature (°C), IQ Score
Ratio	Numeric, ordered, true zero exists.	Mean, Median, Mode	Height, Revenue, Time

Key Definitions:

- **Data quality dimensions:** Measurable aspects of data health, including Completeness, Accuracy, Consistency, Timeliness, Validity, and Uniqueness.

Table 15 The Six Core Dimensions of Data Quality

Dimension	Key Question It Answers	Example Metric
Completeness	Is all the necessary data present?	"% of records with non-null values for critical fields"
Accuracy	Does the data reflect the real-world truth?	"% of records matching a verified source"
Consistency	Is the data uniform across systems?	"% of records where 'cust_status' values align across CRM & Billing"
Timeliness	Is the data available when needed?	"Average latency from event to analysis-ready data"
Validity	Does the data conform to defined rules?	"% of records where 'age' is between 18 and 120"
Uniqueness	Are there unintended duplicate records?	"Number of duplicate customer IDs per 10,000 records"

- **Data profiling:** The use of automated tools to analyze data content and structure, revealing patterns and statistics.
- **Exploratory data analysis (EDA):** An approach to analyzing datasets to summarize their main features, often using visual methods.
- **Levels of measurement:** A hierarchical classification that defines the valid operations for various data types:
    - **Nominal** (categories, mode)
    - **Ordinal** (ordered categories, median)
    - **Interval** (numeric, no true zero, mean)
    - **Ratio** (numeric, true zero, all operations)
- **Composite feature:** A new attribute derived through mathematical or logical integration of two or more existing features (e.g., BMI = weight/height^2).

Step-by-Step Method:

1. **Profile the dataset:** Generate summary statistics appropriate for the **level of measurement** (mode for nominal, median for ordinal, mean for interval/ratio). Calculate counts for missing values.

2. **Assess quality dimensions:** Measure each dimension quantitatively.
    - **Completeness:** % of non-missing values.
    - **Validity:** percentage of values that conform to defined rules (e.g., age between 18 and 120).
    - **Uniqueness:** Number of duplicate records.
    - **Accuracy:** Evaluate against a gold standard whenever possible.
3. **Visualize distributions and relationships:** Create plots based on data type:
    - **Histograms and Box plots:** Used for analyzing single numeric (Ratio/Interval) variables to observe shape, center, spread, skewness, and outliers.
    - **Bar charts:** Used for categorical (Nominal/Ordinal) variables.
    - **Scatter plots:** Used to show relationships between two numeric variables.
    - **Heatmaps:** Used for visualizing correlation matrices or cross-tabulations.
4. **Analyze multivariate relationships:** Use correlation matrices for numeric data, pair plots, or clustered heatmaps to observe how variables interact. Correlation describes association. It does not establish causation.
5. **Create insightful composite features:** Use domain knowledge and EDA patterns to engineer new features that capture complex relationships.

Examples:

- **Loan Default Prediction**
    - **Quality assessment:**
        - *Completeness:* 98% for income, 70% for the credit_score fields.
        - *Level of measurement:* Credit_Score is **Interval**, Income is **Ratio**.
    - **EDA visualization:**
        - *Histogram:* Shows debt_to_income_ratio is right-skewed.
        - *Box Plot:* Shows loan_amount has extreme outliers (possible fraud flags).
        - *Scatter Plot:* Demonstrates a positive correlation between income and loan_amount.

- **Multivariate analysis:** The heatmap of the correlation matrix shows a negative correlation between credit_score and default.
- **Composite feature:** Create payment_to_income_ratio = monthly_payment / monthly_income, representing a more straightforward **ratio** measure of the repayment burden.

Common Pitfalls:

- **Confusing correlation with causation:** Observing that ice_cream_sales and pool_drownings are correlated and inferring that one causes the other (both are driven by summer heat).
- **Using invalid statistics:** Calculating the mean for **ordinal** data (e.g., satisfaction ratings).
- **Automation without validation:** Blindly trusting automated profiling reports without performing a domain sense-check.
- **Ignoring context:** Labeling valid business data as an "outlier" without understanding the operational reason behind it.

Lesson 3.7: Data Collection and Experimental Design

Objective:
Plan and execute data collection through observational studies or controlled experiments to establish valid causal relationships between input variables and outcomes.

Detailed Explanation:
While many analytics depend on existing data, some business questions require creating new data-collection initiatives to obtain missing information or establish causal relationships. This process involves choosing between observational studies and controlled experiments. The **Design of Experiments** (**DOE**) is a structured approach for planning experiments to identify cause-and-effect relationships between input variables and output responses. **Response Surface Methodology** (**RSM**) further improves DOE by modeling and optimizing nonlinear relationships.

Key Definitions:

- **Design of Experiments (DOE):** A systematic and efficient method for planning experiments to identify the relationship between input factors (X's) and output responses (Y's).
- **Randomization:** The process of randomly assigning experimental runs to control for lurking variables.
- **Factorial design:** An experimental framework that investigates all potential combinations of factors and their respective levels.
- **Response Surface Methodology (RSM):** A set of DOE techniques used to model, analyze, and optimize a response with a curved (non-linear) relationship, often utilizing a central composite design.
- **Observational data:** Data gathered without interfering with the process, where the analyst acts as a passive observer.

Step-by-Step Method:

1. **Define the objective and response:** Clearly state the goal (e.g., maximize yield, minimize defects) and identify the measurable output variable (Y).
2. **Select input factors and levels:** Choose the key process variables (Xs) to evaluate and assign high and low levels to each.

3. **Select an appropriate experimental design:** Use a **factorial design** for screening purposes. To optimize a suspected nonlinear process, use a **Response Surface Methodology (RSM)** design such as a Central Composite Design.
4. **Randomize the run order:** Run the experiments in a random sequence to prevent confounding from uncontrolled variables.
5. **Conduct runs and gathers data:** Follow the plan while carefully recording responses.
6. **Analyze results:** Use statistical techniques such as ANOVA for factorial designs and regression modeling for Response Surface Methodology (RSM) to identify significant factors and determine the optimal settings.

Examples:

Example 1: Website Conversion Optimization

- **Objective:** Increase sign-up conversion rate (Y).
- **Factors:** Headline (A/B), Button Color (Red/Green), Page Layout (Single/Multi-step).
- **Design:** A full **factorial design** with 2^3 factors, producing 8 unique website versions.
- **Execution:** Randomly assign site visitors to one of the 8 versions within a specified timeframe.
- **Analysis:** ANOVA shows that Headline and Page Layout have a significant interaction effect on the conversion rate.

Example 2: Chemical Process Optimization

- **Objective:** Maximize purity yield (Y).
- **Factors:** Temperature, Pressure, Reaction Time.
- **Design:** After conducting a factorial DOE experiment to identify the most important factors, apply a Response Surface Methodology (RSM) with a Central Composite Design to model the curved relationships and determine the optimal temperature and time settings.

Common Pitfalls:

- **Not randomizing:** Failing to randomize the run order, which allows trends over time to bias results.

- **Confusing observational and experimental data:** Assuming causality from observational data where only association can be claimed.
- **Overlooking interactions:** Employing one-factor-at-a-time experiments rather than factorial designs, thereby overlooking significant factor interactions.

Lesson 3.8: Documenting and Communicating Data Findings

Objective:
Synthesize and communicate findings from data assessment and exploration to both technical and non-technical stakeholders, enabling informed decisions about whether to proceed, adjust scope, or resolve data issues before modeling begins.

Detailed Explanation:
Insights from data assessment are useless if they are not communicated well. A Data Findings Report is essential because it turns technical observations into straightforward, actionable business language. It presents data quality, limitations, and initial findings, helping stakeholders decide whether to proceed with modeling, adjust the project scope, or address critical data issues first. Proper documentation helps bridge the gap between the data team and the business. Effective communication uses clear visualizations, such as **line charts** for tracking trends, **histograms** for data distribution, and **scatter plots** to show relationships.

Key Definitions:

- **Data findings report:** A formal document that summarizes the current data status, identifies quality issues, highlights key patterns, and provides recommendations.
- **Stakeholder transparency:** The practice of openly sharing both the potential and limitations of the data with all project participants.
- **Actionable recommendation:** A clear, data-supported proposal for subsequent project actions (e.g., "proceed," "pause and rectify data," "revise scope").

Step-by-Step Method:

1. **Structure the report:** Use a clear format including Executive Summary, Data Inventory, Quality Assessment, Exploratory Insights, Limitations, and Recommendations.
2. **Tailor the message:** For executives, focus on high-impact recommendations. For technical teams, provide detailed metrics and profiles.

3. **Quantify issues:** Do not simply state "data is messy." Instead, specify: "The customer_region field is 40% incomplete, which will reduce model accuracy for geographic segments."
4. **Highlight key insights:** Include the most revealing charts from EDA.
    - A **Line chart** illustrating a time trend.
    - A **Histogram** or **Box Plot** to display a skewed distribution or outlier issue.
    - A **Scatter Plot** or **Heatmap** to emphasize a key relationship or correlation.
5. **Provide clear and actionable recommendations:** Based on the findings, present a straightforward, binary-compatible suggestion (e.g., "We recommend pausing model development for two weeks to fix a data collection issue with the region field.").

Examples:

- **Report Summary for a Marketing Mix Model:**
    - **Executive Summary:** Data quality is acceptable to move forward, though with some cautions. The digital advertising spend data is thorough. The competitor pricing data is delayed by three weeks, which limits real-time optimization.
    - **Recommendation:** Proceed with Phase 1 modeling using the current data and form a team to improve the competitor data pipeline.
    - **Key Finding (Visual):** A **scatter plot** in the appendix shows a strong correlation (r=0.85) between social media impressions and website visits, and a weak correlation between impressions and final sales. This indicates that social media primarily functions as a top-of-funnel activity.

Common Pitfalls:

- **Hiding problems:** Using mild language to minimize serious data quality issues, which creates a false sense of confidence.
- **Data dumping:** Presenting numerous charts and statistics without context or explanation.
- **Unclear next steps:** Leaving stakeholders unsure of what to do with the information.
- **Using misleading visuals:** selecting an inappropriate chart type that hides the message.

Lesson 3.9: Validating and Refining Problem Statements with Data Evidence

Objective:
To thoroughly reassess the original business and analytics problem statements by considering data findings and to refine them to ensure they remain feasible, relevant, and properly scoped.

Detailed Explanation:
The data assessment phase often reveals that initial assumptions were incorrect. This step formalizes the essential feedback loop where data insights influence the problem definition. Data assessment regularly reveals that the target variable cannot be measured as defined, a key driver is missing from available sources, or the data points to a more urgent issue than originally scoped. Validating and updating the problem statements helps ensure the project remains focused on a meaningful, solvable problem and prevents wasting effort on a flawed analysis. This step completes the loop with the Framing domain.

Key Definitions

- **Validation:** Formal review of initial business and analytics assumptions against data to confirm feasibility, relevance, and scope before modeling.
- **Feasibility:** The practical viability of solving an analytics problem based on available data, considering completeness, representativeness, measurement levels, and quality.
- **Refinement:** The iterative adjustment of the problem statement's scope, target variable, or analytical approach based on data-driven insights from the assessment.

Figure 12 Validating & Refining the Problem Statement

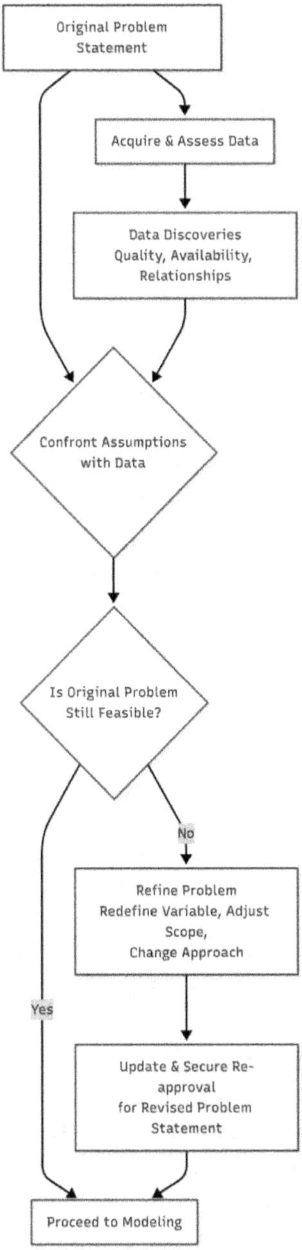

Step-by-Step Method:

1. **Verify assumptions with data:** Review the implicit assumptions made during framing. For each one, ask, "Does the data support this?" and use profiling and exploratory data analysis (EDA) as supporting evidence.
2. **Assess feasibility:** Given the current state of data quality and observed relationships, determine whether the original analytics problem statement remains practically achievable. Evaluate the **levels of measurement** for each variable, the extent and pattern of **missing data**, and whether the available data represents the population the model must serve.
3. **Identify necessary changes:** Determine the specific modifications needed. Options include:
   - **Redefining the target variable** (e.g., from "predict absolute sales" to "predict sales trend").
   - **Refining the scope** (e.g., from "all customer segments" to "only the segment with sufficient data").
   - **Switching the analytical approach** (e.g., from a predictive model to descriptive segmentation).
4. **Update and secure re-approval:** Revise the Business and Analytics Problem Statements along with the Project Charter. Present the data-driven rationale for these modifications to the sponsor and obtain formal endorsement prior to progressing to the modeling phase.

Examples:

- **Example 1: Customer Churn Project**
  - **Original analytics problem:** "Predict churn risk for all customers in the next 90 days."
  - **Data discovery:** The churn flag in historical data is only reliably recorded for subscription customers, not for one-time buyers.
  - **Validation outcome:** The problem is not feasible as stated for the entire customer base.
  - **Refined problem statement:** "Predict the churn risk for subscription customers over the next 90 days." (Scope adjusted to align with data reality)

- **Example 2: Demand Forecasting Project**
  - **Original assumption:** "Historical demand patterns are stable and predictive."

- **Data discovery:** EDA reveals a significant one-time surge in demand approximately 18 months prior, caused by an isolated event that skewed all later historical averages.
- **Validation outcome:** The fundamental forecasting assumption has been breached.
- **Refined approach:** Model demand excluding the anomalous period or redefine the problem as "Identify and forecast demand during exceptional events."

Common Pitfalls:

- **Plowing ahead:** Ignoring clear data signals that indicate the problem is flawed due to **sunk costs** or timeline pressure.
- **Scope creep:** Justifying unrestrained project expansion with data insights (e.g., 'Now that we observe this additional interesting pattern, let's also consider that...').
- **Poor change management:** Making significant alterations to the problem definition without clear communication and realignment with stakeholders.

Summary

Scoping and prioritizing data requirements involve transforming conceptual variables into specific data elements, balancing business value with ease of collection. Each variable is connected to tangible data fields evaluated through a value-feasibility framework, which categorizes sources as critical, strategic investments, quick wins, or deferrals. This process directs data collection efforts toward what really impacts model success, rather than just what is readily available. Additionally, legal, contractual, and technical usage constraints are identified early to avoid rework and compliance problems later.

Data sources are carefully assessed using the 5 Vs, which are Volume, Velocity, Variety, Veracity, and Value, to determine their suitability and guide architecture decisions. An overall data management plan oversees the entire data lifecycle, from collection to disposal, establishing quality standards, security protocols, and stewardship roles. Metadata management supports discoverability, consistency, and lineage tracking, transforming disorganized data into a reliable organizational asset.

Ethical data collection requires careful attention to sampling techniques, bias detection, and handling sensitive information. Sampling bias, such as systematic exclusion or overrepresentation, must be documented and mitigated using methods such as stratified sampling. Privacy measures, including anonymization and pseudonymization, protect personally identifiable information, while data lineage records the sources, transformations, and movements of data to ensure reproducibility and auditability. Data preparation then accounts for most of the project effort, involving cleaning, harmonizing, transforming, and feature engineering, to create useful variables such as ratios, aggregates, or derived attributes that reveal patterns hidden in the raw data.

Quality assessment and exploratory data analysis confirm data fitness through quantitative measures across the dimensions of completeness, accuracy, consistency, timeliness, validity, and uniqueness. Visualizations such as histograms, scatter plots, and heatmaps reveal distributions, relationships, and anomalies. Understanding measurement levels, including nominal, ordinal, interval, and ratio, ensures appropriate statistical treatment. For questions requiring new data collection, experimental designs like factorial designs or response surface methodology establish causal relationships beyond simple observational associations. A data findings report synthesizes these discoveries into actionable recommendations, and the original problem statements are validated against actual data conditions, which helps refine scope, target variables, or analytical approaches before securing sponsor re-approval to proceed.

Chapter 3: Practice Questions

Q1. When using a Value-Feasibility matrix to rank data sources, how should an analyst classify a data source that is essential for model success but is very costly and difficult to integrate?
A) Defer or exclude
B) Quick win
C) Strategic investment
D) Critical

Q2. What is the main risk of choosing a Data Lake architecture for a project that only requires daily standardized financial reporting?
A) High storage cost
B) Architecture misalignment and unnecessary complexity
C) Inability to store unstructured data
D) Poor performance for machine learning

Q3. Within a data management strategy, what is the primary operational responsibility of a Data Steward?
A) Defining the overall data strategy
B) Enforcing data quality standards and governance policies
C) Approving the budget for data tools
D) Writing extraction code for ETL pipelines

Q4. During data acquisition, you find that your main dataset over-represents urban users and under-represents rural ones. What issue does this introduce?
A) Systemic uncertainty (bias)
B) High statistical uncertainty
C) A metadata gap
D) A veracity problem that can be fixed with more data

Q5. In feature engineering, creating a new variable, such as BMI, from weight and height, is known as what?
A) A transformed feature
B) A normalized feature
C) A composite feature
D) An encoded feature

Q6. You are evaluating data quality and discover that 30% of records in the postal_code field are null. Which data quality dimension is being

assessed?
A) Accuracy
B) Validity
C) Completeness
D) Uniqueness

Q7. A stakeholder requests a visualization comparing the central tendency and variability of customer satisfaction scores (on a 1-5 scale) across four retail stores. Which single plot type is most suitable?
A) A set of pie charts
B) A stacked bar chart
C) Side-by-side box plots
D) A single histogram

Q8. In a Designed Experiment (DOE), why is randomizing the run order important?
A) To make the experiment faster
B) To reduce the number of runs needed
C) To control for the effects of lurking variables
D) To ensure a normal distribution of the response

Q9. You have a numeric variable that exhibits a strong positive skew and contains no negative values. To make its distribution more symmetric for a regression analysis, which transformation specifically aims to identify the best power transformation?
A) Min-Max Scaling
B) Z-score Standardization
C) Box-Cox Transformation
D) One-Hot Encoding

Q10. What is the key functional difference between anonymization and pseudonymization of PII?
A) Anonymization is for structured data, pseudonymization for unstructured data.
B) Anonymization is irreversible, pseudonymization is reversible with a key.
C) Pseudonymization is required by GDPR, anonymization is not.
D) Anonymization removes data, while pseudonymization encrypts it.

Q11. You need to merge a customer's table (which contains all customers) with a Purchases table, but you only want to retain records

for customers who have made at least one purchase. What type of JOIN should you use?
A) LEFT JOIN
B) INNER JOIN
C) RIGHT JOIN
D) FULL OUTER JOIN

Q12. When evaluating the veracity of a new external data source, what are two specific actions an analyst should take?
A) Check its cost and assess its volume.
B) Profile the data and assess its provenance.
C) Load it into a lake and test query speed.
D) Stratify it and calculate the margin of error.

Q13. A survey question asks, "How often do you exercise? (Options: Never, Rarely, Sometimes, Often, Always)." What is the level of measurement for this variable?
A) Nominal
B) Ordinal
C) Interval
D) Ratio

Q14. In the context of ETL, what is the primary purpose of the Transform stage?
A) To move data from source to target as quickly as possible.
B) To cleanse, standardize, and apply business logic to the data.
C) To decide which data sources to extract from.
D) To grant users access to the final data.

Q15. You are building a k-means clustering model with annual_salary (range: $40k-$200k) and age (range: 20-65). Why is feature scaling important?
A) To address missing values in both features.
B) To create a combined feature from salary and age.
C) To prevent the variable with the larger range (salary) from dominating the distance calculation.
D) To reduce skewness in the age variable.

Q16. What is the main purpose of stratified sampling?
A) To select individuals from randomly selected geographic clusters.
B) To ensure every individual in the population has an equal chance of

selection.
C) To ensure proportional representation of key subgroups within the sample.
D) To lower data collection costs by sampling pre-existing groups.

Q17. You notice a strong positive correlation in a scatter plot between the number_of_website_visits and total_monthly_sales. Can you conclude causation?
A) Yes, because correlation is a reliable indicator of causation.
B) No, because the association could be due to a confounding variable or reverse causality.
C) Yes, but only if the sample size is very large.
D) No, because scatter plots cannot show correlation.

Q18. Which data architecture is characterized by a "Schema-on-Read" approach?
A) Data Lake
B) Data Warehouse
C) Relational Database
D) Data Mart

Q19. During data preparation, applying a **winsorizing** technique at the 95th percentile to a variable modifies the data. What does this do?
A) It removes the top and bottom 5% of values entirely.
B) It caps the top 5% of values at the 95th percentile value.
C) It normalizes all values to a range between 0 and 1.
D) It replaces missing values with the 95th percentile value.

Q20. After data exploration, you discover that a key driver variable assumed in the problem framing is unavailable. What is a valid option for refining the project?
A) Proceed with the model using only available data, ignoring the missing driver.
B) Adjust the project scope to address a related question that can be answered with the available data.
C) Immediately cancel the project.
D) Use a proxy variable without documenting the substitution.

Chapter 4: Methodology Selection

Introduction

Selecting the right methodology is a defining step in the analytics lifecycle, where theoretical problem framing meets practical solution design. This stage involves selecting appropriate analytical techniques, assessing their suitability under real-world constraints, and developing a technical implementation plan. Proficiency in this area ensures that analytical solutions are theoretically valid, practical, scalable, and aligned with business objectives and technical capabilities. This knowledge helps manage the trade-offs between methodological complexity and practical implementation, a core skill for strategic analytics leaders.

Lesson 4.1: Principles of Analytical Methodology Selection

Objective:

Align analytical techniques with specific problem types, data characteristics, and business objectives through a structured selection process.

Detailed Explanation:

Choosing the right analytical method is a key skill that connects understanding the problem to finding a solution. The process involves identifying the main analytical need, understanding the available data, and matching the data to suitable techniques. This requires a solid grasp of statistical principles to accurately interpret data and the problem structure. The right choice balances analytical rigor with practicality, ensuring the approach addresses the business question directly rather than defaulting to complex techniques without justification.

Table 16 Comparison of Analytical Method Types

Method Type	Key Question	Example Techniques	When to Use
Descriptive	What happened?	Summary statistics, Data visualization, Aggregation, Reporting	Understanding historical patterns, Creating dashboards, KPI tracking
Diagnostic	Why did it happen?	Correlation analysis, Root cause analysis, Drill-down, Hypothesis testing	Investigating causes, Understanding relationships between variables
Predictive	What will happen?	Regression, Classification, Time series forecasting, Ensemble methods (e.g., Random Forest, Gradient Boosting)	Forecasting, Risk assessment, Propensity modeling, Churn prediction
Prescriptive	What should we do?	Optimization, Simulation, Recommendation systems, Decision analysis	Decision support, Resource allocation, Planning, Scheduling

Key Definitions:

- **Descriptive Analytics:** Techniques that summarize and describe historical data patterns to answer, "What has happened?" (e.g., summary statistics, data visualization).
- **Diagnostic Analytics:** Methods that examine data to find causal relationships and answer "Why did it happen?" (e.g., correlation analysis, hypothesis testing).
- **Predictive Analytics:** Approaches that use statistical models and machine learning algorithms to forecast future outcomes, answering 'What is likely to happen?
- **Prescriptive Analytics:** Techniques that recommend the best actions within defined constraints, answering 'What should we do?' (e.g., optimization, simulation).

Step-by-Step Method:

1. **Classify the core analytical need:** Review the problem statement to identify its primary purpose. Is it about understanding the past, explaining causes, forecasting the future, or recommending actions?
2. **Assess data characteristics and foundational statistics:** Evaluate the volume, variety, velocity, and quality of the available data. Conduct initial statistical diagnostics:
   - Calculate **measures of central tendency** (mean, median, mode) to understand the typical value of the data, such as choosing the median for skewed data to avoid the influence of outliers.
   - Calculate **measures of dispersion** such as variance, standard deviation, and interquartile range to quantify uncertainty and risk.
   - Evaluate the distribution shape using **skewness** (asymmetry) and **kurtosis** (tailedness). For example, check for **heteroscedasticity** (non-constant variance) when working with regression models.
3. **Map techniques to problem type:**
   - **Understanding patterns (descriptive/diagnostic):** Use summary statistics, data visualization, segmentation (clustering), association rules (for market basket analysis), and correlation studies. To compare groups, apply **ANOVA** (for three or more group means) or **non-parametric tests** (e.g., Kruskal-Wallis) if data do not meet normality assumptions.
   - **Forecasting outcomes (predictive):** Use regression models such as linear regression for continuous outcomes and logistic regression for binary outcomes. Apply classification algorithms such as decision trees, **k-nearest neighbors (KNN)**, support vector machines, and naive Bayes. For time-dependent data, use time-series methods such as ARIMA and exponential smoothing, and ensemble techniques such as random forests and gradient boosting.
   - **Optimizing decisions (prescriptive):** Use optimization models including linear, integer, and mixed-integer programming, simulation techniques such

as Monte Carlo and discrete-event simulation, decision analysis frameworks such as decision trees and **influence diagrams**, and multi-objective methods to manage trade-offs.

4. **Implement the principle of adequate simplicity:** Select the simplest method that meets business needs and data requirements. Avoid unnecessary complexity that adds costs without enough benefits. A clear **linear regression** model is preferable to a black-box neural network if it provides useful insights and simplifies operations.

Figure 13 Methodology Selection Decision Flow

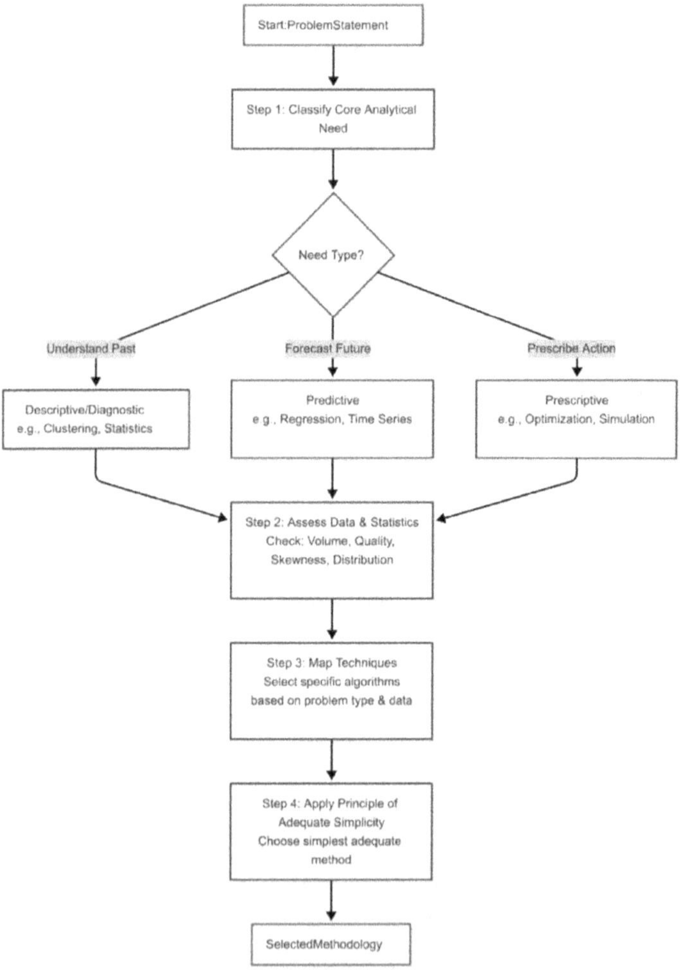

Examples:

- **Example 1: Understanding Customer Base Composition**
  - *Business Need:* "We want to understand the different types of customers in our database to customize marketing messages."
  - *Core Analytical Requirement:* Descriptive (segmentation and profiling).
  - *Appropriate Methodology:* Cluster analysis (e.g., K-means) for behavioral segmentation combined with demographic profiling. Before clustering, apply **Principal Component Analysis** (**PCA**) to reduce dimensionality when many behavioral variables are highly correlated
  - *Rationale:* Clustering is an unsupervised learning technique that identifies natural groups without predefined categories, making it well suited for discovery-based segmentation.

- **Example 2: Forecasting Product Demand**
  - *Business Need:* "We need to forecast next quarter's sales for inventory planning."
  - *Core Analytical Requirement:* Predictive (time-based forecasting).
  - *Appropriate Methodology:* **Time series analysis.** First, decompose the series into trend, seasonality, and residual components. Then, select **SARIMA** (Seasonal Autoregressive Integrated Moving Average) if seasonal, or **Holt-Winters** exponential smoothing based on the components. Validate the model using metrics on a hold-out sample.
  - *Rationale:* These methods explicitly model temporal patterns, including trend, seasonality, and autocorrelation, which standard regression ignores. When reporting average growth rates across multiple forecast periods, use the **geometric mean** rather than the arithmetic mean to avoid overstating performance.

- **Example 3: Optimizing Delivery Routes**
  - *Business Need:* "We need to identify the most efficient daily delivery routes for our fleet to reduce fuel costs and delivery time."
  - *Core Analytical Requirement:* Prescriptive (optimization within constraints).

- *Appropriate Methodology:* Formulate it as a **Vehicle Routing Problem (VRP)**, a type of **combinatorial optimization.** Use **Integer Programming** or a **Metaheuristic** such as Tabu Search for large, complex instances. Conduct a **Sensitivity Analysis** on travel times or demand after finding a solution.
- *Rationale:* These methods are designed to find the optimal solution within specific constraints (vehicle capacity, time windows, driver hours).

Common Pitfalls:

- **A solution in search of a problem:** Opting for a complex, trendy approach like deep learning without first verifying it fits the specific business question and data scenario.
- **Misclassification:** Confusing a predictive problem such as 'will this customer churn?' with a descriptive one such as 'what do churned customers look like?' leads to addressing the wrong question and producing results the business cannot act on.
- **Ignoring method assumptions:** Using techniques without first confirming that the data meet their basic statistical or operational criteria. For instance, using linear regression on non-linear data (violating linearity assumptions), performing a **t-test or ANOVA** without checking for normality and homogeneity of variances, or conducting a **Chi-square test** with expected cell counts less than 5.
- **Correlation versus Causation Fallacy:** Interpreting a correlation coefficient as evidence of a causal relationship without considering confounding variables or establishing temporal precedence.
- **Misinterpreting probabilistic outputs:** Confusing the p-value, which is the probability of observing data as extreme as observed given the null hypothesis is true, with the probability that the null hypothesis itself is true. These are not the same thing. A related error is treating a confidence interval as a statement that there is a 95% probability the true parameter falls within a specific range. The interval is fixed once calculated. The probability statement refers to the long-run behavior of the method.

Lesson 4.2: Evaluating Methods Against Practical Constraints

Objective:
Select the most suitable methodology by assessing analytical benefits alongside practical resource limitations and business requirements.

Detailed Explanation:
The most theoretically optimal approach is often not the most practical. This lesson emphasizes the shift from academic ideals to real-world application. It requires a clear evaluation of constraints, including data quality, timeline, budget, expertise, and computational resources, alongside an honest assessment of trade-offs among performance, interpretability, cost, and speed. The aim is to select a technique that delivers enough business value within practical limits. This process should also consider inferential requirements, such as the need for **confidence intervals** or hypothesis testing to support decision-making.

Key Definitions:

- **Technical merit:** The inherent capabilities of a method, such as its predictive accuracy, ability to handle complex patterns, and computational efficiency.
- **Business fit:** The alignment of a method with organizational needs, including interpretability for stakeholders, actionability of results, implementation speed, and maintenance costs.
- **Implementation feasibility:** The realistic ability to deploy a methodology using current resources, skills, and technology infrastructure.
- **Inferential rigor:** The methodological soundness required to draw valid conclusions about populations from samples, including the proper design of confidence intervals and hypothesis testing.

Step-by-Step Method:

1. **Define practical and inferential constraints:** Clearly document limitations related to the timeline, budget, data availability, in-house expertise, technological infrastructure, and the necessary level of statistical confidence (e.g., 95% confidence intervals, $\alpha=0.05$).

2. **Generate candidate methods:** Choose 2-3 practical methodological approaches from the initial screening process.
3. **Perform a constraint-based evaluation:** For each candidate, evaluate:
   - **Data requirements versus availability:** Does the method need labeled data, large amounts, specific data types such as images for CNNs, or clean, stationary time series? Does the data meet the method's distribution assumptions, such as normality for parametric tests?
   - **Expertise, development, & analytical time:** Does the team have the skills to implement it and interpret it correctly? How long will development take? Does the timeline include proper validation, such as train-test splits and cross-validation?
   - **Computational and operational costs:** What are the hardware and software expenses? What is the long-term burden of maintenance and monitoring (e.g., retraining neural networks versus maintaining a logistic regression)?
   - **Output interpretability and actionability:** Can stakeholders understand and trust the results? A **random forest** provides feature importance but is less interpretable than a **decision tree**. A **Bayesian network** illustrates probabilistic reasoning. A **deep learning** model typically acts as a black box. In regulated industries, the ability to explain individual predictions to auditors or customers is a non-negotiable requirement, not a preference
   - **Inferential needs:** Does the business decision require a measure of uncertainty (e.g., a confidence interval for a forecast) or a hypothesis test (e.g., did the new website design increase conversion)? Methods must support this.
4. **Make the trade-off decision:** Select the method that offers the best balance between adequate performance and high feasibility. A slightly less powerful but more interpretable and maintainable approach is often the best business choice. Use simulation-based optimization only when the system is too complex for analytical models and the necessary computational resources are confirmed.

Examples:

- **Example 1: Building a Credit Risk Model**
  - *Business Need:* Predict the chance of loan default.
  - *Candidate Methods:* Logistic Regression, Random Forest, Neural Network.
  - *Key Constraints:* Regulatory requirement for model explainability. Moderate-sized historical dataset. Six-month timeline. Requirement to provide reasoning for individual credit denials.
  - *Evaluation:*
    1. *Logistic Regression:* High interpretability (coefficients show feature impact) works well with moderate data and is quick to implement. Provides well-understood confidence intervals for coefficients. Lower potential maximum accuracy.
    2. *Random Forest:* Delivers higher accuracy by capturing non-linear relationships. Shows feature importance but lacks clear reasoning for individual predictions, resulting in a 'black box' nature. Less suitable for providing straightforward explanations to customers.
    3. *Neural Network:* Offers the highest potential accuracy. It has very low interpretability, requires large datasets, and takes the longest to develop and tune.
  - *Selection Rationale:* **Logistic Regression** is selected. Although it may have slightly lower accuracy, its high interpretability meets regulatory requirements, and its speed fits the timeline. The business and legal costs of an unexplained model rejection outweigh the marginal improvement in accuracy.

Table 17 Model Trade-off

Model Type	Interpretability	Data Needs	Best Use Case
Logistic Regression	High	Moderate	Regulated industries, when explanations are required
Random Forest	Medium (feature importance)	Large	Complex/non-linear patterns, some explainability needed
Neural Network	Low (black box)	Very Large	Maximum accuracy critical, Image/Text data

- **Example 2: A/B Testing a Web Page Change**
  - *Business Need:* Assess whether a new webpage layout boosts the click-through rate (CTR).
  - *Candidate Methods:* Two-proportion **z-test** (large sample), **Fisher's Exact Test** (small sample).
  - *Key Constraints:* Traffic is limited. The experiment may yield only approximately 50 clicks per variant.
  - *Evaluation:* The **z-test** depends on a normal approximation, which is invalid when expected cell counts fall below 5. **Fisher's Exact Test** calculates the exact p-value without relying on this approximation and is the correct choice when sample sizes are small.
  - *Selection Rationale:* **Fisher's Exact Test** is selected to ensure the statistical validity of the inference due to the small sample size constraint.

Common Pitfalls:

- **Pursuing marginal gains:** Investing disproportionate resources to improve accuracy from 90% to 92%, despite such precision having no impact on business decisions.
- **Underestimating the last mile of deployment:** Focusing only on model development while failing to account for the effort required to implement, monitor, and maintain the model in a live production environment. This includes building retraining pipelines for models whose performance degrades over time, which is often more work than the initial build.
- **Overlooking stakeholder needs:** Selecting a method that yields results that stakeholders find confusing or untrustworthy, leading to rejection of the solution regardless of its technical advantages.
- **Ignoring sample size in inferential planning:** Conducting a **Mann-Whitney U test** or developing a complex model with an inadequate sample size can yield underpowered, inconclusive results.

Lesson 4.3: Designing Technical Architectures for Analytics

Objective:
Design a complete technical framework that supports the implementation, execution, and maintenance of the chosen analytical method.

Detailed Explanation:
A well-designed technical architecture is the blueprint for transforming a methodological concept into a dependable, scalable, and secure analytical solution. This lesson shifts from discussing "what to build" to focusing on "how to build it," highlighting the systems, data flows, and components needed. Architectural design covers the entire data lifecycle, from ingestion to insight delivery, and ensures the solution integrates with existing business processes and technological ecosystems. The design must also support the computational patterns of the chosen methodology, whether that involves batch training a model or real-time transaction scoring.

Key Definitions:

- **Technical architecture:** A detailed description of the software, hardware, network components, and their interactions needed to implement an analytical solution.
- **Data pipeline:** A sequence of automated processes that extract, transform, and load data from source systems to a destination for analysis.
- **Processing paradigm:** The overall data computation approach involves **batch processing** (scheduled tasks on large datasets, such as nightly model retraining), **stream processing** (real-time analysis of live data streams, such as fraud detection), or a combination of these methods.
- **Simulation architecture:** The setup used for conducting computational experiments, which may involve specialized engines tailored for **Discrete Event Simulation (DES)**, **Agent-Based Modeling (ABM)**, or **Monte Carlo** simulation.

Figure 14 Analytics Solution Architecture

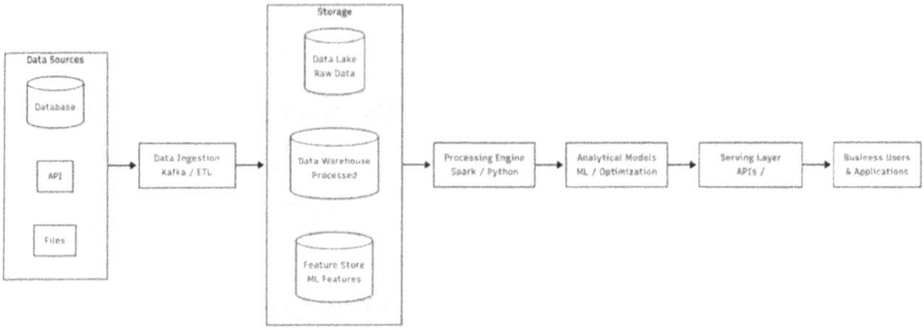

Step-by-Step Method:

1. **Define the data and analytical journey:** Map the entire process flow. Where does raw data originate? How is it ingested? Where is it stored, processed, and modeled? How are results such as predictions, optimized plans, and simulation outputs communicated to end-users or subsequent systems?
2. **Select core processing components:** Choose technologies for key tasks aligned with methodological needs:
    - **Data ingestion:** Tools for extracting data from sources such as APIs, databases, files, and streams.
    - **Storage & management:** Use databases (SQL, NoSQL) or data lakes that suit the data's structure, size, and access requirements, such as fast key-value stores for real-time features.
    - **Transformation and computation:** Frameworks used for data cleaning, feature engineering, and model execution, such as Spark for large-scale data processing, Python or R for modeling, and specialized software for simulations.
    - **Model serving & integration:** Techniques for providing results through REST APIs, embedded libraries, dashboards, or direct updates to operational databases.
3. **Design for integration, scalability, and analytical fidelity:** Plan how the new architecture connects to existing enterprise systems. Ensure the design can accommodate projected growth. Verify that the architecture maintains the integrity of the analytical process, for example, confirming **time series** data is processed in order without look-ahead bias, or

that a **DES model** has a dependable random number generator and a defined warm-up period.

4. **Incorporate foundational requirements from the beginning**: Security measures such as access controls and encryption, monitoring for model performance drift, pipeline errors, and simulation convergence, and reliability measures such as backups and failover mechanisms.

Examples:

- **Example 1: Architecture for a Real-time Personalization Engine**
  - *Business Need:* Deliver personalized product recommendations on a website within milliseconds of a user's click.
  - *Methodology:* A collaborative filtering or lightweight **neural network** model.
  - *Architecture Design:*
    - *Ingestion:* A streaming platform such as Apache Kafka captures real-time user clickstream events.
    - *Storage:* A high-speed key-value repository, such as Redis, maintains user profiles and precomputed features to ensure low-latency access. A dedicated data warehouse stores historical data to support batch retraining of models.
    - *Processing:* A lightweight scoring service (e.g., a Python microservice) retrieves user features and applies a pre-trained model.
    - *Serving:* The recommendation score is provided to the website's front-end through a REST API.
    - *Orchestration:* A workflow manager schedules nightly jobs to retrain models on new data and update the feature store.

Figure 15 Real-time Personalization Engine Architecture

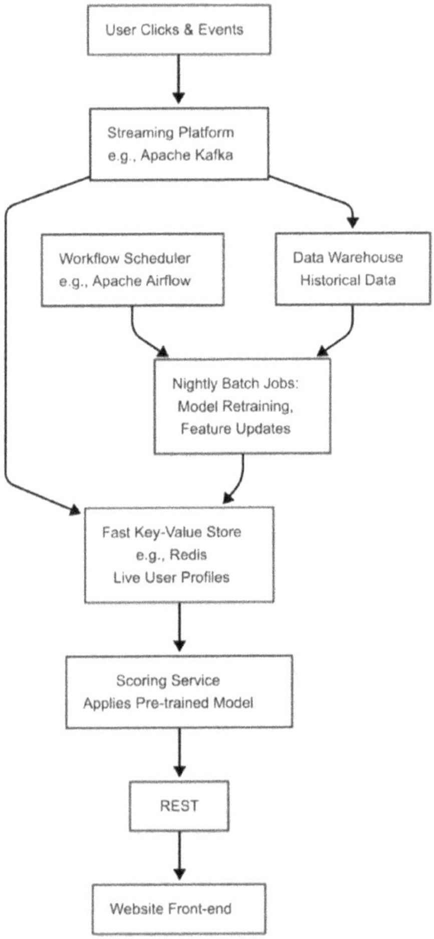

- **Example 2: Architecture for a Supply Chain Simulation**
  - *Business Need:* Run "what-if" scenarios for warehouse layout and inventory policy.
  - *Methodology:* **Discrete Event Simulation (DES)** or **Agent-Based Modeling**.
  - *Architecture Design:*
    - *Ingestion/Data Prep:* Batch jobs extract historical order and shipment data from ERP systems and convert it into a structured format for the simulation model.
    - *Computation:* A specialized simulation engine (e.g., AnyLogic, Simio, custom Python with SimPy) executes

the stochastic model. The architecture must support the execution of thousands of **Monte Carlo** replications, potentially on parallel cloud instances.

- *Storage:* Results from each simulation run, for example, average **cycle time** and resource **utilization,** are recorded in a database for analysis.
- *Serving:* A dashboard retrieves data from the results database to show performance distributions and compare scenarios.

Common Pitfalls:

- **Architecture astronautics:** Designing an excessively complex system that exceeds current and foreseeable needs, raising costs and failure points without providing comparable benefits.
- **Ignoring the production environment:** Building a solution that functions in a data scientist's notebook but cannot be deployed, monitored, or scaled in a production IT setting. This issue is common with complex **deep learning** or large-scale **optimization** models.
- **Creating data silos:** Designing a new system that duplicates data or functions of existing systems without a plan for integration, leading to inconsistency, redundant maintenance effort, and conflicting results across teams.
- **Neglecting simulation execution needs:** Failing to allocate enough computational resources to perform enough simulation replications for statistically meaningful results, which can result in unreliable conclusions.

Lesson 4.4: Selecting and Evaluating Technology Stacks

Objective:
Choose and justify specific software tools, platforms, and infrastructure components that implement the technical architecture.

Detailed Explanation:
This lesson shifts the focus from fundamental architectural principles to the selection of specific technologies. It involves comparing various tools, such as programming languages, databases, analytics platforms, and simulation software, based on factors including functionality, cost, ecosystem, and strategic fit. The assessment should also consider each tool's suitability for implementing the selected analytical methods, including its statistical libraries, optimization solvers, or simulation features. An important part of this process is recognizing the limitations of common but unsuitable tools, such as spreadsheets, for production analytics.

Key Definitions:

- **Technology stack:** The combination of programming languages, frameworks, libraries, databases, and infrastructure tools used to develop and run an application or analytical solution.
- **Open-Source software:** Software with publicly accessible source code, usually available at no cost and open to modification, driven by community development (e.g., Python, R, PostgreSQL, Apache Spark).
- **Proprietary software:** Commercial software in which the source code is owned and controlled by a vendor, usually requiring licensing fees (e.g., certain data science platforms, simulation packages, optimization solvers).
- **Total Cost of Ownership (TCO):** The complete cost of a technology during its lifecycle, covering acquisition, development, deployment, operation, maintenance, and retirement.

Step-by-Step Method:

1. **Translate architecture and methodology into specific requirements:** List the necessary functionalities from the technology stack, such as "must support real-time streaming," "must include a reliable linear programming solver," "must have libraries for ARIMA and neural networks," and "must offer a DES modeling environment."
2. **Research and create a shortlist of options:** For each component (database, processing engine, modeling environment, solver, etc.), identify 2-3 leading open-source and proprietary candidates.
3. **Perform a multi-dimensional evaluation:** Compare candidates with a weighted scorecard. Key dimensions include:
    - **Functional & analytical fit:** Does it fulfill the technical and *methodological* criteria? (e.g., Does it include the necessary statistical tests? Can it handle mixed-integer problems? Does it support agent-based modeling?)
    - **Cost (TCO):** Licensing/subscription fees, development effort, and operational overhead.
    - **Ecosystem and community:** The quality of documentation, availability of talent, third-party integrations, and the strength of libraries supporting chosen methods (e.g., scikit-learn for machine learning, statsmodels for statistical analysis).
    - **Strategic alignment:** Is it consistent with the organization's existing technology standards and future directions?
4. **Recognize tool limitations:** Identify when common tools, such as spreadsheets, are insufficient for the task, typically because of requirements for scale, automation, collaboration, or statistical rigor or robustness.

Table 18 Technology Evaluation Dimensions

Dimension	Open Source	Proprietary	Key Consideration
Functional Fit	High (customizable)	Varies (vendor roadmap)	Does it meet all technical & analytical requirements?
Cost (TCO)	Low (no license fees)	High (annual subscriptions)	Total cost over 3-5 years including support & training
Ecosystem & Community	API-driven, community connectors	May include pre-built integrations	Quality of documentation and availability of talent
Strategic Alignment	Require integration effort	May align with enterprise standards	Fits organization's existing tech and future direction

Examples:

- **Example 1: Selecting an Analytics Platform for a Mid-sized Company**
  - *Requirements:* Support for predictive modeling, collaborative development, dashboard creation, and deployment of models as APIs.
  - *Candidate Evaluation:*
    - *Option A (Open-Source Stack):* Python (pandas, scikit-learn, statsmodels) complemented by Jupyter, FastAPI, and Superset. Strengths include low licensing costs, high flexibility, a large talent pool, and a wide range of supported methodologies. Weaknesses include the need for more deliberate integration work and less centralized governance compared to proprietary platforms.
    - *Option B (Proprietary Platform):* A commercial, all-in-one data science platform. Its strengths include an integrated environment, built-in governance, vendor support, and, in some versions, drag-and-drop modelers. Its weaknesses involve high licensing costs, potential vendor lock-in, and possible delays in supporting the newest algorithms.

- *Selection Driver:* A company with strong in-house engineering capabilities that prioritizes cost management and flexibility should select Option A. An organization that values speed-to-market and reproducibility and has limited technical expertise should select Option B.

- **Example 2: Selecting an Optimization Solver**
  - *Problem:* A large-scale **mixed-integer programming** problem for network design.
  - *Candidates:* Open-source solvers (e.g., CBC), commercial solvers (e.g., Gurobi, CPLEX).
  - *Evaluation:* Open-source solvers carry no licensing fees. They may face performance limitations on large and complex problems. Commercial solvers cost more but offer faster performance, advanced algorithms, and reliable vendor support. For high-stakes, time-sensitive problems, the cost of a commercial solver is justified by the performance and reliability it provides.

- **Example 3: Limitations of Spreadsheet Models**
  - *Scenario:* A finance team develops a complex forecasting and **Monte Carlo** risk model in Excel.
  - *Inherent Weaknesses:*
    - *Scalability & Performance:* Experiences crashes or significant slowdowns when handling large datasets or thousands of simulation iterations.
    - *Error-Prone:* Relying heavily on manual cell references can lead to undetected errors. There is no formal testing framework to validate formula logic.
    - *Poor Version Control & Collaboration: Challenges in* tracking changes and merging work.
    - *Limited Analytical Rigor:* Difficult to implement proper probabilistic distributions, perform **sensitivity analysis**, or generate accurate confidence intervals.
    - *Security & Auditability: Inadequate* access controls and insufficient change tracking.

Table 19 Limitations of Spreadsheet Models

Limitation Area	Specific Issues and Risks
Scalability & Performance	Crashes or becomes unusably slow with large datasets (typically >100,000 rows)
Error Control	Formula errors hard to trace and debug. No built-in data validation or testing framework
Collaboration & Version Control	Version conflicts when multiple users edit. Poor audit trail for changes
Automation & Integration	Manual processes, no scheduling. Poor API connectivity with modern data systems
Security & Auditability	Difficult to implement granular access controls, Hard to reproduce analyses over time
Production Readiness	Not designed for 24/7 operational use. No monitoring, alerting, or failover

Common Pitfalls:

- **Vendor lock-in:** Choosing a proprietary suite that makes switching vendors expensive or difficult later, which limits strategic flexibility.
- **Chasing "Shiny objects":** Selecting new and trendy technologies that lack a solid ecosystem or proven methodologies, which can cause instability and skilled personnel shortages.
- **Underestimating hidden costs:** Focusing only on initial license fees without recognizing substantial expenses for training, integration, customization, and ongoing operations, such as cloud computing costs for training large models.
- **Method-tool mismatch:** Choosing a tool that does not suit the core methodology, such as trying to perform complex **time series forecasting** or discrete event simulation (**DES**) primarily with a standard business intelligence (BI) tool.

Lesson 4.5: Basic Principles of Statistics

Objective:
Apply fundamental statistical and probabilistic concepts to assess data characteristics and select appropriate analytical methods.

Detailed Explanation:
Before selecting a method, accurately diagnose the data itself. This process entails applying fundamental statistical techniques to summarize and describe the dataset and to test assumptions about it. These concepts serve as prerequisites for preventing significant errors in subsequent modeling and for effectively communicating the reliability of the findings.

Key Definitions:

- **Central Tendency:** The **mean** (average), **median** (middle value), and **mode** (most frequent value). The median is resistant to outliers.
- **Dispersion: Variance** (the average of squared deviations from the mean), **standard deviation** (expressed in the original units), and **range**. The **Mean Absolute Deviation (MAD)** is less sensitive to outliers compared to variance.
- **Skewness & Kurtosis:** Skewness measures asymmetry in the distribution. A positive skew indicates a longer right tail. Kurtosis measures the tailedness of the distribution. High kurtosis (leptokurtic) indicates heavy tails and a greater likelihood of outliers.
- **Probability distributions:** Models for data generation, including the
    - **Normal distribution** (Bell Curve)
    - **Binomial distribution** (count of successes in fixed trials)
    - **Poisson** distribution (number of events within an interval)
    - **t-distribution** (used for inference with small sample sizes or unknown population variance)

Table 20 Key Probability Distributions

Distribution	Description	Common Use Case
Normal (Gaussian)	Symmetric, bell-shaped curve defined by mean (μ) and standard deviation (σ).	Modeling natural phenomena (e.g., heights, test scores), Foundation for inferential statistics.
Binomial	Number of successes in *n*independent trials, each with success probability *p*.	Modeling binary outcomes (e.g., defective items in a batch, survey yes/no responses).
Poisson	Number of events occurring in a fixed interval, given a known average rate (λ).	Modeling counts of rare events over time/space (e.g., customers per hour, system failures).
Student's t	Similar shape to Normal but with heavier tails. Defined by degrees of freedom.	Inference for population means when sample size is small and population variance is unknown.

- **Confidence Interval:** A range of plausible values for a population parameter (e.g., mean), derived from sample data at a specified confidence level (e.g., 95%). It measures the uncertainty in estimation.
- **Hypothesis Testing:** A formal process used to evaluate a claim about a population based on sample data. The **p-value** is the probability of obtaining results as extreme as or more extreme than the observed data, assuming the null hypothesis is true.

Step-by-Step Method:

1. **Summarize:** Calculate measures of central tendency and variability (dispersion).
2. **Visualize:** Plot histograms and boxplots to examine shape, central tendency, spread, and outliers.
3. **Assess distribution:** Check for significant skewness or kurtosis. Use Q-Q plots to evaluate normality.
4. **Formulate inferences:** When estimating a population mean from a sample, create a **confidence interval** with the t-distribution for small samples. To compare groups, perform a **hypothesis test** by checking assumptions such as normality and equal variances to decide whether to use parametric tests (t-

test, ANOVA) or non-parametric tests (Mann-Whitney, Kruskal-Wallis).

5. **Interpret correctly:** A 95% confidence interval means that 95% of such intervals obtained from repeated sampling would contain the true parameter. A p-value below α indicates that the observed data are inconsistent with the null hypothesis at that significance level. This is grounds to reject the null hypothesis. It is not proof that the alternative hypothesis is true.

Examples:

- **Example 1: Skewed Data and the Mean:**
  For home prices: $300K, $350K, $400K, $450K, $2,000K. The mean is $700K, distorted by the outlier. The median is $400K, a more representative typical value. Reporting the mean alone would be misleading.

- **Example 2: Confidence Interval for a Mean:**
  A sample of 30 customers has an average spend of $85 with a standard deviation of $15. Using the t-distribution with 29 degrees of freedom, the 95% CI for the true population average spend is approximately $79.40 to $90.60. This provides a range of plausible values rather than a single point estimate.

- **Example 3: Misapplication of Hypothesis Testing:**
  Using a **t-test** to compare customer satisfaction scores (rated on a 1-5 Likert scale, which is ordinal) between two stores.
  A **Mann-Whitney U test** (a nonparametric alternative) is more appropriate, since the data may not meet the assumptions of interval-level measurement and normality required for the t-test.

Common Pitfalls:

- **Using the mean for skewed data:** It can give a misleading view of the "typical" value.
- **Misunderstanding the p-value:** Thinking it is the probability that the null hypothesis is true. It is not. It is the probability of observing data as extreme as or more extreme than the observed results, given that the null hypothesis is true.
- **Confidence interval confusion:** Stating "there is a 95% probability the true mean is in [79.4, 90.6]." The interval is fixed, the probability statement refers to the long-term process.

- **Neglecting test assumptions:** Using a Chi-square test of independence when one or more expected cell counts fall below 5, rather than switching to Fisher's Exact Test. Applying ANOVA without checking for homogeneity of variances using Levene's test or a similar procedure.
- **The Geometric/Harmonic Mean trap:** Using the arithmetic mean to evaluate average growth rates or speeds.
  The **geometric mean** applies to multiplicative processes (e.g., compound annual growth rate), while the **harmonic mean** is suitable for averaging rates (e.g., average speed over equal distances).

Lesson 4.6: Core Predictive and Pattern-Discovery Methods

Objective:
Understand the mechanics, applications, and selection criteria for primary predictive modeling and unsupervised learning techniques.

Detailed Explanation:
This lesson offers a detailed overview of the main algorithms used for prediction and discovery. Predictive (supervised) methods learn a mapping from inputs to a known output, while unsupervised techniques identify underlying structures in the data without depending on a target variable. Each approach has its own advantages, limitations, and specific data needs that influence the choice of method.

Key Definitions:

- **Supervised learning:** Learning from labeled data (input-output pairs). It includes **regression** (for continuous outputs) and **classification** (for categorical outputs).
- **Unsupervised learning:** Identifying patterns in unlabeled data. Includes clustering (grouping) and **dimensionality reduction** (e.g., PCA).
- **Regularization:** Techniques that prevent overfitting by penalizing model complexity.
  - **L1 regularization (Lasso)** can shrink coefficients to exactly zero, removing features from the model and aiding feature selection.
  - **L2 regularization (Ridge)** shrinks coefficients toward zero without eliminating them, reducing the influence of less important features.

Table 21 Regularization Techniques: Lasso (L1) vs. Ridge (L2)

Characteristic	L1 Regularization (Lasso)	L2 Regularization (Ridge)
Penalty Term	λΣ|β| (Sum of absolute coefficients)	λΣβ² (Sum of squared coefficients)
Effect on Coefficients	Can shrink coefficients to exactly zero.	Shrinks coefficients toward zero, but not to exactly zero.
Primary Use	Feature selection (creates sparse models).	Handling multicollinearity, general overfitting reduction.
Model Interpretability	Can produce simpler, more interpretable models.	Retains all features, but with reduced weights.

- **Ensemble learning:** Combining multiple models to improve performance
    - **Bagging** (e.g., Random Forest) reduces variance by averaging results.
    - **Boosting** (e.g., Gradient Boosting) lowers bias by sequentially correcting errors.

Figure 16 Supervised vs. Unsupervised Learning Decision Flow

Step-by-Step Method:

1. **Is the target variable defined and available?** If yes, use supervised learning. If no, use unsupervised learning.
2. **For supervised learning:**
   - *Is the target variable continuous?* Use regression techniques. Start with **linear regression**. If the relationship is non-linear, apply regression trees, support vector regression, or feature transformations.
   - *Is the target variable categorical?* If so, use classification techniques. For binary outcomes, start with logistic regression for its interpretability. For more complex decision boundaries, use decision trees, random forests, or gradient boosting algorithms. For high-dimensional data such as text, apply naive Bayes. For simple instance-based learning, use k-Nearest Neighbors (KNN), ensuring features are properly scaled.
3. **For unsupervised learning:**
   - Is the goal to find natural groups in the data? Use clustering methods such as K-means and hierarchical clustering.
   - Is the goal to reduce the number of features or to visualize high-dimensional data? If so, use dimensionality reduction techniques such as PCA.
   - *Is the goal to find association rules?* Association Rule Mining (Apriori algorithm).
4. **Address overfitting:** Apply regularization techniques such as L1 or L2 to linear or logistic models. For tree-based models, limit depth or use ensemble methods. Always validate the model's performance using holdout data or cross-validation to confirm it generalizes to unseen data.

Examples:

- **Example 1: Logistic Regression vs. KNN:**
  - *Problem:* Classify emails as spam or ham based on word frequencies.
  - *Logistic Regression:* provides probabilistic output, with coefficients indicating which words increase or decrease the likelihood of spam. It is highly interpretable.
  - *KNN:* Classifies instances based on their similarity to the k nearest neighbors (emails). There is no model to interpret,

performance depends heavily on the choice of k and the distance metric. It requires storing all training data.
    - *Selection:* For enhanced interpretability and efficiency, logistic regression may be preferred. If the decision boundary proves highly irregular and interpretability is less important, K-Nearest Neighbors (KNN) could be considered for testing.

- **Example 2: PCA for Data Compression:**
    - *Issue:* A dataset contains 100 highly correlated sensor readings, resulting in model instability and reduced computational speed.
    - *Solution:* Apply **Principal Component Analysis** (PCA) to generate new, uncorrelated components. In this case, ten components may capture 95% of the variance. Use these ten components as inputs to the predictive model to reduce noise and computational complexity.

Common Pitfalls:

- **Not scaling features for distance-based methods:** KNN and SVM rely on distance calculations. If features are on different scales, for example, age ranging from 0 to 100 versus income ranging from 0 to 200,000, the variable with the larger range will dominate the distance calculation. Always standardize features using z-score normalization before applying these methods.
- **Overfitting a decision tree:** Allowing a tree to grow until it perfectly fits the training data. It will fail on new data. Control it with max depth, minimum samples per leaf, or pruning.
- **Black Box reliance:** Using complex models like **Random Forest** or **Neural Networks** when stakeholders require explanations for predictions. This approach trades interpretability for potential accuracy gains.
- **Ignoring the Bias-Variance trade-off:** Simple models like linear regression tend to have high bias but low variance. In contrast, complex models such as deep trees usually show low bias but high variance. **Ensemble methods**, such as bagging, primarily reduce variance, whereas boosting primarily reduces bias.

Lesson 4.7: Time Series and Forecasting Methodology

Objective:
Choose and implement appropriate methods for analyzing and forecasting data collected sequentially over time.

Detailed Explanation:
Time series data require specialized methods because observations are correlated with earlier values (autocorrelation). The main components include Trend (T), Seasonality (S), and Residual/Irregular (I). Selecting an appropriate model depends on the presence and characteristics of these components (additive or multiplicative).

Key Definitions:

- **Stationarity:** A series where statistical properties like mean and variance remain constant over time. Many models, such as ARIMA, require stationarity, which is often achieved through differencing.
- **ARIMA (Autoregressive Integrated Moving Average):** A model for non-seasonal series defined by (p, d, q), where p is the autoregressive lag, d is the differencing order, and q is the moving average lag.
- **SARIMA:** Extends ARIMA to forecast trends with seasonal components (P, D, Q) to handle data that repeats over time and model seasonal patterns.
- **Exponential smoothing:** A forecasting method that assigns exponentially decreasing weights to past observations. The **Holt-Winters** method considers both trend and seasonality.
- **Decomposition:** Breaks down a time series into its T, S, and I components (e.g., using STL decomposition).

Step-by-Step Method:

1. **Visualize and decompose:** Plot the series and break it down to identify trend and seasonality.
2. **Check stationarity:** Use statistical tests such as the Augmented Dickey-Fuller (ADF) test. If the data are non-stationary due to a trend, apply regular differencing. If non-stationarity is seasonal, apply seasonal differencing. Apply both if both forms of non-stationarity are present.

3. **Select model family:**
    - *No clear trend or seasonality:* Use **Simple Exponential Smoothing** or **ARIMA** with low parameter orders as the starting point.
    - *Trend but no seasonality:* **Holt's Linear Trend** method or **ARIMA** with differencing (d >= 1).
    - *Trend and seasonality modeling:* **Holt-Winters** (additive or multiplicative) or **SARIMA**.
4. **Fit, Validate, Forecast:** Fit the model and check that residuals are random (white noise). Use a hold-out period to validate forecast accuracy before making future predictions.

Examples:

- **Example 1: Retail Sales Forecasting**
    - *Data:* Monthly sales exhibiting a yearly seasonal pattern and a slight upward trend.
    - *Analysis:* Decomposition reveals an additive seasonal pattern where the seasonal variation remains roughly consistent year after year.
    - *Candidate Models:* **Holt-Winters Additive** and **SARIMA**.
    - *Selection:* **Holt-Winters** is often easier to implement and interpret for this common business scenario. **SARIMA** may be preferred if the autocorrelation structure is more complex.

- **Example 2: Predicting Daily Energy Demand**
    - *Data:* Has daily and weekly cycles (seasonality) and is non-stationary.
    - *Action:* Apply seasonal differencing at lag 7 for the weekly pattern to achieve stationarity, then fit a **SARIMA** model.

Figure 17 Time Series Model Selection Flow

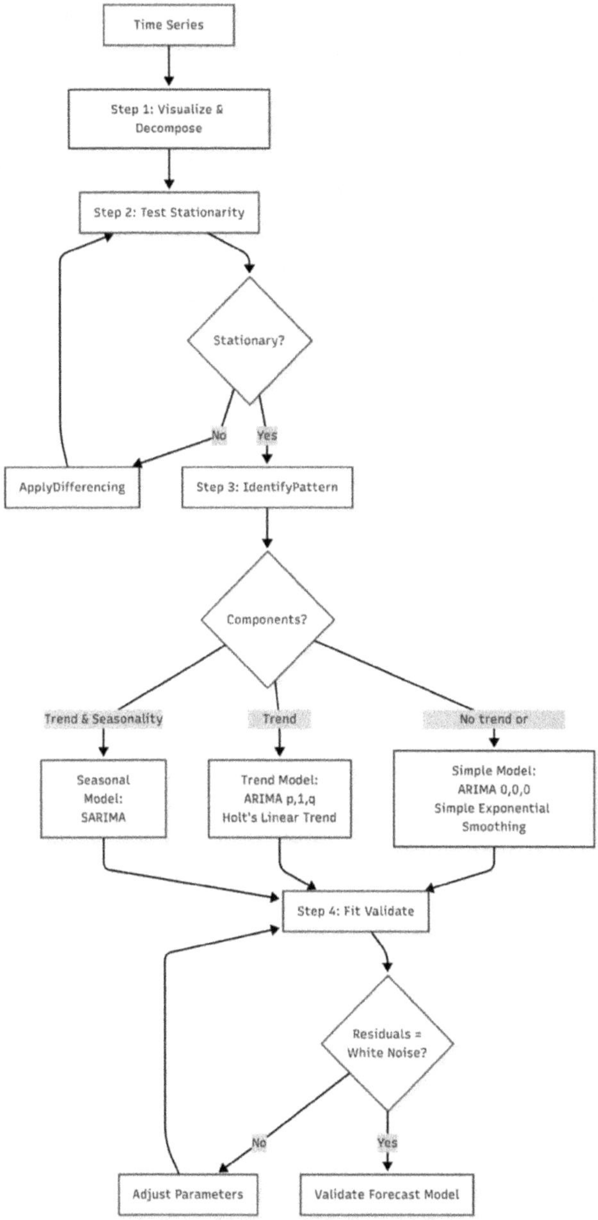

Common Pitfalls:

- **Using non-time series methods:** Applying standard regression to time series data without accounting for autocorrelation violates the independence assumption and produces invalid results.
- **Ignoring seasonality:** Failing to model a clear seasonal pattern results in inaccurate forecasts.
- **Forecasting too far ahead:** Extending a trend or seasonal pattern deep into the future with high confidence. Forecast uncertainty grows rapidly as the forecast horizon lengthens.
- **Data leakage:** Using information not available at prediction time, including future values or target-derived fields, when training or evaluating a model, which produces over-optimistic results.

Lesson 4.8: Simulation Methodology

Objective:

Select and develop simulation methods for analyzing complex systems under uncertainty and conducting structured what-if scenario analysis.

Detailed Explanation:

Simulation is a prescriptive method that models systems too complex for analytical solutions, especially when randomness is involved. It involves creating a computational model of a process, running experiments, and analyzing the results to understand system behavior and support decision-making.

Key Definitions:

- **Monte Carlo simulation:** A method that uses random sampling from probability distributions to model uncertainty and determine the range of possible outcomes for a static system.
- **Discrete Event Simulation (DES):** Models a system in which state changes occur at discrete points in simulated time, triggered by events such as customer arrivals and service completions. The simulation clock advances to the time of the next scheduled event rather than progressing in fixed increments.
- **Agent-Based Modeling (ABM):** This approach constructs a system from the ground up by defining autonomous agents that interact with one another and with their environment according to simple, predefined rules.
- **System Dynamics:** A top-down, **continuous simulation** approach focusing on stocks (accumulations) and flows (rates) to model feedback loops and delays in complex systems.
- **Key Performance Indicators (KPIs): Cycle Time** (total time per unit), Throughput (units completed per unit time), **Utilization** (proportion of time a resource is actively engaged).

Figure 18 Simulation Methodology Selection Flow

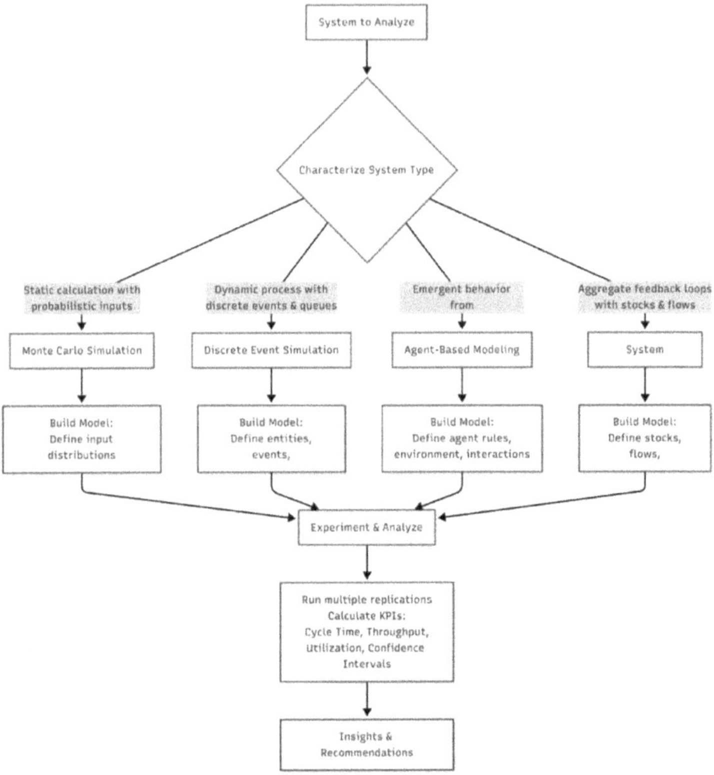

Step-by-Step Method:

1. **Characterize the System:**
   - Is this a static calculation with uncertain inputs? **Monte Carlo** (e.g., for financial risk).
   - Is it a dynamic process involving queuing, resources, and entities, such as in a call center or manufacturing setting? Use Discrete Event Simulation (DES).
   - Does system behavior emerge from interactions among heterogeneous (diverse) agents? **ABM** (e.g., pedestrian flow, market dynamics).
   - Is it focused on aggregate-level feedback loops and delays? **System Dynamics** (e.g., project dynamics, market growth).
2. **Build the model:** Define entities, events, logic (DES), agents and rules (ABM), or stocks and flows (System Dynamics). For

Monte Carlo, specify the input distributions and the output calculations.

3. **Experiment and analyze:** Run multiple replications (for stochastic simulations) to account for randomness. Calculate confidence intervals for output KPIs. Use **simulation-based optimization** to identify input parameters that maximize or improve an output.

Examples:

- **Example 1: Monte Carlo for Project Cost**
  - *Problem:* Estimate the total project cost when task durations and material costs are uncertain.
  - *Method:* Define triangular or PERT distributions for each uncertain input. The model sums the costs. Run 10,000 iterations.
  - *Output:* A probability distribution of total cost (e.g., mean=$1.2M, 90% CI: $1.0M - $1.5M). This provides more information than a single-point estimate.

- **Example 2: DES for Clinic Layout**
  - *Problem:* Test whether adding a nurse or changing the room layout decreases patient wait times.
  - *Method:* Build a DES model with patients as entities, steps (check-in, triage, doctor) as activities, and nurses/doctors as resources.
  - *Output:* Compare average patient **cycle time** and staff **utilization** across different scenarios.

- **Example 3: Little's Law Application**
  - *Scenario:* A coffee shop sees an average of 12 customers in line (L), and the arrival rate, or throughput, is 2 customers per minute (λ).
  - *Analysis:* **Little's Law** ($L = \lambda W$) shows the average time a customer spends: $W = L/\lambda = 12 / 2 = 6$ minutes. This core relationship helps identify bottlenecks.

Common Pitfalls:

- **Not achieving steady state:** In DES, collecting statistical data during the warm-up phase, when the system starts in an empty or unrealistic state, introduces bias into results. Exclude warm-up period data from all performance calculations.

- **Insufficient replications:** Running a stochastic simulation only once. Outputs are random variables. Multiple replications are necessary to accurately estimate their mean and variance and to calculate meaningful confidence intervals for output KPIs.
- **Over-complexity:** Building an excessively detailed model that is difficult to validate and slow to run. Start with the simplest model that can answer the decision question and add complexity only where it materially affects the output.
- **Disregarding common random numbers:** When comparing scenarios, using independent random streams introduces variance into the comparison that is unrelated to the scenarios themselves. Using synchronized random number streams across scenarios reduces this variance and improves the precision of the comparison.

Lesson 4.9: Optimization and Prescriptive Methodology

Objective:
Formulate business problems as mathematical optimization models and select appropriate solution methods.

Detailed Explanation:
Optimization provides a structured framework for prescriptive analytics. It involves establishing an objective function to maximize or minimize (e.g., profit, cost, or time) while considering constraints (such as resource limits or business rules). The specific model type (linear, integer, or nonlinear) determines the solution approach.

Key Definitions:

- **Linear Programming (LP):** A model in which all objectives and constraints are linear functions and all decision variables are continuous.
- **Integer/Mixed-Integer Programming (IP/MIP):** Some or all variables must assume integer values (e.g., yes/no decisions, number of machines).
- **Combinatorial Optimization:** Problems where the solution is a discrete structure, such as the shortest path or the traveling salesperson.
- **Heuristic/Metaheuristic:** Approximation algorithms used for complex problems where exact methods are too slow (e.g., Genetic Algorithm, Tabu Search for complex scheduling).
- **Sensitivity Analysis & Shadow Price:** The shadow price of a constraint indicates how much the objective function would improve with one additional unit of that resource, valid within a specific range.

Step-by-Step Method:

1. **Formulate the problem:** Define the decision variables, the objective function, and all constraints before selecting a solution method.
2. **Classify the model:**
    - Are all relationships linear and variables continuous? Use **LP** and solve it using the **Simplex Method** or an interior-point method.
    - Are some variables discrete (integer/binary)? Use MIP and solve with **Branch and Bound**.
    - Are the objectives or constraints nonlinear? **Nonlinear Programming (NLP)** requires specialized, often iterative, solvers.
    - Is the problem a common type (e.g., assignment, routing, knapsack)? Use its established formulas and specialized algorithms.
3. **Evaluate the size and complexity:** Small- to medium-sized LP/MIP problems can be solved to optimality using exact methods. Larger, more complex, or nonlinear problems require **heuristics** such as **greedy algorithms** for rapid feasible solutions, or **metaheuristics** such as **genetic algorithms**, which deliver high-quality solutions without guaranteeing global optimality.
4. **Analyze the solution:** Conduct **sensitivity analysis** to assess how changes in key parameters affect the optimal solution. Use **shadow prices** to evaluate constraint tightness and resource value. For multi-objective problems, identify the **Pareto frontier** to understand the trade-offs involved.

Figure 19 Optimization Model & Solution Selection Flow

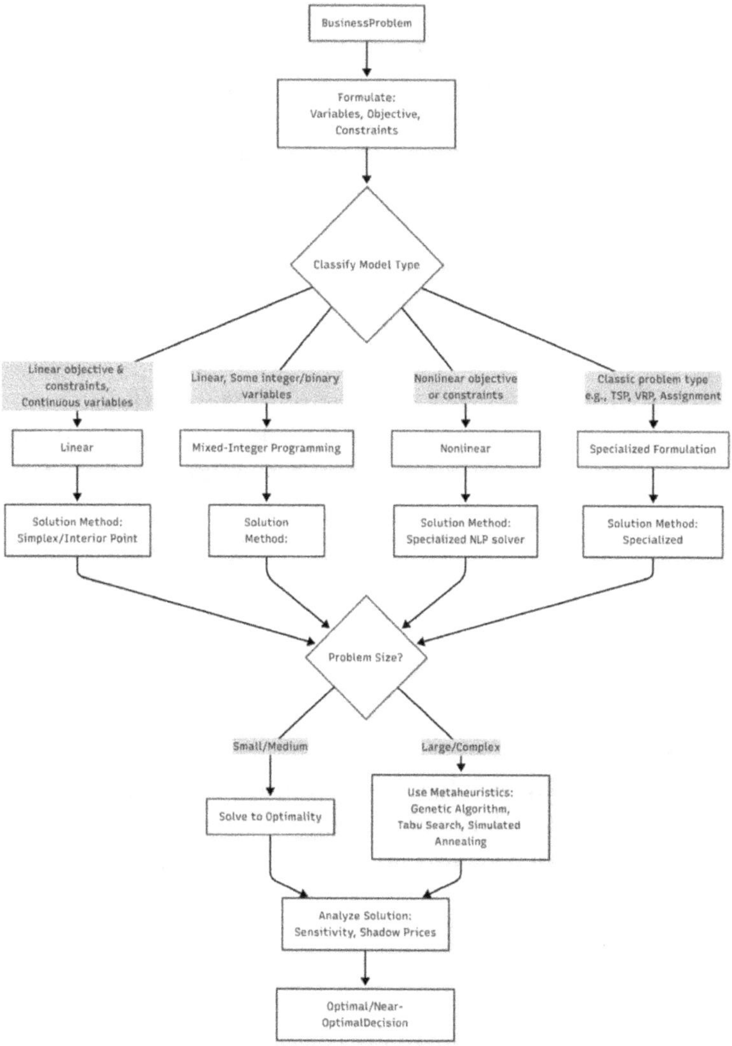

Examples:

- **Example 1: Production Mix LP**
  - *Problem:* Maximize profit from products A and B, given limited labor and materials.
  - *Formulation:* Continuous variables (units of A, B). Linear objective (profit per unit). Linear constraints (labor hours, material pounds).

- *Solution:* The **Simplex Method** provides the optimal production plan and shadow prices for labor and materials.

- **Example 2: Facility Location MIP**
  - *Problem:* Determine the optimal selection of warehouses to open (binary yes/no) and the corresponding shipment quantities (continuous flows) to minimize the total cost.
  - *Formulation:* Mixed-integer program.
  - *Solution:* Implement the **Branch-and-Bound** algorithm. The linear programming (LP) relaxation is solved at each node, and branches are generated based on the integer variables.

- **Example 3: Vehicle Routing with Heuristics**
  - *Problem:* Route 50 delivery trucks from a central depot to 200 customers, representing a complex combinatorial challenge.
  - *Solution:* An exact optimal solution is computationally prohibitive at this scale. Use a **metaheuristic** such as **Tabu Search**, or a specialized construction and improvement **heuristic**, to produce a high-quality solution within a practical timeframe.

Common Pitfalls:

- **Misformulation:** Incorrectly translating a business rule into a constraint, which results in an invalid model.
- **Solving an IP as an LP:** This can lead to infeasible or very suboptimal solutions. The algorithm must enforce integer constraints.
- **Ignoring sensitivity analysis:** The optimal solution depends on fixed parameters such as costs and demands. Not knowing the **allowable increase or decrease** for these parameters introduces a risk if they change.
- **Unnecessarily using a metaheuristic:** Deploying a genetic algorithm for a problem that can be solved to optimality with an LP/MIP solver. This approach wastes time and sacrifices the mathematical guarantee of optimality that exact methods provide.

Lesson 4.10: Advanced Decision and Probabilistic Analysis

Objective:
Apply Bayesian and decision-analytic methods to reason under uncertainty and support complex, sequential decision-making.

Detailed Explanation:
When decisions involve significant uncertainty, probabilistic models provide the structure needed to reason through possible outcomes before committing to an action. Bayesian methods regularly update beliefs based on new data. **Decision analysis** offers a structured way to make choices with multiple, uncertain results. These approaches are well suited to high-stakes, one-time decisions where uncertainty must be quantified before a commitment is made.

Key Definitions:

- **Bayes' Theorem:** Updates the probability of a hypothesis (H) given evidence (E): $P(H|E) = [P(E|H) * P(H)] / P(E)$.
- **Bayesian Network:** A graphical model illustrating variables and their conditional dependencies, used for diagnostic reasoning and probabilistic inference.
- **Decision Tree (Analysis):** A diagram that maps out sequential decisions, chance events, and outcomes with payoffs or utilities. It is solved using **backward induction** (rolling back) to identify the strategy with the highest **Expected Monetary Value (EMV)** or **Expected Utility**.
- **Influence Diagram:** A brief visual alternative to a decision tree that shows decisions, chance variables, and objectives.
- **Sensitivity/Specificity:** Performance metrics for binary classifiers. Sensitivity = True Positive Rate. Specificity = True Negative Rate.

Step-by-Step Method:

1. **Diagnostic reasoning** (What is the most likely cause?):
    - Use **Bayes' Theorem** for straightforward cases (e.g., interpreting a medical test given disease prevalence).
    - Use a **Bayesian Network** for complex problems with many interdependent variables, such as fault diagnosis

in engineering. **Conditional Probability Tables (CPTs)** define the network's quantitative relationships.

2. **Prescriptive decision-making** (What is the best action?):
   - For a multi-stage decision under uncertainty, create a **Decision Tree** or an **Influence Diagram**.
   - Determine probabilities for chance nodes and payoffs/utilities for outcomes.
   - Solve by **backward induction** to find the optimal policy.
3. **Value-focused thinking:** Begin by defining core objectives, then develop alternatives around those objectives. This ensures the analysis is anchored to what matters rather than simply comparing whatever options happen to be available.

Examples:

- **Example: Bayesian Diagnostic Reasoning**
  - *Scenario:* A disease has a 1% prevalence (Prior P(D)=0.01). A test is 99% sensitive (P(+|D)=0.99) and 95% specific (P(-|Healthy)=0.95).
  - *Application of Bayes' Rule:* For a positive test result, the posterior probability P(D|+) is approximately 0.17. This clarifies the common mistake of assuming a positive test means you probably have the disease.

Figure 20 Bayesian Diagnostic & Prescriptive Decision Flow

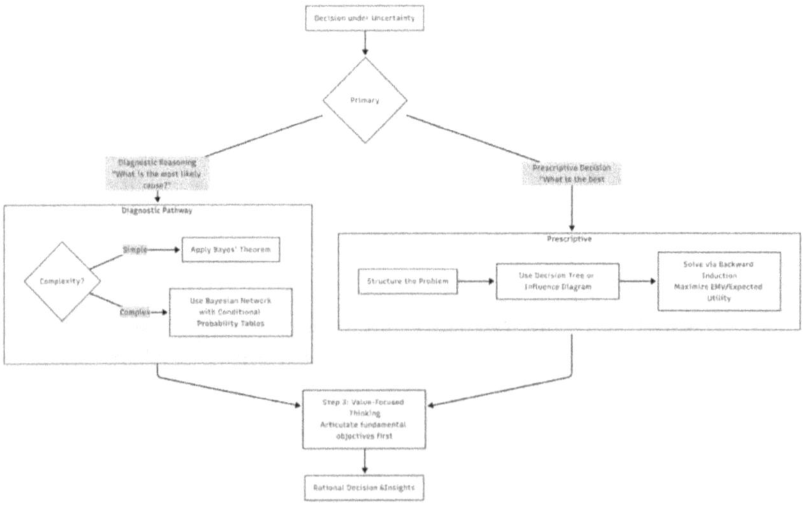

- **Example: Decision Tree for Product Launch**
  - *Decision:* Launch now, test the market first, or abandon.
  - *Tree Structure:* If "test market," a chance node for test results (Good/Poor), influences the subsequent "full launch" decision and its associated market outcome probabilities (Success/Failure).
  - *Analysis:* Roll back the tree to determine the EMV of each initial choice. Backward induction may show that 'Test Market, then launch only if the result is Good' produces the highest EMV, making it the optimal initial strategy.

Common Pitfalls:

- **Base rate neglect:** Ignoring the prior probability (prevalence) when evaluating evidence, leading to a significant overestimation of the posterior probability.
- **Confusing EMV with utility:** EMV applies to risk-neutral decisions. For high-stakes situations where outcomes have non-linear effects, such as bankruptcy, use a utility function that captures the decision-maker's risk aversion rather than relying on expected monetary value alone.
- **Ignoring non-monetary objectives:** Decision analysis focused only on profit will overlook strategic, social, or environmental goals that matter to stakeholders. **Value-focused thinking** and **multi-objective optimization** with **Pareto frontier** analysis provide the structure to include these priorities explicitly
- **Mis-specifying conditional dependencies:** Incorrectly configuring a Bayesian Network or the arcs in an Influence Diagram, resulting in flawed probabilistic reasoning.

Summary

Choosing the right analytical approach starts with identifying the main analytical goal, whether it is descriptive, diagnostic, predictive, or prescriptive. That goal is then matched to data characteristics through basic statistical diagnostics. Measures of central tendency, dispersion, and distributional shape aid initial evaluation, while the principle of adequate simplicity ensures that the selected method balances thoroughness and practicality. Descriptive methods summarize historical data, diagnostic techniques explore causal relationships, predictive models estimate future results, and prescriptive strategies suggest the best actions within given constraints.

Practical constraints often outweigh theoretical optimality when choosing methods in real-world scenarios. Regulatory demands for interpretability may favor logistic regression over black-box neural networks, while limited sample sizes might require nonparametric tests rather than traditional parametric methods. Implementation feasibility also shapes the final decision. This includes data availability, in-house skills, development time, computational costs, and inferential requirements such as confidence intervals or hypothesis testing. The aim is not to achieve maximum theoretical accuracy but to provide sufficient business value within operational limits.

Technical architecture converts methodological concepts into deployable systems, covering the entire data process from ingestion to serving. Processing methods, whether batch, stream, or hybrid, must match methodological needs such as real-time scoring for fraud detection or large-scale replications for simulation. The technology stack choice involves evaluating open-source options versus proprietary ones based on functional fit, total cost of ownership, ecosystem strength, and strategic fit. Recognize the limitations of common tools. Spreadsheets lack the scalability, error control, and analytical rigor required for production analytics.

Predictive and pattern-discovery methods are divided into supervised learning for labeled data and unsupervised learning for uncovering hidden structures. Regression predicts continuous outcomes, while classification deals with categorical targets, and clustering finds natural groupings. Regularization techniques such as Lasso for feature selection and Ridge for managing multicollinearity help prevent overfitting.

Ensemble methods such as bagging and boosting enhance performance. Time series forecasting requires specialized handling of autocorrelation through techniques like decomposition, stationarity checks, and models such as ARIMA, SARIMA, or exponential smoothing.

Simulation methodologies analyze complex systems through computational experiments. Monte Carlo simulation models static uncertainty using random sampling from probability distributions. Discrete-event simulation models dynamic processes where state changes happen at specific time points, such as queueing systems or manufacturing lines. Agent-based modeling builds systems from autonomous agents whose interactions produce emergent behavior. Each approach addresses different system characteristics and analytical questions.

Optimization models mathematically formulate decision problems to maximize or minimize an objective function subject to given constraints. Linear programming deals with continuous variables and linear relationships, while mixed-integer programming handles discrete choices, such as yes/no decisions or integer quantities. For problems that are too large or complex for exact methods, heuristics and metaheuristics deliver high-quality approximate solutions. Sensitivity analysis shows how changes in parameters affect the optimal solution, and shadow prices reveal the marginal value of constrained resources.

Advanced probabilistic methods support structured reasoning under uncertainty. Bayesian networks revise beliefs as new evidence emerges, supporting diagnostic reasoning in complex fields. Decision trees outline sequences of decisions and chance events and are solved via backward induction to find strategies with the highest expected value. These techniques are well-suited to high-stakes, one-time decisions where understanding uncertainty and its effects directly shape the outcome.

Chapter 4: Practice Questions

Q1. A business must categorize its customer base into distinct groups to support targeted marketing campaigns. Since no pre-existing labels are available for these groups, which methodological paradigm is most suitable?
A) Supervised Learning
B) Reinforcement Learning
C) Unsupervised Learning
D) Prescriptive Optimization

Q2. In evaluating a new drug, a clinical trial yields a p-value of 0.04. With a significance level (α) of 0.05, what is the correct interpretation?
A) There is a 4% chance the drug is effective.
B) There is a 4% chance the observed result happened if the drug had no effect.
C) The drug is definitely effective.
D) The null hypothesis is proven false.

Q3. Which measure of central tendency best describes the "typical" income in a city with a highly skewed income distribution caused by a few billionaires?
A) Arithmetic Mean
B) Geometric Mean
C) Median
D) Mode

Q4. A data scientist is developing a model to predict house prices and needs an algorithm that offers explicit interpretability, clearly showing the individual influence of each feature, such as square footage and number of bedrooms, on the price. Which model is the most appropriate initial selection?
A) Random Forest
B) Deep Neural Network
C) Multiple Linear Regression
D) Support Vector Machine with RBF kernel

Q5. A call center simulation model aims to evaluate the effect of increasing staff levels on the average customer wait time. Which performance metric is most directly pertinent to this analysis?
A) Utilization

B) Cycle Time
C) Throughput
D) Shadow Price

Q6. The shadow price for the constraint "labor hours ≤ 100" in a profit-maximization Linear Programming model is indicated as $25. What is the implication of this value?
A) Profit will increase by $25 if precisely 100 labor hours are utilized.
B) The labor cost is $25 per hour.
C) Profit is projected to increase by approximately $25 if the labor hour limit is extended to 101 hours, within the permissible range.
D) It is advisable to be willing to pay up to $25 per hour for additional labor.

Q7. You are forecasting monthly sales that exhibit a distinct upward trend, along with regular seasonal fluctuations every 3 months. Which model is specifically tailored to address this pattern?
A) Simple Exponential Smoothing
B) ARIMA(1,1,1)
C) Holt-Winters (with seasonal period=3)
D) Logistic Regression

Q8. In a Monte Carlo simulation for project cost estimation, what is the primary purpose of running thousands of iterations?
A) To find the single, exact cost of the project.
B) To build a probability distribution of possible total costs, accounting for input uncertainties.
C) To optimize the project schedule.
D) To identify the critical path of the project.

Q9. A corporation faces a strategic decision: either invest in a new, risky product or opt for a secure bond. Although decision tree analysis indicates that the high-risk product possesses a higher Expected Monetary Value (EMV), the company is very risk-averse. What analytical method should be adopted under these circumstances?
A) Sensitivity Analysis
B) Maximin Criterion
C) Expected Utility Theory, employing a concave utility function
D) Goal Programming

Q10. A diagnostic test for a rare disease has an overall accuracy of 99%, with sensitivity and specificity both at 99%. The prevalence of the disease in the population is 1 in 10,000. If an individual receives a positive test result, what is the most accurate assessment of the patient's actual risk?
A) The patient almost certainly has the disease.
B) The probability that the patient has the disease is approximately 99%.
C) The probability that the patient has the disease is approximately 1%.
D) The probability that the patient has the disease is between 10% and 30%.

Q11. When comparing the average delivery times of three different shipping vendors based on a sample of deliveries from each, which statistical test is most suitable if the delivery time data follows a normal distribution?
A) Two-sample t-test
B) Chi-square test of independence
C) One-way ANOVA
D) Kruskal-Wallis test

Q12. The **harmonic mean** is the appropriate average to use in which of the following scenarios?
A) Calculating the average annual investment return over five years.
B) Calculating the average test score of a class.
C) Calculating the average speed for a round trip when traveling equal distances at different speeds.
D) Calculating the average household size in a neighborhood.

Q13. In a **Discrete Event Simulation** (DES) of a hospital emergency room, which of the following would be characterized as an "event"?
A) The average patient wait time.
B) The percentage of time doctors are occupied.
C) A patient's arrival.
D) The total number of beds.

Q14. Principal Component Analysis (PCA) is mainly used for:
A) Predicting a continuous target variable.
B) Reducing the number of features while preserving most of the variance in the data.
C) Classifying emails as spam or not spam.
D) Identifying association rules between products.

Q15. A manufacturing problem involves deciding how many units of several products to produce to maximize profit, while accounting for constraints on machine time and labor. The relationship between production quantities and profit/constraints is linear. Some products can only be produced in whole units. This is best formulated as:
A) A Linear Programming (LP) problem.
B) An Integer Programming (IP) problem.
C) A Nonlinear Programming (NLP) problem.
D) A Dynamic Programming problem.

Q16. Little's Law ($L = \lambda W$) applies to a stable queuing system. If the average number of customers in the system (L) is 15 and the average arrival rate (λ) is 3 customers per hour, what is the average time a customer spends in the system (W)?
A) 5 hours
B) 0.2 hours
C) 45 hours
D) 12 hours

Q17. Regularization techniques like Lasso (L1) and Ridge (L2) are mainly used to:
A) Increase the model's complexity to better fit the training data.
B) Reduce overfitting by penalizing large coefficients.
C) Ensure all assumptions of linear regression are satisfied.
D) Convert a classification problem into a regression problem.

Q18. The **Pareto frontier** in a multi-objective optimization problem represents:
A) The single solution that maximizes all objectives simultaneously.
B) The set of solutions where no objective can be improved without worsening another.
C) The solution obtained by weighting all objectives equally.
D) The result of converting all objectives into constraints.

Q19. A data scientist observes that the residuals (errors) spread out more as the predicted value increases in her linear regression model. This suggests a violation of which key assumption?
A) Linearity
B) Independence
C) Homoscedasticity (constant variance)
D) Normality

Q20. Fisher's Exact Test is preferred over the **Chi-square test of independence** when:

A) The sample size is very large.

B) The expected cell counts in the contingency table are small (e.g., less than 5).

C) The variables are continuous.

D) The purpose involves testing for a difference between two group means.

Chapter 5: Model Development and Implementation

Introduction

Model development is the key phase where conceptual business questions are transformed into practical analytical solutions. This process encompasses the entire lifecycle of creating, testing, refining, and communicating analytical models. It begins by turning a clearly defined problem into a technical design, progresses through careful model building and validation, and concludes with successful implementation and stakeholder communication. Mastering this process ensures that analytical work produces reliable, actionable insights that serve the business, meet ethical standards, and remain practically relevant.

Figure 21 Model Development Lifecycle

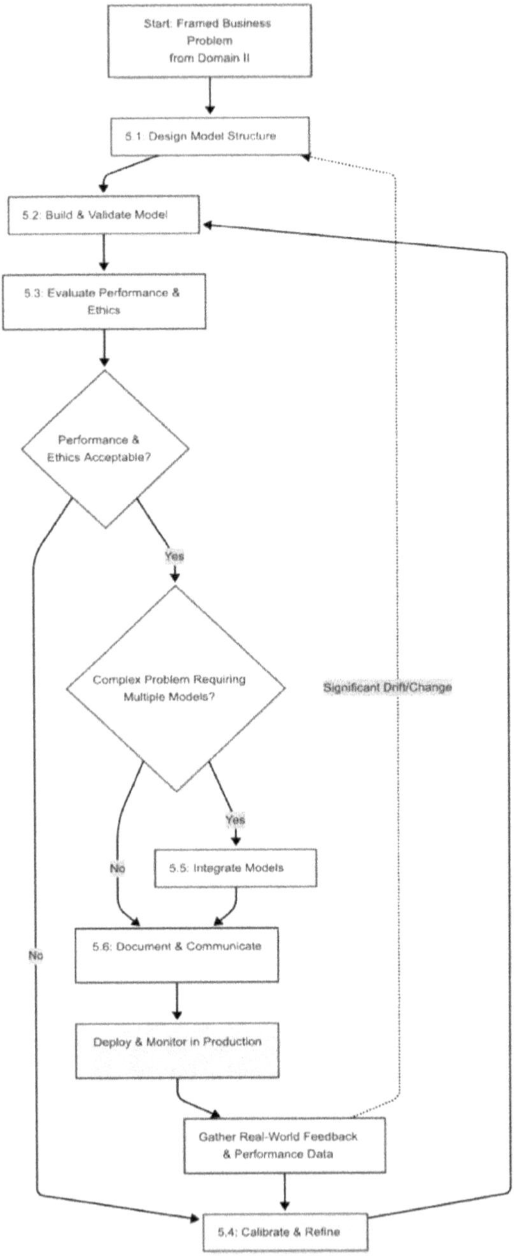

Lesson 5.1: Designing the Analytical Model Structure

Objective:
Create a technical blueprint for analytical models by identifying their key components, specifically inputs, outputs, and their relationships, to serve descriptive, predictive, and prescriptive goals.

Detailed Explanation:
Designing a model's structure is the first step in the development process, where the team translates the previously identified business problem into a technical framework. This architectural phase decides which data will be processed, what results will be produced, and how the transformation will take place. The design approach mainly varies based on the analytical goal: understanding past patterns (descriptive), forecasting future outcomes (predictive), or recommending optimal decisions (prescriptive). A well-designed structure helps prevent wasted effort, guides data preparation, and sets clear criteria for success.

Table 22 Model Architecture Focus by Analytical Type

Analytical Type	Primary Goal	Core Question	Example Output Format	Structural Emphasis
Descriptive	Understand the past	What happened and what are the patterns?	Segments, trends, summary statistics, association rules	Identifying relationships and groupings within historical data
Diagnostic	Identify root causes and drivers	Why did it happen?	Root causes, anomaly detection, segment comparisons, correlation matrices, hypothesis test results	Isolating relationships and comparing sub-groups to explain observed changes or outliers
Predictive	Forecast the future	What is likely to happen?	Probabilities, class labels, continuous value forecasts	Mapping input features to a target output variable using historical patterns

Analytical Type	Primary Goal	Core Question	Example Output Format	Structural Emphasis
Prescriptive	Recommend optimal action	What should we do?	Specific decisions, allocation, schedules, actionable recommendati ons	Defining decision variables, an objective function, and operational constraints

Key Definitions:

- **Model architecture:** The detailed blueprint outlining data inputs, processing steps, expected outputs, and underlying assumptions of an analytical system.
- **Feature variables:** The quantifiable data elements used by the model as the foundation for its calculations or predictions.
- **Target variable:** The main output or result the model aims to produce, such as a classification, forecast, or suggested action.
- **Functional relationship:** The mathematical or logical process that transforms input features into the target output.
- **Model parameters:** Internal coefficients or values learned from data during training that define the specific relationships the model has identified. These are distinct from hyperparameters, which are settings configured before training begins to control the learning process, such as learning rate or tree depth.

Step-by-Step Method:

1. **Clarify the analytical goal:** Clearly specify what the model needs to accomplish, whether it is description, prediction, or prescription.
2. **Define the target output:** Clarify the exact format and type of the model's main result, ensuring it aligns with the business objective.
3. **Identify potential inputs:** List all relevant data elements that could logically influence or explain the target output.
4. **Determine the analytical approach:** Choose the general methodological category (e.g., clustering, regression, optimization) that effectively links inputs to outputs.

5. **Document governing assumptions:** Clearly specify the conditions that must hold true for the model to remain valid and reliable.

Examples:

- **Example 1: Descriptive Model for Website Traffic Analysis:**
    - *Goal:* Understand visitor behavior patterns.
    - *Target:* User journey categories.
    - *Inputs:* Page visit sequences, time on page.
    - *Relationship:* A sequence analysis algorithm groups similar navigation paths.

- **Example 2: Predictive Model for Equipment Maintenance:**
    - *Goal:* Forecast machinery failure likelihood.
    - *Target:* A failure probability score.
    - *Inputs:* Sensor readings, maintenance history.
    - *Relationship:* A classification algorithm estimating probability based on sensor data patterns.

- **Example 3: Prescriptive Model for Marketing Budget Allocation:**
    - *Goal:* Recommend how to allocate funds to maximize leads.
    - *Target:* Specify the ideal dollar amount for each channel.
    - *Inputs:* Historical cost-per-lead data and channel budget constraints.
    - *Relationship:* An optimization algorithm that maximizes total leads while staying within the budget and limits.

Common Pitfalls:

- **The "Everything but the kitchen sink" approach:** Including all available data points without clear justification, which makes the model more complicated and adds noise.
- **Output ambiguity:** Failing to specify the model's output in a clear, measurable, and business-actionable format.
- **Ignoring practical constraints:** Designing a prescriptive model without accounting for business, regulatory, or physical limitations that define the boundaries of acceptable solutions.

Lesson 5.2: Constructing and Validating Models

Objective:
Implement the designed model structure by selecting and applying specific algorithms, thoroughly validating the process, and identifying and preventing common errors in specifications, implementation, and data.

Detailed Explanation:
This lesson shifts from architectural design to practical implementation. It involves choosing an appropriate algorithmic technique, preparing data in the required format, and training the model to learn from historical patterns. A key part is thoroughly validating the construction process through methods such as data splitting and cross-validation to ensure the model's generalizability. The team must actively avoid errors that undermine the model's effectiveness or fairness, including technical specification mistakes, data leakage, and inherent data flaws such as survivor bias.

Key Definitions:

- **Algorithm selection:** The process of choosing a specific computational method (e.g., decision tree, **linear regression**, simulation) suitable for the data and problem type.
- **Model training:** The process during which a model learns patterns or parameters from past data to make predictions or decisions.
- **Data leakage:** A major mistake in which information from future data or external sources not meant to be used is inadvertently included during model training, leading to overly optimistic performance estimates.
- **Infeasible formulation:** A state in prescriptive modeling where no possible solution can meet all constraints, indicating an overly restrictive or contradictory problem setup.
- **Survivor bias:** A logical error where a model is built only with data from entities that have "survived" a selection process (such as current customers or successful funds), while ignoring data from failures or dropouts. This method leads to overly optimistic and flawed conclusions.
- **Feature selection:** The process of automatically or manually choosing the most relevant features for model building to

simplify the model, improve interpretability, and reduce overfitting. Common techniques include forward selection (starting with no features and adding the most significant one at each step), backward elimination (starting with all features and removing the least significant one at each step), and stepwise selection (a hybrid that combines both forward and backward steps).

- **High bias (Underfitting):** A condition where a model is too simple to accurately identify the true pattern in the data, resulting in strong but incorrect assumptions and systematic mistakes on both training and new data.
- **High variance (Overfitting):** A situation where a model is too complex, capturing noise in the training data as if it were a true pattern, which causes it to perform well on training data but poorly on new, unseen data.

Table 23 Comparison of High Bias vs. High Variance

Characteristic	High Bias (Underfitting)	High Variance (Overfitting)
Definition	Model is too simple to capture the underlying pattern in the data.	Model is too complex and captures noise in the training data as a pattern.
Cause	Overly simplistic model, too few features, incorrect assumptions.	Excessively complex model, too many features, trained on noise.
Performance on Training Data	Poor performance (high error).	Excellent performance (very low error).
Performance on New/Test Data	Poor performance (high error).	Poor performance (high error, does not generalize).
Visual Analogy	A straight line forced through a curved data pattern.	A complex, wiggly line that passes through every training data point.
Primary Remedy	Increase model complexity, add relevant features, use a more powerful algorithm.	Simplify model, reduce features, use regularization, gather more training data.

Step-by-Step Method:

1. **Select the appropriate algorithm:** Choose a modeling technique suitable for your data characteristics, problem structure, and business objectives.
2. **Prepare and partition data:** Format the data for the chosen algorithm and split it into separate sets for training, validation, and final testing to ensure fair evaluation.
3. **Set initial parameters: Define** the initial parameters and hyperparameters that control the algorithm's learning behavior and complexity.
4. **Perform model training:** Run the algorithm on the training data to develop the model's internal logic or find the best decision variables.
5. **Apply feature selection:** Use methods such as backward elimination or regularization to identify and retain only the most influential variables, simplifying the model and reducing the risk of overfitting.
6. **Diagnose construction errors:** Systematically identify common issues such as data leakage, overfitting (high variance), underfitting (high bias), infeasible formulations, and survivor bias in the training data.

Examples:

- **Example 1: Predictive model with data leakage:** A subscription renewal model uses "final month usage data" to predict renewal, even though the decision should be made at the 10-month mark without knowing the last two months.

- **Example 2: Prescriptive model with infeasibility:** A university exam scheduler requires all third-year engineering students to take five exams within three consecutive days while also demanding a 24-hour gap between exams, a mathematically impossible situation.

- **Example 3: Survivor bias in model data:** A churn prediction model built solely with data from current customers ignores the traits of those who have already left, skewing the model toward characteristics of "having survived" rather than real indicators of loyalty.

Common Pitfalls:

- **Overfitting (high variance)/Underfitting (high bias):** See the definitions above and Table 24 for a detailed breakdown of overfitting and underfitting.
- **Misspecification:** Wrongly defining the functional relationship between inputs and output, such as applying a linear model to a distinctly non-linear phenomenon. This causes systematic errors that neither more data nor parameter tuning can fix.
- **Ignoring survivor bias:** Using non-representative data that only includes successful or existing cases, which leads to flawed insights and predictions.

Table 24 Common Model Construction Errors

Error	Description	Primary Consequence	Key Mitigation Strategy
Data Leakage	Using information during training that would not be available in a real-world prediction scenario.	Creates deceptively high-performance during testing that will not hold in production, leading to model failure.	Implement strict time-based data splits and conduct feature validity checks with domain experts.
Overfitting (High Variance)	Creating a model so complex it memorizes noise and specific details of the training data.	Excellent performance on training data but poor generalization to any new, unseen data.	Use techniques like cross-validation, regularization, and simplify the model architecture.
Infeasible Formulation	Defining a set of constraints in a prescriptive model that are contradictory or impossible to satisfy simultaneously.	The model fails to produce any solution, halting the decision-making process.	Review constraint logic with stakeholders, use soft constraints, and prototype with a simplified model first.
Underfitting (High Bias)	Creating a model too simple to capture the underlying trend in the data.	Poor performance on both training and new data, failing to provide useful insights or predictions.	Increase model complexity, engineer additional relevant features, or select a more powerful algorithm.
Survivor Bias	Training a model only on data that has "survived" a selection process, ignoring failures or dropouts.	Model learns traits of "survival" rather than true predictive relationships, leading to over-optimistic and flawed predictions.	Ensure training data is representative of the entire population, including failed/non-respondent cases.

Lesson 5.3: Evaluating Model Performance and Ethical Implications

Objective:
Assess developed models for accuracy, reliability, and fairness using a range of statistical methods and metrics, and review outputs for ethical concerns before deployment.

Detailed Explanation:
Creating a model is just part of the process. Thorough evaluation verifies accuracy, reliability, and fairness before the model is deployed. This includes testing the model on new data and measuring its performance against predefined success metrics. The chosen metric must align with the business context, such as whether false positives are more costly than false negatives, or whether percentage error provides more useful insight than absolute error. Evaluation must also include an assessment of model fidelity, which is the degree to which the model accurately reflects the real-world system it represents. Structured ethical audits to identify unintended bias or unfair outcomes across demographic groups are a standard requirement in responsible model development.

Key Definitions:

- **Validation:** The process of evaluating a model's performance using data not involved in training, providing an estimate of how it will perform in real-world scenarios. Key techniques include **train-test-validation splits** and **cross-validation methods such as K-fold and LOOCV**.
- **Performance metric:** A measurable value used to assess a model's effectiveness (e.g., accuracy, precision, recall, R-squared, RMSE, MAPE, F1 Score, AUC).
- **Model fidelity:** The degree to which a model accurately represents the real-world system or processes it is designed to simulate, assessed through face validity, historical data validation, and predictive validation.
- **Confusion matrix:** A table that summarizes the performance of a classification model by comparing actual class labels against predicted labels across four outcomes: True Positive (TP), True Negative (TN), False Positive (FP, analogous to Type I Error), and False Negative (FN, analogous to Type II Error). Key metrics

derived from it include **Precision** = TP/(TP+FP), **Recall** (Sensitivity) = TP/(TP+FN), and **Specificity** = TN/(TN+FP).

Table 25 Model Evaluation Metric Selection Guide

Analytical Task	Primary Metric(s)	Business Context for Selection
Binary Classification (e.g., Fraud Detection)	Precision, Recall, F1-Score	Use Precision to minimize false alarms. Use Recall to ensure most cases are caught. The F1-Score balances the two when both are equally important.
Forecasting / Regression (e.g., Sales Forecast)	RMSE, MAPE	Use RMSE to heavily penalize large errors. Use MAPE for an intuitive percentage-based error, but not when actual values can be near zero.
Prescriptive Optimization (e.g., Resource Scheduling)	% Improvement vs. Baseline	The ultimate measure is tangible improvement over the current process (e.g., "15% cost reduction" or "20% faster service").
Descriptive Clustering (e.g., Customer Segmentation)	Business Utility & Silhouette Score	Statistical cohesion (Silhouette Score) is helpful, but validation by domain experts on the actionability of segments is paramount.

F1 score: The harmonic mean of Precision and Recall, calculated as 2 × (Precision × Recall) / (Precision + Recall). It provides a single metric that balances both and is preferred over accuracy when class distributions are imbalanced because accuracy alone can be misleading when one class dominates.

- **ROC curve & AUC:** A graphical plot that shows the trade-off between the True Positive Rate (Sensitivity) and False Positive Rate at various classification thresholds. The Area Under the Curve (AUC) measures the model's ability to rank predictions correctly.

Figure 22 The Confusion Matrix for Binary Classification

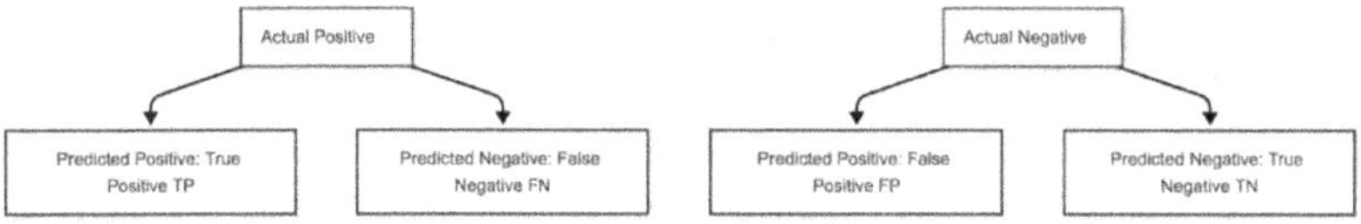

Figure 23 The ROC Curve Concept

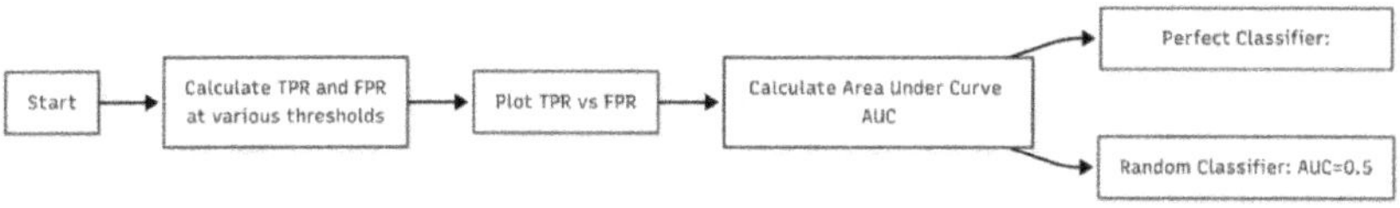

- **Lift and gain charts:** Evaluation tools used in marketing to measure the effectiveness of a predictive model compared to random selection. They show the "lift" in response rates achieved by targeting segments ranked by the model.

Figure 24 Process for Creating Lift and Gain Charts

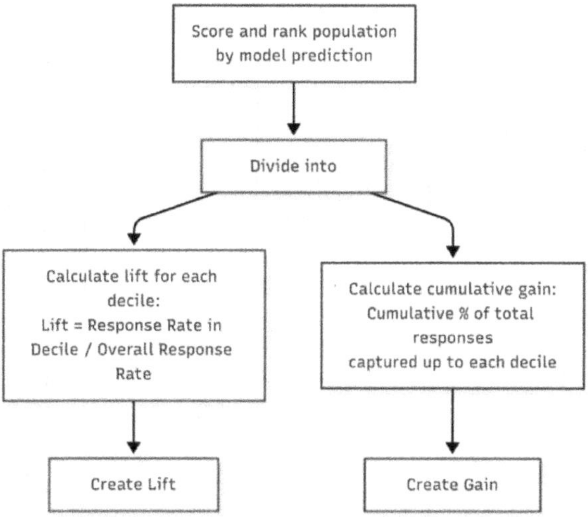

- **R-squared (Coefficient of determination):** A statistical measure that indicates the proportion of variation in the dependent variable explained by the independent variables in a regression model.

- **MAPE (Mean Absolute Percentage Error):** A metric used to measure prediction accuracy, expressed as a percentage, by averaging the absolute percentage errors.
- **RMSE (Root Mean Squared Error):** A common measure of the difference between predicted and observed values, expressed in the original units of the variable, highlighting larger errors.
- **Algorithmic bias:** Systematic and unfair discrimination in model outputs against individuals or groups based on protected attributes such as race, gender, or age.
- **Model selection criteria:** Quantitative methods such as the **AIC (Akaike Information Criterion)** and **BIC (Bayesian Information Criterion)**. These methods are used to choose between candidate models by balancing goodness-of-fit with model complexity, measured by the number of parameters. Lower values signify a better balance.

Table 26 Comparison of Model Selection Criteria: AIC vs. BIC

Criterion	**Name**	**Formula (Simplified)**	**Penalty for Model Complexity**	**Primary Use Case & Philosophy**
AIC	Akaike Information Criterion	-2*log(Likelihood) + 2*k	2 * (number of parameters, k)	Prediction-focused. Seeks the model that will perform best on new data, favoring better fit but penalizing complexity.
BIC	Bayesian Information Criterion	-2*log(Likelihood)* + *k*log(n)	(number of parameters, k) * log(sample size, n)	"True Model" identification. More heavily penalizes complexity, especially with large n, favoring simpler models. Tends to select more parsimonious models than AIC.

Step-by-Step Method:

1. **Partition data carefully:** Split data into separate training, validation, and final hold-out test sets. Use the training set to fit the model, the validation set for hyperparameter tuning and

model selection, and the hold-out test set only once for final performance estimation. Cross-validation can replace the validation set during tuning to maximize data usage, but the final hold-out test set must remain untouched until the model is fully finalized.

2. **Execute on hold-out data:** Run the final model on the reserved test dataset that it has never seen before during training or tuning.
3. **Calculate contextual performance metrics:** Compute metrics that align with the business goal and analytical task.
4. **Assess model fidelity:** Evaluate face validity (eyeball test) with experts, verify the reproduction of historical outcomes, and confirm predictions against new data.
5. **Apply statistical validation and selection:** Use techniques such as cross-validation to get reliable estimates and apply criteria such as AIC/BIC for objective model comparison.
6. **Conduct ethical auditing:** Evaluate model outcomes across different population groups to identify significant disparities that could indicate bias.
7. **Verify practical feasibility:** For prescriptive models, ensure that recommended actions are logical, executable, and compliant with all real-world constraints.

Examples:

- **Example 1: Evaluating a Hiring Tool:** Use stratified k-fold cross-validation to ensure consistent results. An ethical audit reveals the tool's "recommended for interview" rate is disproportionately low for one gender, indicating bias learned from historical data.

- **Example 2: Choosing a Forecasting Model:** Two time-series models have been created. Model A has a lower RMSE but a higher MAPE than Model B. The choice depends on the business context, specifically whether reducing large absolute errors or understanding relative percentage errors is more important for the decision being supported.

- **Example 3: Evaluating a Campaign Targeting Model:** A gain chart shows that contacting only the top 20% of customers ranked by the model captures 65% of the overall probable responders, demonstrating significant lift and efficiency.

Common Pitfalls:

- **Test set snooping:** Repeatedly testing and adjusting the model based on test set performance. Each time the test set is used to guide a decision, it becomes part of the training process in effect. This undermines the set's role as an independent performance estimate and produces overly optimistic results.
- **Misuse of metrics:** Using R-squared to compare models with different numbers of predictors (instead of Adjusted R-squared) or relying solely on accuracy for imbalanced classification problems.
- **Misinterpreting correlation as causation:** Treating a descriptive model's identified relationship as conclusive proof that one variable causes a change in another.
- **Neglecting edge cases:** Failing to evaluate the model's performance during rare but important situations, like market disruptions.

Lesson 5.4: Model Refinement Through Stakeholder Feedback

Objective:
Learn how to diagnose and resolve issues identified by model users or clients, thereby refining both data and model components to better align with operational realities and expectations.

Detailed Explanation:
A model's initial version is rarely perfect in real-world use. Calibration is an ongoing process that improves a model through feedback from actual application. Stakeholders might say the outputs seem "off," impractical, or not aligned with their domain expertise. This feedback surfaces hidden issues, such as data that no longer reflects current conditions (concept drift) or model assumptions that ignore key practical realities. Good calibration connects the technical model to the business context it serves, keeping it relevant and accurate over time.

Key Definitions:

- **Model calibration:** The process of fine-tuning a model's parameters, thresholds, or structure after the initial deployment to improve its accuracy or better satisfy user expectations.
- **Concept drift:** A phenomenon where the underlying relationship between input variables and the target variable changes over time, making the model's learned patterns less relevant to current conditions. This differs from data drift, where input distributions change but the underlying relationship remains stable. Both require monitoring and can trigger retraining.
- **Stakeholder feedback:** Direct input from end-users, clients, or domain experts regarding the model's usability, relevance, and output quality in real-world conditions.

Step-by-Step Method:

1. **Solicit structured feedback:** Gather specific, actionable concerns from users, such as 'The demand forecast is consistently 15% low for new product categories.'
2. **Perform a root cause analysis:** Determine whether the problem originates from the data (such as missing variables,

outdated information, or concept drift) or the model itself (such as incorrect assumptions or missing constraints).

3. **Implement targeted adjustments:** Update data sources, add or remove features, tweak model parameters, or change constraints based on the root cause.
4. **Reassess performance:** Test the recalibrated model to confirm the issue has been effectively resolved without affecting other performance metrics.
5. **Document and communicate changes:** Clearly note what was modified, why, and how it affects stakeholders and future maintainers.

Examples:

- **Example 1: Improving a Retail Demand Model:** Feedback shows underestimation for viral products. Root Cause (Data): Training data lacks records of non-linear, viral demand spikes. Action: Add early-velocity metrics or use algorithms tailored to exponential growth.

- **Example 2: Refining a Hospital Staffing Model:** Feedback indicates staffing levels are insufficient during shift changes. Root Cause (Model): The model relies on average arrival rates and lacks peak-capacity buffers. Action: Add time-varying capacity constraints or use stochastic programming to address uncertainty.

Common Pitfalls:

- **Overfitting to anecdotes:** Making significant model changes based on isolated feedback without verifying if it indicates a systematic issue.
- **Ignoring user expertise:** Dismissing stakeholder concerns as "not understanding the model," which could overlook important flaws in real-world use.
- **Creating undocumented adjustments:** Making calibration changes without documenting the rationale, which makes the model's evolving behavior difficult to understand, audit, or replicate.

Lesson 5.5: Integrating Multiple Models for Complex Solutions

Objective:
Combine different analytical models into a coordinated system to solve complex business problems that no single model can address effectively.

Detailed Explanation:
Many real-world business problems are too complex for just one analytical method. Model integration involves carefully combining descriptive, predictive, and prescriptive models into a coordinated pipeline or ensemble. For example, a descriptive model might segment customers, a predictive model might forecast each segment's behavior, and a prescriptive model might recommend the best action for each segment. Effective integration expands the analytical capability of the solution but requires careful planning to manage complexity, prevent errors from propagating between models, and keep the system interpretable.

Figure 25 An Analytical Model Pipeline for Integrated Solutions

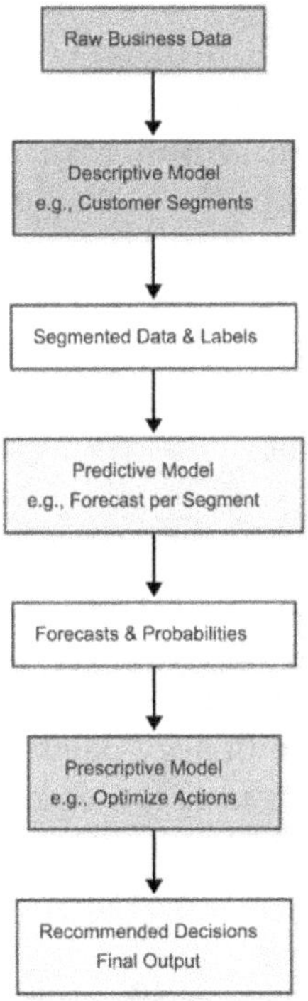

Key Definitions:

- **Model ensemble:** A technique that combines predictions from multiple models to produce a single output that is typically more accurate and reliable than any individual model. Ensembles may combine models of the same type, as in bagging and boosting, or different types, as in stacking, where a meta-model learns to combine the outputs of diverse base models.
- **Analytical pipeline:** A sequence of models where each model's output serves as the input for the next, with each step handling a specific part of the analysis.
- **System integration:** The technical and architectural process of connecting different models to enable data exchange and operate as a unified analytical solution.

Step-by-Step Method:

1. **Decompose the problem:** Break the main business problem into specific sub-problems, either sequential or parallel.
2. **Map models to sub-problems:** Assign the most appropriate model type (descriptive, predictive, prescriptive) to each sub-problem.
3. **Design the data flow:** Clearly specify how information will move between models, making sure that the output formats of earlier models match the input formats of later models.
4. **Build and test components:** Develop and validate each model separately using the evaluation and validation techniques from Lessons 5.2 and 5.3 before connecting them.
5. **Test the integrated system:** Validate the entire pipeline end-to-end to confirm accuracy, performance, and that errors in one component do not propagate through the system and corrupt downstream outputs.

Examples:

- **Integrated System for Dynamic E-commerce Pricing:** A descriptive clustering model groups products based on price elasticity. A predictive time-series model forecasts demand for each cluster at different price points. A prescriptive optimization model uses these forecasts to recommend prices that maximize profit.

Common Pitfalls:

- **Increased system opacity:** As models are sequential, it becomes harder to understand how final decisions are made. This reduced transparency weakens trust and makes debugging more difficult.
- **Error propagation:** Inaccuracies or biases in an initial model, such as a flawed segmentation, are amplified and spread through all subsequent models.
- **Unmanageable complexity:** Building an overly complicated system that becomes impossible to debug, maintain, update, or explain.

Lesson 5.6: Documenting and Communicating Model Results

Objective:
Create complete model documentation and translate technical findings into clear, actionable insights tailored to diverse audiences.

Detailed Explanation:
The value of a model only becomes clear when its insights are understood, trusted, and acted upon. This involves two main activities: thorough documentation and audience-specific communication. Documentation acts as the technical record of the model, covering its purpose, data sources, architecture, performance, and validation, enabling reproduction, auditing, and ongoing maintenance. Effective communication means translating technical details into engaging narratives for different stakeholders, emphasizing business impact, assumptions, and limitations. Tailoring the message for the audience supports informed decisions and builds organizational trust.

Table 27 Audience-Tailored Communication Focus

Audience	Primary Need	Communication Focus	What to Avoid
Technical Team	Reproducibility & Maintenance	Detailed methodology, code, parameters, validation data, version control.	Vague business statements without technical backing.
Business Managers	Actionable Decisions	Clear recommendations, impact on KPIs, required actions, resource implications.	Deep technical jargon and algorithmic details.
Executive Leadership	Strategic Impact & ROI	Alignment with strategy, high-level benefits, risk summary, investment rationale.	Operational minutiae and lengthy technical reports.
End-Users / Clients	Usability & Trust	How to use the output, what it means for them, feedback channels, limitations for safe use.	Overwhelming them with assumptions or technical limitations unless critical for correct use.

Key Definitions:

- **Model documentation:** A living record that describes every stage of a model's lifecycle, from initial business goals and data sources through algorithmic specifics, validation outcomes, and deployment guidance.
- **Assumptions log:** A detailed and clear list of the conditions, beliefs, and data features on which the model's validity and reliability depend.
- **Limitations statement:** An honest and transparent disclosure of the model's recognized shortcomings, potential edge cases where failure may occur, and the boundaries defining its proper use.

Step-by-Step Method:

1. **Prepare technical documentation:** Document the business objective, data sources, feature definitions, rationale for algorithm selection, parameter settings, and full validation reports that include all performance metrics and selection criteria.
2. **Document performance and validation:** Include all evaluation results, test data performance metrics, ethical audit findings, and comparisons to baseline models.
3. **Explicitly list assumptions and limitations:** Create a dedicated section that details what the model assumes to be true and where it should not be used.
4. **Draft an executive summary:** Create a one-page overview that explains the business problem, the key finding or recommendation of the model, the anticipated impact on the business, and any major caveats.
5. **Customize communications based on audience:** Emphasize methodology and validation for technical teams, and highlight insights, recommendations, ROI, and risk management for business decision-makers.

Examples:

- **Communicating a Customer Lifetime Value (CLV) Model:** For Data Scientists, explain the BG-NBD model, its MAPE on holdout data, and main predictors. For Marketing Executives, highlight the high-value customer segment and projected profit gain from targeted retention.

Common Pitfalls:

- **Documentation as an afterthought:** Creating documentation only at the end of the project, leading to incomplete or inaccurate records.
- **Jargon-heavy communication:** Using technical terms that alienate business stakeholders and obscure the main message.
- **Overselling the model:** Failing to clearly communicate limitations and assumptions, which can result in misuse and loss of trust.

Summary

Model architecture converts business challenges into technical frameworks. Descriptive models detect patterns in historical data, predictive models link inputs to forecasts or classifications, and prescriptive models set decision variables and constraints to suggest optimal actions. Each framework outlines the desired output format, specifies relevant input variables, and explains the relationships that govern how inputs become results.

Model construction turns designs into algorithms through careful implementation. Algorithm choice matches data traits, with data split into training, validation, and test sets. Feature selection simplifies models while keeping accuracy. Watch out for errors: data leakage uses future info, overfitting captures noise, underfitting misses true patterns, infeasible formats break real-world rules, survivor bias ignores failures, skewing outcomes.

Model evaluation assesses performance against business-aligned metrics using unseen data. For classification tasks, precision, recall, F1-score, and confusion matrices are used, with the choice of metric guided by whether false positives or false negatives incur a higher cost. Regression and forecasting employ RMSE to penalize large errors or MAPE for percentage-based accuracy. Prescriptive models demonstrate value by quantifying improvements over the current baseline process, expressed as cost reductions, efficiency gains, or other business-aligned outcomes. Ethical auditing examines outcomes across population groups to detect bias. Stakeholder feedback prompts refinement through root-cause analysis, distinguishing between data issues (e.g., concept drift) and model problems (e.g., missing constraints).

Complex problems often need integrating models into coordinated pipelines. Descriptive models segment customers, feeding into predictive models that forecast behavior, which inform prescriptive models that recommend actions. Documentation records objectives, data sources, rationale, and validation. Assumption logs and limitations prevent misuse by clarifying conditions. Communication adapts content: methodology for technical teams, recommendations and KPIs for managers, strategic impact for executives, and usability guidance for end users.

Chapter 5: Practice Questions

Q1. When designing a prescriptive model architecture, what is the main structural focus?
A) Analyzing relationships within historical data.
B) Mapping input features to a target output variable.
C) Defining decision variables, an objective function, and constraints.
D) Grouping similar data points into segments.

Q2. A predictive model for loan default uses a borrower's "future credit score update from next month" as a feature during training. This is a classic example of which model construction error?
A) Overfitting
B) Underfitting
C) Infeasible Formulation
D) Data Leakage

Q3. When evaluating a binary classification model for a rare disease, where missing a positive case is highly costly, which metric should be prioritized?
A) Precision
B) R-squared
C) Recall (Sensitivity)
D) Specificity

Q4. A model designed to analyze the traits of top salespeople uses data only from current employees who have not been fired or quit. This model is most vulnerable to:
A) High Variance
B) Survivor Bias
C) Concept Drift
D) Data Leakage

Q5. The F1 Score is best described as:
A) The proportion of variance explained by a regression model.
B) The harmonic mean of Precision and Recall.
C) The square root of the average of squared errors.
D) A measure of lift compared to a random baseline.

Q6. Which technique involves dividing data into k subsets, using each one as a validation set while training on the others to maximize data

usage for performance evaluation?
A) Train-Test Split
B) K-Fold Cross-Validation
C) Backward Elimination
D) AIC Calculation

Q7. For a regression model, you need a single metric that penalizes large errors more heavily. Which should you choose?
A) Mean Absolute Error (MAE)
B) R-squared
C) Root Mean Square Error (RMSE)
D) Mean Absolute Percentage Error (MAPE)

Q8. When presenting model results to executive leadership, the main focus should be on:
A) Detailed algorithmic parameters and code.
B) The strategic impact, ROI, and high-level recommendations.
C) Step-by-step instructions for daily use.
D) The complete statistical validation report.

Q9. In a prescriptive optimization model for delivery routing, if no solution can satisfy all constraints (such as delivery times and vehicle capacities), the model is said to be:
A) Overfit
B) Leaking data
C) Infeasible
D) Unbiased

Q10. The process of starting with all candidates' features and iteratively removing the least significant one until a stopping criterion is met is called:
A) Forward Selection
B) Stepwise Selection
C) Backward Elimination
D) Cross-Validation

Q11. An ROC curve plots the True Positive Rate against what?
A) Precision
B) Recall
C) False Positive Rate
D) R-squared

Q12. Which of the following is used to select among statistical models by balancing goodness-of-fit with a penalty for the number of parameters, with a stronger penalty for larger sample sizes?
A) F1 Score
B) Adjusted R-squared
C) Akaike Information Criterion (AIC)
D) Bayesian Information Criterion (BIC)

Q13. A stakeholder reports that a demand forecasting model consistently underestimates sales for products featured in social media campaigns. The most appropriate first step in calibration is to:
A) Immediately add more complexity to the model.
B) Dismiss the feedback as anecdotal.
C) Conduct a root cause analysis to see if the data lacks viral product history.
D) Rebuild the model from scratch with a different algorithm.

Q14. In a customer management model pipeline, a descriptive segmentation model feeds into a predictive lifetime value model, which in turn feeds into a prescriptive marketing action model. This is an example of:
A) An Ensemble
B) An Analytical Pipeline
C) High Fidelity
D) Survivor Bias

Q15. Which evaluation tool is specifically designed to show how many times better a model is at identifying positive cases in a ranked list compared to random selection?
A) Confusion Matrix
B) ROC Curve
C) Lift Chart
D) MAPE Chart

Q16. A model that is too simple, failing to capture non-linear relationships in the data and performing poorly on both training and test sets, is suffering from:
A) High Variance (Overfitting)
B) Data Leakage
C) High Bias (Underfitting)
D) Infeasibility

Q17. The primary purpose of maintaining a formal "Assumptions Log" as part of model documentation is to:
A) Show how clever the model design is.
B) Provide a clear record of the conditions required for the model to remain valid.
C) List all the software libraries used.
D) Hide the model's potential weaknesses.

Q18. Mean Absolute Percentage Error (MAPE) is a useful metric because it:
A) Is not affected by outliers.
B) Expresses error as an easy-to-understand percentage.
C) Can be used even when actual values are zero.
D) Penalizes under-forecasts more heavily than over-forecasts.

Q19. When combining multiple models, a major risk where a small mistake in an early model leads to a large error in the final output is called:
A) Increased Opacity
B) Error Propagation
C) Model Fidelity
D) Algorithmic Bias

Q20. The coefficient of determination (R-squared) in a linear regression model shows:
A) The statistical significance of each predictor.
B) The proportion of variance in the target variable explained by the model.
C) The strength of the relationship between each predictor and the target.
D) The prediction error on new data.

Chapter 6: Deployment of Solutions and Operational Integration

Introduction

The final stage of the analytics lifecycle involves turning a validated model into a dependable and valuable business asset. This step is structured within an iterative project framework such as the Cross-Industry Standard Process for **Data Mining** (CRISP-DM). CRISP-DM outlines six interconnected, repeating phases: Business Understanding, Data Understanding, Data Preparation, Modeling, Evaluation, and Deployment. This chapter emphasizes the Deployment phase, which involves planning for maintenance, monitoring, final reporting, and handoff to make sure the solution is sustainably integrated into business operations. The process includes confirming business value through thorough validation, communicating results clearly for stakeholder decisions, defining production requirements, and overseeing testing and monitoring in live environments. Mastering this phase connects analytical potential to real-world business impact. It ensures solutions are technically effective, operationally sustainable, and ethically sound.

Figure 26 CRISP-DM Deployment Phase

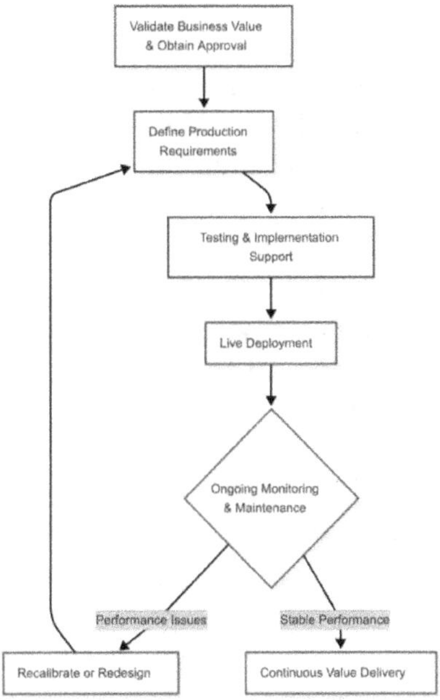

Lesson 6.1: Conducting Business Value Validation

Objective:
Confirm that an analytical solution adequately solves the initial business challenge and delivers measurable benefits before scaling, using structured validation methods.

Detailed Explanation:
Business value validation acts as a key checkpoint before deployment, extending beyond technical assessment to evaluate real-world impact. It confirms that the solution effectively addresses the problem, provides measurable benefits, and aligns with organizational goals and ethical standards. The DMAIC (Define, Measure, Analyze, Improve, Control) framework originated in Six Sigma as a structured problem-solving method. It defines the problem and success metrics, measures current performance against a baseline, analyses data to identify root causes of variation, implements targeted improvements, and establishes ongoing control through monitoring to sustain results. Validation also includes structured testing in a controlled pilot environment that simulates real operations, evaluating both quantitative results and qualitative factors such as usability and integration readiness. This ensures resources are committed only to solutions that clearly demonstrate value.

Key Definitions:

- **Value validation:** The structured process of verifying that an analytical solution delivers measurable business benefits and effectively solves the key problem it targets.
- **Pilot environment:** A controlled, production-like setting where a solution is tested with real users and data, but with a limited scope to reduce risk.
- **Ethical compliance review:** An evaluation of a solution's adherence to principles of fairness, transparency, privacy, and social responsibility.
- **Success criteria:** The specific, measurable conditions that must be met for the solution to be considered successful, directly linked to the original business objectives.

Table 28 Business Validation Assessment Framework

Validation Dimension	Key Questions to Answer	Metrics & Evidence	Stakeholders Involved
Business Impact	Does the solution deliver the promised value? Does it solve the original problem?	ROI calculation, KPI improvement vs. baseline, cost savings/revenue impact.	Business Sponsors, Finance, Department Heads.
Technical Performance	Does the solution meet technical requirements in a real-world setting?	Model accuracy on live data, system response time, error rates, integration success.	Data Scientists, IT/Engineering Teams.
User Adoption & Usability	Will target users adopt and effectively use the solution?	User task completion rates, satisfaction scores, training completion, feedback on ease of use.	End-Users, UX/Design Teams, Training Specialists.
Operational Viability	Can the solution be reliably operated, supported, and maintained?	System uptime during pilot, support ticket volume, maintenance procedure validation.	Operations Teams, IT Support, System Administrators.
Ethical & Compliance	Does the solution operate fairly and within regulatory boundaries?	Bias audit results, privacy impact assessment, regulatory checklist completion.	Legal/Compliance Officers, Ethics Board, Data Privacy Team.

- **DMAIC**: A five-phase, data-driven improvement framework consisting of Define (establish the problem and success criteria), Measure (quantify current performance), Analyze (identify root causes), Improve (implement and test solutions), and Control (monitor and sustain results). It provides a structured approach to validating and embedding analytical solutions within existing business processes.

Step-by-Step Method:

1. **Define validation metrics and scope:** Clearly identify the business problem and the specific, measurable success criteria (e.g., "reduce process time by 20%" or "increase conversion by 5%") to ensure clarity and focus.
2. **Design and execute a pilot:** Implement the solution in a small, representative area of the business using real users and operational data.
3. **Measure quantitative impact:** Gather data on the predefined success metrics during the pilot period and compare performance to the established baseline.
4. **Analyze results and root causes:** Use data analysis to determine whether success criteria are met and investigate the underlying causes of any deviations or unexpected results.
5. **Assess qualitative factors and improve:** Evaluate user adoption, ease of use, workflow integration, and user confidence. Refine the solution based on feedback.
6. **Conduct an ethics and compliance review and create a control plan:** Audit for bias, privacy issues, and regulatory compliance. Develop a plan for ongoing monitoring during the Control phase of DMAIC after deployment.

Examples:

- **Example 1: Validating a Predictive Inventory System using DMAIC:**
  - *Define:* The goal is to reduce stockouts by 15% without increasing holding costs.
  - *Measure:* Pilot in 10% of stores shows a 15% reduction in stockouts and a 10% decrease in excess inventory costs.
  - *Analyze:* Analysis confirms that the optimization does not systematically disadvantage suppliers from specific regions.
  - *Improve:* Fine-tune the model to more accurately identify promotional items.

  - *Control:* Plan to monitor weekly stockout rates after deployment.

- **Example 2: Validating a Customer Service Chatbot:**
  - *Pilot:* The bot handles Tier-1 inquiries for a single product line over two months.
  - *Business Value Measured:* The bot handles 40% of inquiries without human help, reducing average handle time by 30%.
  - *Qualitative Assessment:* Feedback highlights ease of use, but complex queries are not handled well, underscoring the need for clear escalation procedures (an improvement action).

Common Pitfalls:

- **Validating the incorrect aspect:** Solely focusing on model accuracy (e.g., 95% AUC) while neglecting the actual business outcome (e.g., cost savings).
- **Insufficient pilot duration:** Running a test for too short a period to capture relevant business cycles or long-term user behavior. A pilot that misses seasonal patterns, month-end spikes, or other cyclical events cannot produce reliable validation results.
- **Neglecting the human element:** Failing to assess how the solution fits into user workflows or whether adequate change management is in place. A technically sound solution can fail at scale if users are not prepared, trained, or willing to adopt it.
- **Omitting DMAIC phases:** Not fully completing the Measure and Analyze stages, resulting in solutions that only address symptoms instead of root causes.

Lesson 6.2: Reporting Validation Findings for Decision-Making

Objective:
Compile and communicate validation results in a clear, actionable report that enables stakeholders to make informed deployment decisions.

Detailed Explanation:
The validation report serves as the primary tool for transforming technical and operational findings into a compelling business case for action. Its goal is not to document every minor detail but to deliver the key information decision-makers need to approve, reject, or modify the deployment plan. An effective report balances thoroughness with brevity, combining data-driven evidence with a clear explanation of risks, benefits, and recommended next steps. It must be tailored to its audience, offering strategic insights for executives and specific operational details for planning teams.

Key Definitions:

- **Decision-focused report:** A document created to support a particular business decision (e.g., "Should we deploy this solution?") by highlighting implications instead of detailing the methodology.
- **Executive summary:** A concise opening section that addresses three key stakeholder questions: What was found? What do the results mean? What actions are recommended?
- **Actionable recommendation:** A clear and straightforward suggestion for the next steps, supported by evidence in the report.

Step-by-Step Method:

1. **Start with the conclusion (Executive Summary):** Include a brief section outlining the main finding, business impact, and key recommendation.
2. **Summarize methodology and scope:** Clearly explain what was tested, how it was tested (pilot design), and the limitations of the validation process.
3. **Present key findings:** Report quantitative results (impact on KPIs) and qualitative insights (user feedback, integration observations) with clear visuals such as charts and tables.

4. **Analyze business impact:** Translate findings into business language, potential ROI, cost savings, revenue impact, risk reduction, or strategic advantage.
5. **Assess risks and limitations:** Honestly identify potential downsides, operational risks, ethical considerations, and the solution's boundaries.
6. **Provide clear recommendations:** State a definitive suggestion (Proceed, Do Not Proceed, Proceed with Modifications) along with a rationale and recommended next steps or conditions.

Examples:

- **Example 1: Report for a Fraud Detection System:**
    - *Executive Summary:* The pilot achieved a 92% fraud detection rate with a 1.5% false-positive rate, preventing an estimated $250K in monthly losses. We recommend full deployment accompanied by an enhanced six-month monitoring plan.
    - *Key Finding:* The system identified 15% more fraudulent transactions than the current rule-based system, while reducing manual review workload by 60%.

- **Example 2: Report for a Staff Scheduling Optimization Tool:**
    - *Recommendation:* Proceed with a phased deployment. The pilot demonstrated a 12% improvement in schedule efficiency. Do not deploy until the designated training program is complete.

Common Pitfalls:

- **Burying the lead:** Hiding the main recommendation deep inside the report.
- **Overwhelmed by data:** Including all raw data points without context hides the main story behind technical detail. Present only the findings that directly support the recommendation.
- **Avoiding hard truths:** Ignoring or downplaying significant risks or negative feedback can erode trust and lead to poor decisions.

Lesson 6.3: Securing Stakeholder Alignment for Deployment

Objective:
Secure formal organizational commitment and resources by aligning stakeholders around a shared understanding of the deployment plan, its benefits, and its requirements, using tools such as process mapping.

Detailed Explanation:
Even the most thoroughly validated solution can fail if the necessary organizational support is lacking. This lesson highlights the importance of human and procedural factors in moving from approval to implementation. A useful tool for establishing early shared understanding is the SIPOC (Suppliers, Inputs, Process, Outputs, Customers) diagram. It provides a high-level view of the process in which the solution will operate, clarifying key boundaries and interfaces. This clarity supports proactive stakeholder management, secures formal sign-off, and ensures all stakeholders, from end users to IT support, understand their roles in deployment. The goal is to turn passive agreement into active commitment and shared ownership.

Key Definitions:

- **Formal sponsorship:** Clear, documented support from an executive or business leader with the authority to allocate resources and resolve organizational obstacles.
- **Deployment charter:** A short document that defines the agreed scope, timeline, success criteria, roles, and resources for the deployment phase.
- **Stakeholder map:** A visual tool that identifies all individuals or groups affected by the deployment, their level of influence, and their main concerns.
- **SIPOC:** A high-level process mapping tool that identifies Suppliers, Inputs, the Process (four to seven steps), Outputs, and Customers. It helps define the project scope and align stakeholders on process boundaries.

Step-by-Step Method:

1. **Map the process using SIPOC:** Define the high-level process that the solution will impact. Identify Suppliers (data sources), Inputs (data, triggers), the main process steps, Outputs

(predictions, reports), and Customers (decision-makers, end users).

2. **Identify and analyze stakeholders:** Use the SIPOC outputs (particularly Customers and Suppliers) to determine all affected parties. Understand their interests, influence, and possible objections.

Figure 27 Stakeholder Map

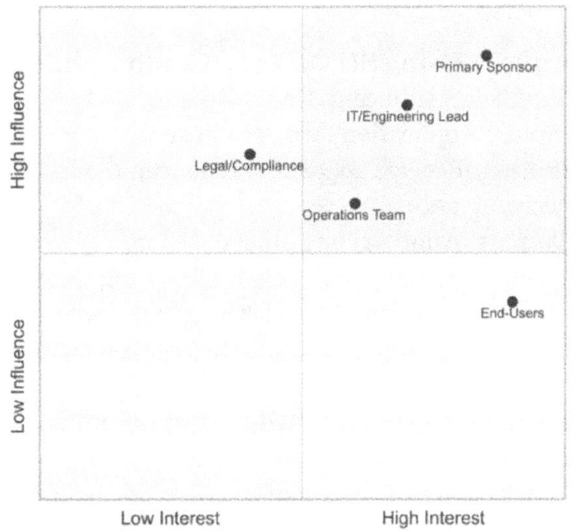

3. **Present the validation case:** Share the validation report findings, highlighting benefits and addressing concerns specific to each stakeholder group.
4. **Negotiate and finalize the deployment plan:** Work together to determine the rollout scope, timeline, resource needs, and success metrics.
5. **Formalize the commitment:** Secure documented approval for the deployment charter from the primary sponsor and key stakeholder representatives.
6. **Establish governance:** Define clear communication channels, decision-making authority, and escalation procedures for deployment issues.

Figure 28 Three-Phase Process for Securing Stakeholder Alignment

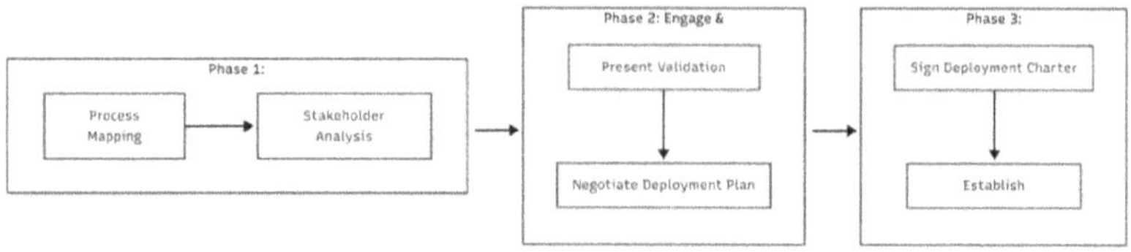

The three-phase process for stakeholder alignment moves from understanding to engagement, then to formal agreement and governance.

Examples:

- **Example 1: Using SIPOC for a Credit Application Model:**
  - *Suppliers:* Applicant, Credit Bureau.
  - *Inputs:* Application form, credit score.
  - *Process:* Receive app, verify data, run model, make a decision, notify.
  - *Outputs:* Approval or Denial decision.
  - *Customers:* Applicant, Legal, Marketing Department.
  - *Alignment Action:* This SIPOC clarifies where IT should integrate the model and who in Legal receives the outputs.

- **Example 2: Addressing Objections in a Process Automation Deployment:**
  - *Concern:* Operations staff are worried about losing their jobs.
  - *Alignment Action:* The team revised the deployment plan to include a reskilling program that emphasizes the tool's role in eliminating repetitive tasks, enabling users to focus on higher-value activities.

Common Pitfalls:

- **Confusing agreement with alignment:** Assuming silence means full buy-in during meetings.
- **Neglecting key stakeholders:** Failing to include an important department or individual who could later hinder the rollout.
- **Vague commitments:** Accepting verbal agreements or unclear promises of resources.
- **Over-detailing SIPOC:** Including too much detail in the Process column diminishes its purpose. SIPOC provides a high-level overview for alignment purposes, not for detailed process design.

Lesson 6.4: Defining Robust Production Requirements

Objective:
Define the complete set of functional, technical, and operational criteria a solution must meet to operate effectively and sustainably in a live business setting, with emphasis on maintainability through proper documentation.

Detailed Explanation:
Transitioning a solution from pilot to full-scale production demands strict criteria. These extend beyond model accuracy to cover the entire system's performance, security, usability, and maintainability. Systematic **model documentation and versioning** underpin long-term upkeep. Clear requirements serve as the implementation blueprint and the shared agreement among analytics, business, and IT teams. Complete documentation ensures future reusability by recording the solution in a form that is understandable, modifiable, and adaptable as business needs evolve.

Key Definitions:

- **Production readiness criteria:** The conditions a system must meet across stability, performance, security, and supportability before it goes live.
- **Operational requirements:** Specifications for how the system will be operated, monitored, and maintained daily (e.g., uptime, backup procedures, support model).
- **Reusability documentation:** Detailed records that include business goals, data sources, feature definitions, model algorithms, hyperparameters, performance metrics, assumptions, and limitations.
- **Model versioning:** The practice of using systems to track, manage, and control changes to the model's code, data, configuration, and trained binary by assigning unique version IDs to each artifact.

Table 29 Production Readiness Requirements Checklist

Requirement Category	Specification Examples	Verification Method	Owner
Functional	"System must generate daily forecast reports by 6 AM local time." "Users must be able to override model recommendations with manual input."	User Acceptance Testing (UAT), business scenario testing.	Product Owner, Business Lead.
Performance & Scalability	"API response time < 200ms for 95% of requests at peak load of 1,000 requests/sec." "System must scale to handle 2x current transaction volume within 4 hours."	Load testing, stress testing, performance benchmarking.	DevOps, Engineering Lead.
Security & Compliance	"All customer PII must be encrypted in transit and at rest." "Model predictions must be logged for audit trails to meet regulation X."	Security audit, penetration testing, compliance review.	Security Officer, Compliance Lead.
Reliability & Availability	"System availability of 99.5% during business hours (8 AM - 8 PM, Mon-Fri)." "Automated failover to backup data center within 15 minutes of primary failure."	Disaster recovery (DR) drill, historical uptime monitoring (if applicable).	Operations, SRE Lead.
Maintainability & Support	"Full model retraining pipeline must complete within 4 hours." "Complete documentation for Level 1 & 2 support teams must be approved."	Documentation review, runbook validation, support handoff session.	Data Science Lead, Support Manager.

Step-by-Step Method:

1. **Define functional and usability requirements:** Specify what the system must do and how users will interact with it.
2. **Establish technical and performance requirements:** Specify system performance metrics, integration points, data security protocols, scalability, and infrastructure needs.
3. **Document operational and support requirements:** Outline monitoring, disaster recovery plans, maintenance windows, and support structure.

4. **Capture model-specific requirements:** Specify schedules for model retraining, thresholds for performance degradation, and monitoring for data drift.
5. **Create and manage reusability documentation:** Develop clear, version-controlled records that detail the model's purpose, assumptions, input data schemas, and retraining instructions. Make sure each trained model is associated with the specific code and data snapshot used.

Examples:

- **Requirements for a Real-Time Pricing Engine:**
    - *Performance:* Provide a price quote within 100 milliseconds for 99.9% of requests during peak load.
    - *Operational:* Retrain the model weekly and send an alert if the average prediction confidence drops below 85%.
    - *Documentation & Versioning:* The model is saved as "v2.1.3" in a model registry. The configuration file outlines feature weights, and a companion document details steps for adapting the model to new regions.
- **What Does NOT Belong:** Specific programmer names or experimental code snippets are implementation details, not system requirements.

Common Pitfalls:

- **Ambiguous language:** Using vague terms such as "fast" or "user-friendly" without specific measurements.
- **Neglecting "ilities":** Overlooking key aspects like maintainability, scalability, and security.
- Creating documentation that is never maintained: Producing lengthy, static documents at project close that become outdated and unused. Documentation must be treated as a living record and updated whenever the model, data schema, or business rules change.
- **Inadequate version** control: Not properly tracking model artifacts, leading to confusion about which model is in production and making it hard to revert to a previous stable version.

Lesson 6.5: Supporting Implementation and Deployment Testing

Objective:
Participate actively in the technical implementation process and design structured tests, including A/B testing and User Acceptance Testing (UAT), to verify that the solution functions correctly before launch.

Detailed Explanation:
Deployment testing is the final verification that all components function together as intended under real-world conditions. The analytics team must shift to a support-and-validation role. This includes designing tests that go beyond unit functionality to assess integration, performance, and business fit. **User Acceptance Testing (UAT)** is the critical phase in which end users verify that the solution meets their needs in a simulated production environment. To compare a new solution against an existing one, **A/B testing** (also called Champion/Challenger testing) provides a controlled, randomized experiment to measure incremental impact with statistical rigor before a full rollout.

Key Definitions:

- **Integration testing:** Confirming the analytics solution properly exchanges data and operates correctly with other existing systems.
- **User Acceptance Testing (UAT):** A validation process where end-users test realistic business scenarios to ensure the solution meets business requirements and is usable in the operational environment. It answers the question, "Are we building the right thing?"
- **Performance and load testing:** Evaluating the system's performance and stability during both normal and peak usage conditions.
- **A/B testing:** A controlled experiment that compares two versions (A and B) of a single variable to see which performs better using a specific metric.
- **Champion model:** The current production version or system (the control group in an A/B test).
- **Challenger model:** The new or modified version being tested (the treatment group in an A/B test).

- **Rollback plan:** A series of procedures to quickly revert the system to its prior state if major problems occur.

Step-by-Step Method:

1. **Develop a complete test plan:** Include tests for functionality, integration, performance, security, and UAT. Where a comparison against a current solution is needed, include an A/B test design.
2. **Support environment configuration:** Assist teams in setting up test and production environments and ensure model dependencies are properly installed.
3. **Conduct and oversee integration tests:** Verify data pipelines and system connectivity.
4. **Support user acceptance testing:** Provide business-scenario test cases, assist users throughout the process, and record their feedback and any defects identified. Obtain formal UAT approval from the designated business sponsor before proceeding.
5. **Design and execute A/B tests:** Formulate a hypothesis (e.g., "Challenger increases conversion by 2%"), randomly assign users to Champion (A) or Challenger (B) groups, run the test simultaneously, collect metric data, and use statistical testing to determine if the difference is significant.
6. **Verify performance benchmarks and rollback plan:** Confirm the system meets performance requirements under load and that the rollback process functions correctly.

Examples:

- **Example 1: A/B Testing a New Recommendation API:**
  - *Test:* 50% of users receive recommendations from the Champion model. The other 50% receive suggestions from the Challenger model.
  - *Result:* After two weeks, the Challenger shows a statistically significant 2% increase in click-through rate and is rolled out to all users.

- **Example 2: UAT for a Demand Forecasting Dashboard:**
  - *Action:* Supply chain planners test the dashboard by entering historical scenarios to verify forecast accuracy and test report generation.
  - *Outcome:* Formal approval is required prior to the launch.

Common Pitfalls:

- **Testing in isolation:** Assessing the analytics model independently, without any integration.
- **Insufficient test data: Relying on** small, clean datasets that fail to represent real-world production data variability.
- **Confusing UAT with Quality Assurance (QA):** Treating UAT as a technical sign-off rather than recognizing it as a business validation activity performed by real end-users verifying that the right solution was built for their needs.
- **A/B testing errors:** Peeking at results and stopping the test prematurely, which raises the risk of false positives, or failing to run the test long enough to encompass complete business cycles.

Lesson 6.6: Validating Production Deployment and Data Flows

Objective:
Monitor and verify the proper functioning of a new solution in the live environment, with emphasis on the quality and consistency of production data feeds to prevent silent failures.

Detailed Explanation:
The deployment phase is not the final step. Initial validation in the live environment is crucial for identifying issues that occur only in production. The most common failure point is not the model's logic but the data it receives. This emphasizes the importance of post-deployment activities to ensure the entire system, especially data pipelines, functions correctly. This includes proactive monitoring for data drift, schema changes, and integration errors that can silently reduce model performance and business value. This continuous oversight aligns with the Control phase of the DMAIC methodology and is central to preserving the solution's long-term value.

Table 30 Post-Deployment Monitoring & Response Framework

Monitoring Layer	What to Monitor	Alert Threshold (Example)	Initial Response Action
Infrastructure Health	Server CPU/Memory, API endpoint status, database connectivity.	CPU > 85% for 10 min, HTTP error rate > 1%.	Notify DevOps/SRE team, check auto-scaling.
Data Pipeline Integrity	Data freshness (latency), record counts vs. expected, schema validation errors.	Data delayed by > 1 hour, record count drop > 20%.	Investigate ETL/ingestion jobs, check source system.
Model Input Drift	Statistical distribution of key input features (mean, standard deviation, missing rate).	Feature distribution shift (KL divergence) > predefined threshold.	Investigate data source change, assess impact on model.
Model Performance	Business KPI linked to model (e.g., conversion rate), model-specific metrics (accuracy, precision) on live data.	KPI degrades by > 10% for 3 consecutive days, precision drops below SLA.	Execute diagnostic checklist, check for data issues first.
Business Outcome	Ultimate business goal metrics (e.g., total revenue, cost savings, customer satisfaction).	Negative trend vs. projected business case for 2 consecutive reporting periods.	Convene business & analytics stakeholders for review.

Key Definitions:

- **Production validation:** The immediate post-launch activities to confirm that the system is working properly and delivering value in the live environment.
- **Data flow verification:** The process of confirming data moves accurately from source systems through the analytics solution, maintaining proper quality, format, and timing.

- **Silent failure:** A malfunction that does not cause an immediate system error but results in a gradual decline in output quality (e.g., a data feed providing outdated information).
- **Proactive monitoring:** Implementing automated checks and alerts for key health indicators (data freshness, distribution shifts, outlier counts) instead of relying on user reports.
- **Data drift:** A change in the statistical properties of input data features over time, such as shifts in mean, variance, or distribution shape, that can degrade model performance. Data drift differs from concept drift, where the underlying relationship between inputs and the target variable changes. Both require monitoring and can trigger model retraining.

Step-by-Step Method:

1. **Implement Initial Health Monitoring:** Set up dashboards and alerts for system metrics (e.g., latency and error rates) and model performance indicators (e.g., input distributions and output scores).
2. **Verify Data Pipeline Integrity:** Ensure that live data matches the expected schema, remains within the anticipated value ranges, and arrives at the scheduled frequency.
3. **Perform initial output validation:** Manually review a sample of the system's outputs during the initial hours or days to confirm they are logically plausible and consistent with expected ranges.
4. **Establish a Hypercare Support Protocol:** Have a dedicated team prepared to quickly diagnose and resolve any immediate post-launch issues.
5. **Transition to Long-Term Monitoring:** After reaching stability, hand over primary monitoring duties to the operational teams, with clear escalation procedures to refer back to the analytics team for model-specific concerns, such as data drift.

Examples:

- **Example 1: Root Causes of Production Data Issues:**
  - *Source System Change:* An update to the CRM changes the "customer tenure" field from days to months, disrupting the model's expected input format.
  - *Failed Integration Job:* A nightly data pipeline silently fails, causing the model to process outdated data.

    - *Schema Drift:* An optional field was added to the transaction data, leading to ingestion errors.

- **Example 2: Validation Action for a Shipping Cost Model:** In the first week, the analytics team compares the model's recommended carriers for 100 randomly selected orders with the old manual method to spot significant, unexplained differences.

Common Pitfalls:

- **"Set it and forget it" mentality:** Assuming that successful deployment testing guarantees flawless ongoing operation without proactive monitoring.
- **Monitoring lagging indicators:** Only tracking overall business KPIs (e.g., monthly revenue), which take a long time to reveal data quality issues, instead of using leading indicators like input data distribution.
- **Lack of understanding of data lineage:** Not knowing the full path of data from source to model, making it hard to trace and identify root causes.

Summary

Business value validation ensures analytical solutions deliver tangible benefits before full deployment. Using frameworks such as DMAIC, business value validation assesses business impact through ROI and KPIs, technical performance in real-world scenarios, user adoption and usability, operational feasibility, and ethical standards. Pilot testing in controlled environments with actual users and data enables quantitative comparisons against baselines and qualitative evaluation of workflows. Success relies on confirming business results over a period that captures key cycles, focusing on outcomes rather than model accuracy alone.

Validation findings must translate into clear, actionable reports for deployment decisions. Decision-focused reports begin with executive summaries that address key questions such as what was found, what it means, and what steps to take next. Findings include quantitative results and qualitative insights expressed in business language, emphasizing ROI, cost savings, or strategic advantages. An honest assessment of risks and limitations builds trust. Definitive recommendations, such as proceeding, not proceeding, or proceeding with modifications, provide clear guidance. Reports customize content for different audiences, providing strategic insights for executives and operational details for planning teams.

Stakeholder alignment transforms approval into active commitment by fostering a shared understanding of deployment plans. SIPOC diagrams illustrate the high-level process involving Suppliers, Inputs, Process steps, Outputs, and Customers. They define the boundaries and interfaces where the solution operates. Formal deployment charters specify the agreed-upon scope, timeline, success criteria, roles, and resources. Production requirements extend beyond model accuracy to include functional specifications, performance and scalability targets, security and compliance standards, reliability benchmarks, and maintainability considerations. Complete documentation and version control support these requirements by tracking changes to code, data, and model artifacts.

Deployment testing ensures all components work together under real-world conditions. Integration testing verifies proper data exchange with existing systems. User acceptance testing confirms the solution meets business needs through end-user validation of realistic scenarios. A/B testing evaluates champion and challenger models through controlled, randomized experiments that measure incremental impact with statistical rigor. Post-deployment validation monitors live production feeds for silent failures such as data drift, schema changes, and integration errors that can degrade performance without immediate alerts. Proactive monitoring of infrastructure health, data pipeline integrity, model input drift, and business outcomes enables quick responses and supports sustainable operations.

Chapter 6: Practice Questions

Q1. Within the CRISP-DM framework, which of the following activities is primarily involved in the Deployment phase?
A) Selecting the final modeling algorithm after evaluating multiple options.
B) Cleaning and transforming raw data into a modeling dataset.
C) Planning for maintenance, monitoring, and handoff to business owners.
D) Formulating the initial business objectives and project goals.

Q2. A team is applying the DMAIC methodology to validate a new analytics solution. In the "Measure" phase, what is the primary focus?
A) Developing and testing potential improvements to the solution.
B) Identifying the root causes of process variation.
C) Measuring the current process performance and the pilot impact of the solution.
D) Implementing control charts for ongoing monitoring.

Q3. The primary purpose of a SIPOC diagram in the deployment context is to:
A) Provide a detailed, step-by-step flowchart of the new analytical algorithm.
B) Define the high-level process boundaries and key interfaces for stakeholder alignment.
C) Document the hyperparameters and code version of a machine learning model.
D) Serve as the final user acceptance test script for business stakeholders.

Q4. During User Acceptance Testing (UAT), the main responsibility of end-users is to:
A) Verify that the API integrations are technically functional.
B) Perform load tests to identify system breaking points.
C) Ensure the solution meets business needs in real-world scenarios.
D) Review the source code for optimization and efficiency.

Q5. Which of the following is a required characteristic of a valid A/B test for comparing a Champion and Challenger model?
A) The test groups are assigned based on user demographics to ensure fairness.
B) The Challenger model is exposed to all traffic while the Champion is

paused.
C) Users are randomly assigned to either the Champion or Challenger group.
D) The test is concluded as soon as the Challenger shows any positive improvement.

Q6. Comprehensive model documentation for reusability MUST include:
A) The names of the data scientists who developed the model.
B) The business objective, data sources, key assumptions, and performance metrics.
C) Speculative notes on the model's potential performance in future, unseen markets.
D) The hourly wage of the operations staff responsible for monitoring the model.

Q7. In the context of production requirements, "operational requirements" specifically refer to specifications about:
A) The mathematical accuracy and precision of the predictive model.
B) The user interface design and color scheme of an application.
C) How the system will be run, monitored, and maintained daily.
D) The cost-benefit analysis and projected ROI of the solution.

Q8. A "silent failure" in a deployed analytics system is best described as:
A) A complete system crash that triggers multiple automatic alerts.
B) A gradual decline in output quality caused by an undetected data feed issue.
C) A user accidentally deletes a critical database table.
D) A network switch failure that isolates the production server.

Q9. The "Control" phase of the DMAIC methodology, when applied to solution deployment, is most closely associated with which ongoing activity?
A) Designing the pilot study for business value validation.
B) Writing the final project report and presentation.
C) Implementing proactive monitoring and alerting systems.
D) Conducting the initial data collection and exploration.

Q10. The most significant risk of "peeking" at interim results during an A/B test and stopping early is:
A) Increasing the computational cost of the experiment.
B) Inflating the probability of falsely concluding a difference exists (Type

I error).
C) Annoying users with frequent changes to the system.
D) Guaranteeing that the Challenger model will be selected for deployment.

Q11. When creating a SIPOC diagram, a common mistake is:
A) Starting by defining the Outputs and Customers.
B) Including 4-7 high-level steps in the Process column.
C) Listing the internal IT department as a Supplier for data inputs.
D) Providing excessive, granular detail for each process step.

Q12. The main difference between Quality Assurance (QA) testing and User Acceptance Testing (UAT) is that UAT specifically emphasizes:
A) Technical verification that the system was built correctly according to specifications.
B) Business validation that the right system was developed to meet user needs.
C) The security and penetration testing of the application.
D) The system's performance under extreme stress loads.

Q13. Model versioning is critically important because it:
A) Allows different models to be trained simultaneously on the same data.
B) Provides a way to roll back to a previous model artifact if a new deployment fails.
C) Automatically improves the accuracy of a model over time.
D) Is a legal requirement for all software developed in the United States.

Q14. In a business value validation report, the "Executive Summary" section should primarily:
A) Provide a detailed appendix with all raw data collected during the pilot.
B) List every stakeholder who was interviewed during the project.
C) State the main finding, business impact, and core recommendation concisely.
D) Explain the complex statistical methods used in model evaluation.

Q15. Proactive monitoring of a deployed model should ideally track leading indicators such as:
A) Quarterly corporate revenue reports.
B) Statistical distributions of key input features for signs of data drift.

C) Annual customer satisfaction survey results.
D) The project's initial budget versus actual spend.

Q16. A formal "Deployment Charter" is mainly used to:
A) Promote a new analytics capability to potential customers.
B) Define the agreed scope, resources, and success criteria for the rollout.
C) Train end-users on the functionalities of a new software tool.
D) Record the detailed technical steps for the go-live event.

Q17. The ethical compliance review during business value validation should evaluate:
A) The computational efficiency of the model's code.
B) The model's adherence to fairness, privacy, and regulatory standards.
C) The user interface's compliance with brand style guidelines.
D) The return on investment (ROI) compared to other projects.

Q18. A team is planning a pilot for a store inventory optimization model. To avoid the pitfall of "insufficient pilot duration," they should ensure the pilot:
A) Runs in only one store to minimize disruption.
B) Uses synthetic data to accelerate testing.
C) Captures at least one full business cycle, such as a complete quarter.
D) Is supervised directly by the data science team at all times.

Q19. The main goal of the "Hypercare Support Protocol" immediately after deployment is to:
A) Assign the development team permanently to maintain the system.
B) Have a dedicated team ready to quickly diagnose and fix initial live issues.
C) Start planning the next analytics project in the portfolio.
D) Perform a post-mortem analysis to identify causes of any problems.

Q20. When translating technical findings into a business impact analysis for a validation report, the most appropriate metric to emphasize would be:
A) The F1-score of the model on the hold-out test set.
B) The reduction in manual review hours, translated into estimated cost savings.
C) The Python library versions used in the development environment.
D) The number of features used in the final model.

Chapter 7: Overseeing and Managing the Analytics Lifecycle

Introduction

Implementing an analytical solution is just the start, marking the beginning of a phase focused on continuous value delivery. Analytics Lifecycle Management involves ongoing monitoring to keep solutions accurate, relevant, and effective. This includes tracking performance, updating and recalibrating models, supporting users and maintainers, validating the business case, and identifying unintended consequences. Analytical assets require regular maintenance and adjustment to remain accurate and relevant as business conditions change. Mastering this process ensures that analytical investments deliver sustained benefits while maintaining ethical and professional standards.

Figure 29 The Analytics Lifecycle Management Framework

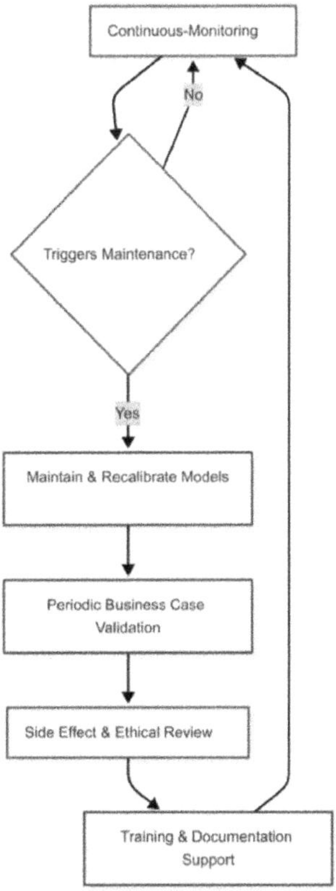

Lesson 7.1: Monitoring Solution Performance and Value

Objective:
Build and apply a monitoring framework that tracks the technical performance and business impact of a deployed analytics solution, ensuring it continues to deliver **expected value**.

Detailed Explanation:
Continuous performance monitoring is crucial for running a live analytics system. It systematically collects data on the system's technical functioning and on how well it meets business goals. This goes beyond just detecting system errors, it involves tracking metrics directly related to the success criteria established during the problem-framing stage. Proper monitoring provides early warnings of performance problems and demonstrates ongoing return on investment. This enables proactive management rather than reactive responses. Monitoring should be customized for different stakeholder groups, considering each group's unique information needs and review schedules.

Table 31 Performance Monitoring Framework by Audience

Audience	Monitoring Focus	Key Metrics to Track	Alert Response Owner
Business Leadership	Strategic value & ROI	Business KPI impact, ROI trend, cost vs. benefit, strategic alignment.	Business Sponsor / Product Owner
Operations Management	Operational efficiency & process impact	Process efficiency gains, user adoption rates, support ticket volume, error rates affecting workflows.	Operations Manager
Technical/IT Team	System health & technical performance	System uptime, API response times, data pipeline latency, compute resource utilization, model performance scores.	DevOps / SRE Lead
Data Science Team	Model health & predictive quality	Model accuracy/precision/recall, data/concept drift indicators, feature importance stability, retraining effectiveness.	Data Science Lead
End-Users	Usability & decision support	Task completion time, user satisfaction scores, frequency of manual overrides, perceived value of insights.	UX/Business Analyst

Key Definitions:

- **Performance dashboard:** A centralized visual display of key metrics that show the health and value of an analytics solution, often updated in real time or near-real time.
- **Leading Indicator:** A metric that provides an early warning of potential future performance issues (such as changes in input data patterns) before they impact key business results.
- **Service Level Agreement (SLA):** A formal commitment that defines the expected service level for the analytics solution, including performance benchmarks, availability, and support response times.

Step-by-Step Method:

1. **Revisit success criteria:** Ensure your monitoring plan aligns with the original business goals and the key performance indicators (KPIs) established for the solution.
2. **Define a comprehensive set of metrics:** Select technical metrics such as model accuracy, latency, and system uptime, business metrics such as ROI, cost savings, and revenue impact, and operational metrics such as user adoption rates and support ticket volume.
3. **Establish baselines and thresholds:** Document the expected performance levels at deployment and define clear, actionable alert thresholds that prompt investigation or intervention.
4. **Set up monitoring infrastructure:** Automate the collection, calculation, and visualization of these metrics with dashboards accessible to relevant stakeholders.
5. **Set regular review intervals:** Plan periodic business and technical reviews (e.g., weekly, monthly, or quarterly) to track trends over time rather than focusing on one-time statuses.
6. **Develop an alert response protocol:** Outline explicit steps for handling alerts, encompassing diagnosis, escalation, and resolution.

Examples:

- **Example 1: Monitoring a Predictive Maintenance System for Manufacturing:**
  - *Technical Metric:* Model precision for failure prediction must remain above 88%, alerts are triggered if it drops below 85% for three consecutive days.

- *Business Metric:* Overall Equipment Effectiveness (OEE) must reach a sustained 8% increase from the pre-deployment baseline within three months of go-live.
- *Operational Metric:* Reduce the mean time to repair (MTTR) for flagged equipment by 15%.

- **Example 2: Monitoring a Customer Recommendation Engine:**
  - *Leading Indicator:* Monitor the click-through rate (CTR) for recommendations. If it consistently drops despite stable model accuracy, it could indicate a change in customer preferences.
  - *Business Metric: Monitor the average order value (AOV) for sessions where recommendations are shown compared to sessions without recommendations.*

Common Pitfalls:

- **Dashboard paralysis:** Creating overly complex dashboards with dozens of metrics, making it difficult to identify what truly matters.
- **Chasing vanity metrics:** Focusing on numbers that seem impressive but do not reflect core business value (e.g., number of predictions made versus revenue influenced by those predictions).
- **Ignoring the human element:** Failing to monitor user satisfaction and adoption rates, which are direct indicators of whether a solution is delivering value in practice. A technically accurate model that users distrust or ignore produces no business benefit.
- **Alert fatigue:** Setting monitoring thresholds too sensitively, causing a flood of false alarms that desensitize the response team to real problems.

Lesson 7.2: Maintaining and Recalibrating Analytical Models

Objective:
Apply structured processes and defined triggers to update, retrain, and adjust analytical models, ensuring they remain accurate and relevant as business conditions evolve.

Detailed Explanation:
Analytical models are not fixed. They represent the world as it was when they were developed. As markets shift, consumer behaviors change, and companies evolve, the relationships a model has learned can become outdated, a phenomenon called **model or performance drift**. Maintenance and recalibration include both scheduled activities and triggered responses to detected decline. This includes scheduling regular reviews, setting clear criteria for unscheduled updates, and choosing suitable retraining strategies. Identifying the root cause of drift is necessary for selecting the correct response. **Data drift (covariate shift)** occurs when the statistical distribution of input data changes while the underlying relationship with the target variable remains stable. **Concept drift** is deeper, involving a change in the statistical relationship between inputs and the target variable. Effective maintenance protects the value of the analytical investment and prevents gradual performance degradation over time.

Key Definitions:

- **Model degradation / Performance drift:** The general term for a decline in a model's predictive ability, as shown by its performance metrics (e.g., decreasing accuracy, rising error rate).
- **Data drift (Covariate shift):** A shift in the statistical distribution of the input data over time, with the relationship between inputs and outputs staying constant.
- **Concept drift:** A shift in the fundamental relationship between input features and the target variable being predicted.
- **Drift detection:** The methods and procedures used to automatically or semi-automatically identify when model, data, or concept drift has occurred, serving as an early warning system.

Figure 30 Model Drift Taxonomy and Relationships

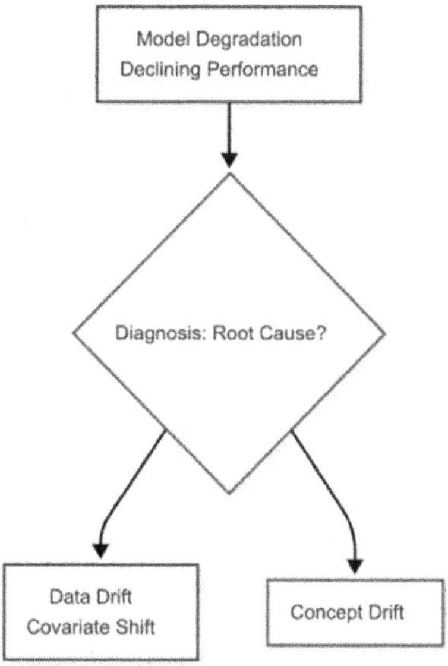

- **Scheduled retraining:** The practice of consistently updating a model with new data according to a regular schedule (e.g., monthly, quarterly), regardless of performance changes.
- **Triggered retraining:** The process of retraining a model after specific events or alerts, such as a major decline in performance metrics, a drift detection alert, or a significant business change.
- **Model version control:** The systematic tracking of different iterations of a model, including data, code, and parameters for each version, enabling rollback and auditability.

Step-by-Step Method:

1. **Establish a monitoring baseline:** Continuously track model inputs and performance as outlined in Lesson 7.1 to determine what "normal" looks like.
2. **Implement drift detection:** Choose metrics (e.g., statistical tests such as the **Population Stability Index** or the **Kolmogorov-Smirnov test** for data drift, and performance on a holdout set for concept drift) and set thresholds to automatically spot significant changes.
3. **Define recalibration triggers:** Set clear rules for when to retrain models. These can be **performance-based** (accuracy falls below a certain percentage), **drift-based** (a detection

metric exceeds its threshold), **scheduled**, or **event-driven** (such as a new product launch or regulatory change).

Table 32 Model Recalibration Triggers & Response Protocols

Trigger Type	Specific Condition	Leading Indicator	Required Action	Timeframe for Response
Performance Based	Model accuracy drops below SLA by >5% for 3 consecutive evaluation periods	Gradual decline in precision/recall metrics on validation set	Initiate diagnostic analysis, then full retraining with recent data	Within 1 week of trigger
Data Drift	Statistical distribution (K-S test) of 2+ key input features shifts beyond predefined threshold	Automated monitoring alerts from data drift detection system	Investigate data source, then retrain model if drift is real and persistent	Within 72 hours
Concept Drift	Relationship between key feature and target changes significantly (measured via performance on recent data vs. old)	Model performance degrades despite stable input data distributions	Retrain model, consider adding/removing features or changing algorithm	Within 2 weeks
Scheduled/ Calendar	End of fiscal quarter or pre-defined maintenance window	Calendar date	Execute full retraining pipeline with latest available data as preventive maintenance	On schedule
Business Event	Major product launch, new regulation, market disruption, or merger/ acquisition	Business announcement or external event	Convene review team to assess impact, retrain or adjust model as needed	Within 1 month of event

4. **Select a retraining strategy:** Choose a method for updating the model.
    - **Full retraining:** Developing a brand-new model from scratch using all available historical data.
    - **Windowed retraining:** Training only on the most recent N periods of data to adapt to recent trends.
    - **Incremental/Online learning:** Updating the model continuously as new data arrives.
    - **Ensemble retraining:** Adding a new model trained on recent data to an existing group of previous models.

Figure 31 Retraining Strategy Decision Flow

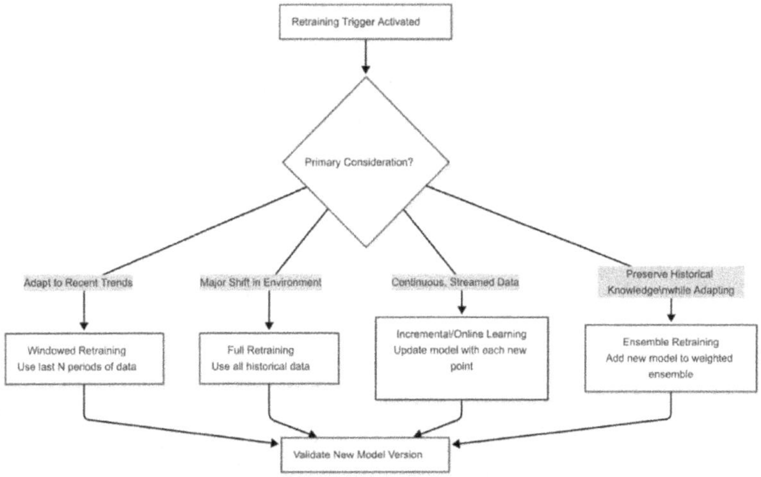

5. **Create a retraining pipeline:** Automate the collection of new data, retrain the model using the selected strategy, and assess its performance.
6. **Implement strict validation:** Ensure each new model version passes tests for accuracy, fairness, and stability before deployment to confirm improvement.
7. **Perform a controlled deployment:** Use methods such as canary releases or A/B testing to gradually introduce a new model version.
8. **Document everything:** Record each retraining event, including the trigger, data, and strategy used, and the resulting performance metrics.

Examples:

- **Example 1: Diagnosing Drift in a Credit Risk Model:**
  - *Data Drift:* The model was trained when the average customer debt was $15,000. Over time, due to economic factors, the average applicant debt has increased to $25,000. The input distribution has shifted.
  - *Concept Drift:* When a major recession begins, it fundamentally alters the relationship between income, employment history, and the likelihood of repaying a loan. The core concept of "credit risk" has shifted.

- **Example 2: Retraining a Dynamic Pricing Model:**
  - *Scheduled Activity:* The model undergoes retraining each Sunday night using data from the past 8 weeks.
  - *Triggered Activity:* A special event (e.g., a major concert) is announced. The team may manually adjust constraints or deploy an event-specific model layer.

Common Pitfalls:

- **Waiting for failure before acting:** Postponing retraining until major performance failures occur leads to prolonged periods of degraded model outputs and poor business decisions. Scheduled and triggered maintenance prevent this.
- **Confusing drift types:** Mistaking data drift for concept drift, or vice versa, leads to an ineffective response. During concept drift, performing full retraining with all historical data can embed outdated relationships into the new model. During data drift, treating the problem as concept drift may trigger unnecessary architectural changes when simply updating the input distribution would suffice. Correctly diagnosing the drift type is the prerequisite to selecting the right retraining strategy.
- **Retraining without validation:** Deploying a newly trained model without adequately testing it against the previous version.
- **Losing model history:** Not saving previous model versions and their training data, which prevents audits or rollbacks.

Lesson 7.3: Designing and Delivering Effective Training Programs

Objective:
Design and implement training programs tailored to different stakeholder groups, including technical maintainers, equipping each group with the knowledge and skills to operate, support, and maintain the analytics solution.

Detailed Explanation:
The most advanced model is useless if people do not understand how to interact with it or maintain it. Training connects technical development with real-world value. Different audiences have different needs: end users must learn to interpret outputs and take action, business stakeholders need to understand the strategic implications, and IT or technical staff require in-depth knowledge to operate, troubleshoot, and improve the system. A one-size-fits-all approach will inevitably fail at least one of these groups. Training is not a one-time event but an ongoing process that adapts to updates and staff turnover.

Key Definitions:

- **Role-based training curriculum:** A collection of learning materials and activities tailored for a specific job role or stakeholder group (e.g., "Analyst User," "System Administrator," "Business Manager").
- **Knowledge transfer plan:** A structured approach for passing expertise from the project development team to the long-term operations and support teams.
- **Continuous learning:** The principle that training is an ongoing process rather than a one-time event at launch, aimed at adapting to system updates, staff turnover, and evolving best practices.

Step-by-Step Method:

1. **Audience segmentation and needs analysis:** Identify all groups that interact with the solution and conduct interviews or surveys to pinpoint their specific knowledge gaps and daily tasks.
2. **Develop custom content:** Create unique training modules for each segment. For IT/Technical audiences, focus on system

architecture, logging, monitoring tools, backup procedures, and diagnostic scripts.

3. **Select suitable delivery methods:** Incorporate a combination of interactive workshops, video tutorials, simulation environments (sandboxes), detailed runbooks, and documentation portals.
4. **Include hands-on practice:** For technical staff, add labs that let them perform real-world maintenance tasks in a safe, non-production environment.
5. **Assess competency and gather feedback:** Use quizzes, practical tests, and feedback forms to evaluate learning effectiveness and identify areas for improvement in the training program.
6. **Plan for sustainment:** Develop a materials repository, designate owners for updates, and schedule refresher courses or "lunch and learn" sessions for major updates.

Examples:

- **Example 1: Training for IT Staff: Maintaining a Real-Time Fraud Detection API**
  - Module 1: System Architecture and Data Flow.
  - Module 2: Operational Monitoring and Alert Response. (Hands-on training with dashboard and triaging common alerts).
  - Module 3: Model Deployment and Version Control Management.
  - Module 4: Troubleshooting and Escalation.

- **Example 2: Training for Marketing Managers Using a Campaign Analytics Dashboard:**
  - Focus: How to navigate the dashboard, interpret the 'ROI by Channel' visualization, and use the 'what-if' simulation tool.
  - Format: A 90-minute interactive webinar with a follow-up quick-reference guide.

Common Pitfalls:

- **Death by PowerPoint:** Relying only on lecture-based presentations without interactive or practical elements leads to poor retention.
- **Ignoring the reasoning behind procedures:** Training technical audiences on the steps alone, without explaining the

purpose behind each procedure, limits their ability to diagnose and resolve problems they have not seen before

- **No training for new hires:** Failing to include training on the solution in the onboarding process for new employees can create knowledge gaps over time.

Lesson 7.4: Validating the Ongoing Business Case

Objective:
Regularly and thoroughly reevaluate the financial and strategic value of an analytics solution, ensuring it remains justified in terms of operational costs and resource use.

Detailed Explanation:
The initial business case that justifies development and deployment is a hypothesis about future value. Ongoing validation involves testing that hypothesis against reality over time. This requires moving beyond simple usage statistics to perform causal **attribution analysis** that isolates the solution's specific impact from other business factors. The aim is to answer a key executive question: 'Does this solution still deliver sufficient return to justify its cost, or should these resources be redirected?' This process guards against solutions that continue consuming resources without delivering commensurate value. It requires a comparative assessment against alternative uses of the same investment.

Key Definitions:

- **Attribution analysis:** The process of determining how much of a business outcome, such as increased sales, is directly attributable to the analytics solution rather than to other initiatives or market forces.
- **Total Cost of Ownership (TCO):** The overall expense of acquiring, operating, and maintaining the analytics solution over its entire lifespan, including indirect costs such as labor and opportunity costs.
- **Comparative value assessment:** An analysis that compares ongoing investment in the current solution with alternative uses of the same resources, including potential new projects or improvements.

Table 33 Business Case Validation Components

Component	Description	Data Sources	Calculation Method	Success Threshold
Attributed Benefit	The portion of observed business improvement directly caused by the analytics solution	A/B test results, controlled experiments, time-series analysis with counterfactual	(Performance with solution) - Performance in control/ baseline scenario)	Benefits exceed pre-defined target (e.g., 10% improvement)
Total Cost of Ownership (TCO)	All direct and indirect costs associated with the solution over a period	Finance records, timesheets, cloud bills, software licenses, allocated overhead	Sum of (Development Amortization + Operational Costs + Support/Maintenance + Infrastructure)	TCO is within original budget + 15% tolerance
Return on Investment (ROI)	The financial return generated per unit of cost	Attributed Benefit value, TCO	(Attributed Benefit - TCO) / TCO * 100%	ROI > Minimum Acceptable Rate of Return (MARR), typically >20%
Strategic Alignment Score	Qualitative assessment of how well the solution supports current strategic priorities	Strategic plan documents, executive interviews, competitive analysis	Scoring rubric (1-5) across dimensions: Revenue Growth, Cost Reduction, Customer Experience, Innovation	Score ≥ 4/5
Opportunity Cost Assessment	Value of the next-best alternative use of the resources consumed by the solution	Project pipeline, resource capacity analysis, potential project ROI estimates	Compare current solution ROI to estimated ROI of most promising unfunded project	Current solution ROI > Next-best alternative ROI

Step-by-Step Method:

1. **Measure actual outcomes:** Quantify the current state of business metrics the solution was designed to influence (e.g., current cost savings, revenue uplift).
2. **Isolate the solution's impact:** Use rigorous attribution methods. This could involve maintaining a control group (A/B testing), analyzing time-series data with counterfactual modeling, or correlating solution usage intensity with improvements in outcomes.
3. **Recalculate total costs:** Include all ongoing expenses, including software licenses, cloud computing, dedicated personnel time for maintenance and support, and allocated overhead.
4. **Calculate the current Return on Investment (ROI):** Compare the attributed benefits to the TCO over a relevant period (e.g., the past year) to determine an updated ROI figure.
5. **Conduct a strategic review:** Assess whether the solution still aligns with current business priorities. Has the strategic context changed since deployment?
6. **Make a renewal decision:** Based on the updated ROI and strategic alignment, intentionally choose to: Continue as-is, Invest to Enhance, Sunset and Retire, or Replace the solution.

Examples:

- **Example 1: Validating a Customer Churn Reduction Model:**
    - *Attribution Method:* The company continuously runs an A/B test where 5% of customers are randomly excluded from the churn intervention campaigns driven by the model.
    - *Analysis:* The "treatment" group (with model) has a 15% lower churn rate than the "control" group (without model). This 15% reduction is directly attributable.
    - *Cost-Benefit:* The annual TCO of the solution is compared to the yearly revenue saved from reduced churn.

- **Example 2**: When Benefits Are Not Attributable: A sales forecasting tool is credited with improving inventory turnover. However, further analysis indicates that a new supply chain vendor was the primary factor, with the tool's role minimal.

Common Pitfalls:

- **Confusing correlation with causation:** Thinking that an increase in a business metric after deployment automatically means the solution caused it.
- **Forgetting hidden costs:** Not including the time business users spend in meetings about the solution or the expense of data engineering support in the TCO.
- **Analysis paralysis:** Developing an overly complicated attribution model that is unmanageable, when a simpler, practical method would produce actionable results faster.

Lesson 7.5: Identifying and Mitigating Unintended Consequences

Objective:
Proactively monitor and systematically address the negative side effects and ethical implications that arise from the ongoing use of an analytics solution, guided by the principles of Fairness, Accountability, and Transparency (FAT).

Detailed Explanation:
Analytics solutions affect complex business and social systems. Even solutions that achieve their primary goal can create ripple effects, some positive and others negative. This lesson emphasizes the importance of developing a disciplined habit of identifying these unintended consequences, especially negative ones. This includes **ethical risks** such as bias and discrimination, operational risks such as overreliance, and strategic risks such as market backlash. A key framework for managing these risks is **FAT**: **Fairness**, **Accountability**, and **Transparency**. **Fairness** means avoiding bias that disadvantages individuals or groups based on protected characteristics. **Accountability** means holding specific parties responsible for system outcomes. **Transparency** (or Explainability) ensures that a system's logic and decisions are understandable to those affected by them. **Algorithmic bias** is a primary ethical risk. It appears at every stage of the analytics lifecycle. Historical bias originates in training data that reflects past inequalities. Representation bias occurs when data collection systematically excludes population subgroups. Measurement bias arises when a chosen feature or label is an imperfect proxy for the real quantity of interest, especially when that proxy is measured differently or less reliably across groups. Aggregation bias arises when heterogeneous groups are treated as homogeneous in model design. Evaluation bias occurs when test data do not represent the deployment population. Deployment bias emerges when a model is used in contexts or for purposes beyond its original design.

Figure 32 The FAT Framework Pillars

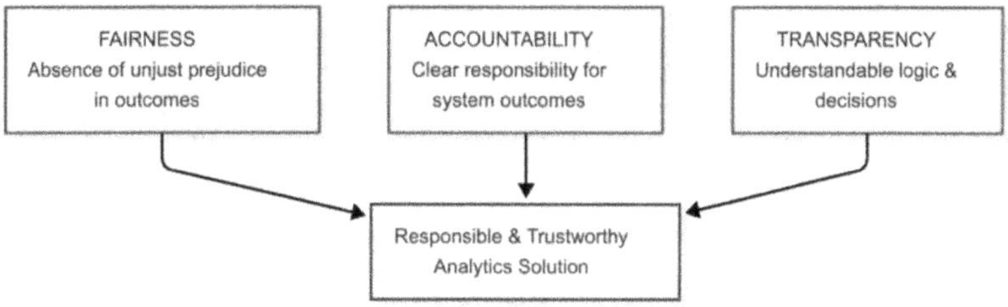

Key Definitions:

- **Ethical audit:** A thorough review of an analytics solution's inputs, processes, and outputs to identify potential harms, such as unfair bias, privacy violations, or lack of transparency.
- **Fairness, Accountability, Transparency (FAT):** A framework for responsible analytics. Fairness ensures model outputs don't unfairly disadvantage protected groups. Accountability means responsible parties must take responsibility for decisions and consequences. Transparency requires the system's logic to be explainable to users or those affected.
- **Algorithmic bias:** Systematic and repeatable errors in an algorithm that cause unfair outcomes, favoring one arbitrary group over others.
- Self-reinforcing error loop: When a model's output causes changes that reinforce and amplify its errors. For instance, a model recommending less policing may result in fewer incidents, seeming to validate its advice, regardless of the true situation.
- **Second-order effect:** An indirect result that stems from the immediate outcome of the solution.

Table 34 Side Effect Identification & Mitigation Matrix

Side Effect Category	Potential Manifestation	Monitoring Signal	Mitigation Strategy
Ethical / Fairness	Algorithmic bias against protected demographic groups.	Disparate impact analysis shows >20% difference in favorable outcomes between groups.	Implement bias mitigation (re-weighting, adversarial debiasing), add human review for edge cases.
Operational Risk	Over-dependence creates single point of failure, staff skill atrophy.	No manual fallback process tested in 6+ months, key person risk (only 1 person understands system).	Develop and regularly test manual fallback procedures, cross-train staff, create detailed runbooks.
Customer/ User Impact	Solution causes friction, perceived as opaque or unfair, leading to distrust.	User satisfaction surveys show decline, increase in complaints or overrides.	Improve explainability (e.g., feature attribution), enhance user communication, establish appeal process.
Systemic/ Market	Optimizing for a local KPI harms broader system (e.g., inventory model damages supplier relations).	Supplier satisfaction scores drop, contract renegotiation difficulties emerge.	Adjust model to include secondary constraints (e.g., order size variability), improve stakeholder communication.
Compliance & Legal	Model drifts out of compliance with new regulations (e.g., privacy laws).	Regulatory change alerts, audit findings.	Establish regulatory watch process, build compliance checks into retraining pipeline.

Step-by-Step Method:

1. **Proactively brainstorm risks:** During the design phase and at regular intervals, systematically identify potential adverse effects and sources of bias.
2. **Establish specific monitoring:** Develop metrics for fairness (e.g., disparity testing across protected groups), accountability (e.g., audit trails), and transparency (e.g., user comprehension scores).

3. **Gather comprehensive feedback:** Actively seek input from all relevant stakeholders, such as end-users, clients, and partners, using methods like surveys, interviews, and focus groups.
4. **Assess the severity and likelihood:** Evaluate the potential harm and the probability of identified consequences to prioritize mitigation efforts.
5. **Develop and implement mitigation strategies:** Design countermeasures that may include technical solutions such as debiasing algorithms and explainability tools, process-oriented approaches such as human-in-the-loop reviews, or policy-based measures such as usage guidelines.
6. **Document and communicate:** Keep a risk register and be open with stakeholders about known limitations and mitigation strategies.

Examples:

- **Example 1: Bias in a Hiring Algorithm:**
    - *Adverse Effect:* The algorithm tends to favor candidates from elite universities based on historical data, which decreases diversity.
    - *Bias Source:* Historical bias.
    - *Mitigation:* Conduct regular fairness audits, remove the university as a feature, and implement "cluster hiring" rules.

- **Example 2: Consequence of a Dynamic Pricing Model:**
    - *Adverse Effect:* The model effectively smooths grid demand but results in disproportionately high electricity costs for low-income households.
    - *Mitigation:* Implementing rate protections and formally modeling "equity of impact" as a constraint.

Common Pitfalls:

- **Focusing on a single metric:** Optimizing the solution to maximize one KPI (e.g., profit) without considering trade-offs with fairness or trust.
- **The "Blind Model" fallacy:** Believing that excluding protected attributes (like race) automatically ensures fairness, while bias still exists through correlated proxy variables (such as zip code).

- **Delegating ethics to engineers:** Believing ethical issues will be handled through technical skill alone, instead of through cross-disciplinary oversight.
- **Treating ethical review as a one-time activity:** Side effects develop gradually as usage increases, data distributions shift, and societal norms change. Ethical audits must be embedded into ongoing lifecycle management, not confined to the initial deployment phase.

Lesson 7.6: Maintaining Complete Solution Documentation

Objective:
Ensure the creation, updating, and maintenance of accurate, accessible, and audience-appropriate documentation throughout the analytics solution lifecycle.

Detailed Explanation:
Documentation acts as the institutional memory of an analytics solution. It prevents critical knowledge from leaving when team members depart and helps new team members become effective contributors. In lifecycle management, documentation is not a static deliverable from the project phase but a **living document** that must evolve with the solution. Different stakeholders require different layers: from high-level business summaries for executives to detailed technical **runbooks** for on-call engineers. Poor documentation is a major source of risk and **documentation debt**, increasing maintenance costs, slowing enhancements, and creating single points of failure.

Key Definitions:

- **Runbook:** A detailed procedural guide for performing a specific operational task, such as restarting a service, deploying a model update, or responding to a particular alert type.
- **Knowledge base:** A centralized, searchable storage for all documentation, FAQs, and troubleshooting guides related to the solution.
- **Living document:** A document intended to be updated regularly as information changes, unlike a static report.
- **Documentation debt:** The accumulated cost and risk that result from postponing the creation or updating of required documentation. As debt grows, maintenance becomes more expensive, knowledge transfer more difficult, and operational risk higher.

Step-by-Step Method:

1. **Inventory documentation needs by audience:** Identify the key information each stakeholder group, namely, Business, End-User, Technical/IT, and Data Science, must understand to perform their roles effectively.

2. **Establish documentation standards and templates:** Create consistent formats for document types (e.g., API specifications, user guides, and architecture diagrams) to enhance usability and maintainability.
3. **Integrate documentation into workflows:** Make updating documentation a required step in key processes such as model retraining, code releases, and incident resolution. It must not be optional or deferred.
4. **Assign clear ownership:** Designate individuals or teams responsible for maintaining the accuracy and completeness of specific documentation sets.
5. **Implement review and sunset procedures:** Schedule regular reviews of documentation to ensure accuracy and archive or remove outdated documents.
6. **Ensure accessibility and discoverability:** Store documentation in a location that is accessible and searchable for all authorized stakeholders.

Table 35 Documentation Taxonomy by Audience and Purpose

Audience	Document Type	Primary Purpose	Key Contents
Executive Leadership	Value Dashboard & Brief	Communicate strategic impact and justify continued investment.	Current ROI, KPI trends, risk register, high-level recommendations.
Business Users	User Guide & FAQ	Enable effective daily use and interpretation of outputs.	Step-by-step task instructions, output interpretation guide, common scenarios, troubleshooting.
IT / DevOps	Runbook & Architecture Guide	Support system operations, troubleshooting, and integration.	System diagrams, deployment procedures, monitoring guide, backup/DR steps, API specs.
Data Science / Stewards	Model Card & Retraining Guide	Enable model understanding, maintenance, and evolution.	Model purpose, training data specs, performance metrics, assumptions, retraining pipeline steps.
Compliance / Auditors	Governance Dossier	Demonstrate regulatory compliance and control effectiveness.	Data lineage, access logs, model validation reports, bias audit results, change records.

Examples:

- **Example 1: Documentation for a Financial Risk Model:**
  - *For Auditors:* A complete model card detailing intended use, training data, performance metrics, and known limitations.
  - *For IT Operations:* A runbook titled "Steps to Redeploy the Q4-2023 Model Version in the Disaster Recovery Environment."
  - *For Trading Desk Users:* A one-page cheat sheet for understanding the "Risk Score" output.

- **Example 2:** What Constitutes "Complete" Documentation: It is about quality, not quantity. Can a competent new hire use it to understand the solution's purpose, use it correctly, and perform common maintenance tasks?

Common Pitfalls:

- **The "myth of self-documenting code":** Relying solely on code comments, which do not capture the reasoning behind the code, the business context, or operational procedures.
- **Centralized obscurity:** Keeping all documentation in one large, disorganized file or a deeply nested folder system where no one can find what they need.
- **Lack of incentive:** Not acknowledging documentation work in performance reviews or project timelines, leading teams to deprioritize it.

Summary

Continuous performance monitoring assesses how deployed analytics solutions perform and impact the business. It tracks technical metrics like model accuracy, latency, and system uptime, alongside business metrics such as ROI, cost savings, and KPI improvements compared to initial targets. Operational metrics monitor user adoption, support volume, and workflow integration. Leading indicators provide early warnings of potential issues before they affect key results. Dashboards display customized metrics for different audiences, including business leaders, operations managers, technical teams, and data scientists.

Analytical models tend to lose accuracy over time as business conditions change. Data drift occurs when the input data distribution shifts, even if the relationship with the target remains stable. Concept drift refers to changes in the fundamental relationship between inputs and the target variable. Scheduled retraining updates models at fixed intervals regardless of performance. Triggered retraining responds to drift-detection alerts, performance drops below defined thresholds, or significant business events. Each retraining cycle must be validated against previous versions and managed carefully before full deployment.

Training programs provide various stakeholder groups with the necessary knowledge to operate and maintain solutions effectively. End users learn to interpret outputs and respond appropriately. Technical staff need a thorough understanding of system architecture, monitoring tools, backup processes, and diagnostic scripts. Business stakeholders must understand the strategic implications and limitations. Role-specific curricula include practical exercises, detailed runbooks, and documentation portals to fill knowledge gaps and lower operational risks.

Ongoing validation of the business case ensures that solutions remain justified investments. Attribution analysis helps identify the solution's specific contribution, independent of other factors, by using control groups or counterfactual models. The total cost of ownership includes all direct and indirect expenses, such as licenses, cloud services, personnel time, and overhead costs. Updated ROI calculations, when compared with alternatives, support renewal decisions. Monitoring for unintended consequences involves proactively evaluating ethical risks such as algorithmic bias, operational risks such as overreliance, and systemic effects such as negative feedback loops. The FAT framework, which stands for Fairness, Accountability, and Transparency, guides responsible analytics.

Complete documentation serves as institutional memory. Audience-specific artefacts, including executive dashboards, user guides, technical runbooks, model cards, and governance dossiers, are maintained as living documents throughout the solution's lifecycle.

Chapter 7: Practice Questions

Q1. A quarterly business review of an analytics solution shows high user adoption and 99.9% system uptime. However, the key business KPI the solution aimed to improve has not changed. What is the most likely monitoring issue?
A) Focusing on technical metrics instead of business metrics.
B) Overlooking user satisfaction scores.
C) Setting alert thresholds too low.
D) Not tracking system latency.

Q2. A predictive maintenance model for industrial printers shows a consistent decline in accuracy over the past 6 months. Analysis indicates that the distribution of the "number of pages printed per day" input feature has shifted significantly, but the link between usage and failure stays valid. What kind of drift is taking place?
A) Concept Drift
B) Performance Drift
C) Data Drift
D) Scheduled Drift

Q3. Which training delivery method is most suitable for ensuring IT staff can effectively perform a controlled rollback of a model version during an incident?
A) A quarterly webinar presentation.
B) An interactive workshop with a simulation environment.
C) A one-page FAQ sheet.
D) A recorded lecture from the project kickoff.

Q4. When validating the ongoing business case for a customer segmentation tool, the analyst finds that customer retention increased by 10% after deployment. However, a major competitor also left the market at the same time. What is the critical next step?
A) Declare the project a success and increase its budget.
B) Perform an attribution analysis to isolate the tool's impact.
C) Recalculate the Total Cost of Ownership (TCO).
D) Schedule an immediate retraining of the model.

Q5. An audit of a loan approval model reveals that it has a significantly lower approval rate for applicants from certain zip codes, which serve as

demographic proxies. Removing 'zip code' as a feature is suggested to promote fairness. What is the main flaw in this argument?
A) It breaches model version control protocols.
B) It will probably improve the model's accuracy.
C) Bias can continue through other correlated proxy variables.
D) It simplifies the model retraining pipeline.

Q6. What is the primary purpose of implementing a drift detection system, such as calculating the Population Stability Index (PSI) on key features?
A) To automatically retrain models on a fixed schedule.
B) To provide an early warning that triggers an investigation before business harm occurs.
C) To replace the need for a performance dashboard.
D) To calculate the final Return on Investment (ROI) of the solution.

Q7. A data science team uses a retraining approach where they train a new model weekly, relying only on data from the past four weeks. What is this approach called?
A) Full Retraining
B) Incremental Learning
C) Windowed Retraining
D) Ensemble Retraining

Q8. Which component of the FAT framework is mainly addressed by using post-hoc explanation tools like SHAP or LIME to show users the top factors influencing a specific model prediction?
A) Fairness
B) Accountability
C) Transparency
D) Fidelity

Q9. A runbook is best described as documentation that provides:
A) High-level strategic alignment and ROI for executives.
B) A step-by-step procedural guide for a specific operational task.
C) A historical archive of all model versions.
D) Legal and regulatory compliance certificates.

Q10. The "Ignoring the Human Element" pitfall in monitoring refers to failing to track which of the following?
A) API response times and server CPU utilization.

B) User adoption rates and satisfaction scores.
C) The statistical distribution of input data.
D) The accuracy of the model on a holdout set.

Q11. A sentiment analysis model for product reviews performs poorly after a viral social media trend shifts the connotation of a key phrase from negative to positive. What type of drift most likely occurred?
A) Data Drift
B) Concept Drift
C) Performance Drift
D) Measurement Drift

Q12. What is the main difference between a *triggered* retraining and a *scheduled* retraining?
A) Triggered retraining is less computationally intensive.
B) Scheduled retraining occurs in response to a specific alert or event.
C) Triggered retraining is based on a predefined calendar.
D) Scheduled retraining happens on a calendar, while triggered retraining responds to an event.

Q13. In the context of unintended consequences, a "Negative Feedback Loop" occurs when:
A) User complaints lead to the model being turned off.
B) Model outputs change the environment in a way that reinforces the model's errors.
C) The cost of monitoring exceeds the value of the solution.
D) A model is retrained too often, causing instability.

Q14. Which of the following is a common source of *historical bias* in an algorithm?
A) The training data reflects past societal inequalities.
B) The data collection sensor is faulty.
C) The model is evaluated on an unrepresentative test set.
D) The deployment environment has different hardware than the testing environment.

Q15. The "Total Cost of Ownership (TCO)" for an analytics solution should include:
A) Only the initial development cost.
B) The development cost and software licenses.
C) All direct and indirect ongoing operational, support, and

infrastructure costs.
D) Only the costs associated with the data science team.

Q16. A model card is a type of documentation primarily aimed at which audience?
A) Executive Leadership
B) Data Scientists and Model Stewards
C) End-Users
D) Compliance Auditors

Q17. What is a leading indicator in the context of solution monitoring?
A) A metric that summarizes overall business value delivered last quarter.
B) A system health metric that alerts after a service is already down.
C) A metric that provides an early signal of potential future performance issues.
D) The final calculation of Return on Investment (ROI).

Q18. A company depends solely on a scheduled, quarterly retraining policy for its customer churn model. What is the main risk of this approach?
A) It is computationally inefficient.
B) It requires too much manual effort.
C) It will miss a necessary retraining event between quarters, leading to extended periods of suboptimal performance.
D) It makes model version control impossible.

Q19. The principle of *Accountability* in the FAT framework most directly requires:
A) That model predictions be explainable to a layperson.
B) That clear roles and responsibilities be assigned for system outcomes.
C) That performance metrics be equal across demographic groups.
D) That all source code be made open source.

Q20. What is the main risk of accumulating "documentation debt"?
A) Higher storage costs on company servers.
B) Increased licensing fees for documentation software.
C) Greater operational risk, maintenance expenses, and knowledge loss.
D) Slower internet speeds for the engineering team.

Chapter 8: Analytics Concepts Reference

1. Data Foundations

1.1 Data Types

Structured Data
Structured data is organized information arranged in predefined rows and columns, with specified data types, used in business systems that need fast querying, consistent reporting, and reliable storage. Analysts use it to run SQL queries, join tables, and calculate metrics directly within relational databases. For example, a retailer maintains daily sales transactions in a table with fields for date, store, product, quantity, and price, an analyst uses this structured dataset to find weekly revenue by region.

Semi-structured Data
Semi-structured data includes tags, key–value pairs, or hierarchical elements, but does not follow a strict table schema. It is used in systems that need flexibility as data attributes change. Analysts process it by parsing JSON, XML, or log files and extracting fields for analysis. For example, a logistics platform records shipment events as JSON objects that include shipment_id, status, timestamp, and an optional delay_reason. An analyst loads these logs into a data lake, extracts the relevant fields, and examines how often "weather_delay" occurs across regions to identify where contingency planning is needed.

Unstructured Data
Unstructured data lacks a fixed format or schema and includes text, images, audio, and video. It is used when organizations need to analyze qualitative or free-form information. Analysts use NLP, transcription tools, or image processing to convert raw content into structured features. For example, a customer service team reviews thousands of complaint emails and call transcripts to identify common phrases such as "late delivery" or "missing item," then connects those insights to order and shipment data to determine which carriers or warehouses are causing the most service issues.

1.2 Data Characteristics (5Vs)

Volume

Volume refers to the total amount of data generated or stored, and it is a key consideration for large enterprises, where data scale influences storage architecture, processing tools, and costs. Analysts apply it using distributed systems such as Hadoop or cloud warehouses to process massive datasets efficiently. For example, a global e-commerce company processes billions of clickstream events each month, analysts rely on distributed computing to aggregate these events into customer journey metrics that guide website optimization and marketing spend.

Velocity

Velocity describes the speed at which data is generated, transmitted, and processed to remain useful, and it is applied in real-time operational settings. Analysts use it to create streaming pipelines that update dashboards or trigger alerts within seconds. For example, a retailer updates inventory levels in real time as barcode scans happen across hundreds of stores, analysts monitor these streams to prevent overselling during peak events like Black Friday.

Variety

Variety refers to the diversity of data formats, structures, and sources, and it is a key consideration in integrated analytics environments where decisions depend on combining data from multiple systems. Analysts do this by merging ERP orders, WMS inventory data, TMS shipment data, GPS feeds, and external weather data into unified models. For example, a supply chain control tower brings together all these sources to predict delivery delays and automatically reroute shipments when storms threaten key transportation routes.

Veracity

Veracity concerns the reliability, accuracy, and consistency of data, which is critical when poor data quality can distort forecasts, KPIs, or operational decisions. Analysts achieve this by profiling data, spotting inconsistencies, and setting validation rules. For example, a planner finds that supplier lead times are recorded differently across plants, leading to inaccurate safety stock calculations. The analyst then launches a data quality initiative to standardize lead-time fields and prevent recurring stockouts.

Value
Value measures how much a dataset contributes to better decisions, cost savings, or revenue growth, and is used to prioritize which data sources to integrate or clean. Analysts evaluate which datasets directly support high-impact use cases. For example, a subscription business prioritizes integrating churn data, support tickets, and product usage logs because these sources enable targeted retention campaigns that reduce customer attrition.

1.3 Data Scales

Nominal Scale
A nominal scale sorts data into separate categories without any inherent order. It is used when analysts need to group or compare categories without suggesting a ranking. Analysts do this by dividing the data by labels and calculating metrics for each group. For example, a logistics analyst classifies shipments by carrier, such as Carrier A, Carrier B, and Carrier C, and compares on-time delivery rates across carriers to identify which partner underperforms consistently.

Ordinal Scale
An ordinal scale categorizes data with a meaningful order but without equal spacing between levels, and it is used in surveys, ratings, and qualitative assessments. Analysts apply it by ranking responses and using medians or non-parametric tests. For example, a delivery service collects customer satisfaction ratings of "poor," "fair," "good," and "excellent", analysts use the ordinal scale to track shifts in satisfaction over time without treating the difference between "fair" and "good" as numerically equal.

Interval Scale
An interval scale uses numeric values with equal spacing but no true zero, and it is used when analysts need to measure differences but not ratios. Analysts apply it by analyzing changes or deviations rather than proportional comparisons. For example, a warehouse monitors temperature in refrigerated zones, comparing 4°C vs. 8°C to detect deviations, knowing that 8°C is not twice as hot as 4°C.

Ratio Scale
A ratio scale has equal intervals and a true zero point, allowing all arithmetic operations and meaningful ratios. It is often used in

operational metrics such as quantities, times, and costs. Analysts use it to calculate averages, growth rates, and ratios. For example, a transportation analyst compares lane costs and determines that one route is "twice as expensive" as another, even though both costs start from a true zero baseline.

1.4 Data Measurement & Uncertainty

Accuracy
Accuracy indicates how close a recorded or measured value is to the true value, and it is used in quality control and regulatory compliance. Analysts apply it by comparing measurements to certified standards. For example, a packaging line must fill 500g cereal boxes. The quality team tests the scale using a certified 500g weight and confirms that readings are within ±1g to prevent underfilled or overfilled products, which could lead to customer complaints or regulatory penalties.

Precision
Precision indicates how consistently repeated measurements agree with each other, regardless of whether those measurements are close to the true value, and it helps evaluate process stability. Analysts assess it by checking the variability in repeated measurements. For example, a filling machine consistently dispenses 495ml instead of 500ml, the process is precise but inaccurate, showing the machine is stable but requires recalibration to hit the target volume.

Uncertainty
Uncertainty indicates the range within which the true value is likely to fall due to limitations in measurement, data, or modeling. It is used in forecasting and risk planning. Analysts express uncertainty by providing estimates with confidence intervals or ranges. For instance, a planner forecasts monthly demand for a new product as 10,000 units ± 2,000 units, helping the operations team set safety stock and capacity buffers that account for risk.

Statistical Uncertainty
Statistical uncertainty arises because analysts use samples rather than entire populations, and it is important to consider this when interpreting survey, experimental, or pilot test results. Analysts implement it by calculating confidence intervals and accounting for sampling error. For example, a company surveys 500 of its 50,000 customers and estimates a

satisfaction score of 4.2, the analyst reports a confidence interval to avoid overreacting to small differences that may arise from sampling variation.

Systemic Uncertainty

Systemic uncertainty arises from the behavior of the entire system rather than from random sampling, and it is used when analyzing complex processes such as supply chains or transportation networks. Analysts apply it by modeling system-level variability and identifying structural constraints. For instance, a company models end-to-end lead-time variability caused by port congestion, customs inspections, and carrier capacity constraints. The analyst concludes that collecting more data will not eliminate delays and recommends redesigning the network or diversifying ports.

1.5 Sampling & Data Sources

Sampling Methods

Sampling methods are techniques for choosing a subset of observations from a larger population, used when full inspection or data collection is too expensive or impractical. Analysts implement them by designing representative samples that reduce bias. For example, a quality engineer selects a random sample of 50 boxes from each production batch instead of inspecting every box, enabling the team to estimate defect rates while keeping inspection costs low.

Data Sources

Data sources are systems, processes, or external providers where data originates, and they are used to create integrated analytics environments. Analysts achieve this by mapping data flows and combining sources into unified datasets. For example, an order visibility dashboard combines ERP order data, WMS inventory data, carrier tracking feeds, and customer service tickets, providing managers with a single view of order status and bottlenecks.

1.6 Data Schemas

Schema-on-Read

Schema-on-read stores raw data without enforcing a structure until analysis time, making it suitable for data lakes that support flexible, exploratory analytics. Analysts define the structure only when querying the data. For example, a factory stores raw IoT sensor logs in a data lake, maintenance teams interpret the logs differently for failure prediction, while energy analysts structure them differently to analyze power consumption patterns.

Schema-on-Write

Schema-on-write enforces a predefined structure before data is stored and is used in data warehouses that require consistency and standardized reporting. Analysts apply it by loading data into fixed tables with strict validation rules. For example, a sales data warehouse requires every transaction to match a defined schema covering date, store, product, quantity, and price, ensuring that dashboards across the company use consistent and comparable data.

1.7 Data Preparation

Data Wrangling

Data wrangling involves cleaning, merging, reshaping, and enriching raw data to make it analysis-ready, and it is used in nearly every analytics project. Analysts do this by resolving duplicates, fixing inconsistent IDs, and joining datasets. For example, an analyst preparing an on-time delivery report merges order and shipment tables with customer master data, corrects mismatched customer IDs, and removes duplicate shipments to create a clean dataset for performance analysis.

Data Transformation

Data transformation alters the format, scale, or structure of data to prepare it for analysis or modeling. It is used in forecasting, machine learning, and financial reporting. Analysts do this by encoding categorical variables, normalizing numeric fields, or converting currencies. For example, a forecasting analyst converts all sales amounts to USD, encodes carrier names as numeric variables, and applies log transformations to skewed demand data before training a predictive model.

Skewness

Skewness measures the asymmetry of a distribution around its mean and helps select statistical methods or prepare data for modeling. Analysts use it to determine whether extreme values skew averages or break model assumptions. For example, a planner examining weekly demand notices a strong right skew caused by occasional bulk orders. They select a forecasting method that is less affected by outliers, such as median-based smoothing or trimmed mean approaches.

Box-Cox Transformation

The Box-Cox transformation is a family of power transformations used to reduce skewness and stabilize variance. It is applied when preparing data for models that assume normally distributed errors. Analysts choose the best lambda parameter and transform the data before modeling. For example, a demand planner applies a Box-Cox transformation to monthly sales volumes to improve the reliability of forecasts and confidence intervals generated by exponential smoothing models.

1.8 Experimental Design

Design of Experiments (DOE)

Design of Experiments is a systematic approach to testing multiple factors simultaneously to understand their individual and combined effects. It is commonly used in manufacturing, quality improvement, and process optimization. Analysts implement it by designing controlled trials that systematically vary factors. For example, a bakery tests different oven temperatures, baking times, and humidity levels using a DOE plan to find the best combination that minimizes product defects while using the fewest tests.

Response Surface Methodology (RSM)

Response Surface Methodology is a set of techniques for modeling and optimizing a response to multiple continuous variables. It is applied when organizations seek to determine the best operating conditions. Practitioners typically fit a predictive model and analyze the response surface to find optimal settings. For example, a chemical plant uses RSM to model yield as a function of pressure and temperature, then identifies the optimal operating point that maximizes output while ensuring safety limits are met.

1.9 Statistical Foundations

P-Value

A p-value is the probability of observing results as extreme as or more extreme than those in the sample, assuming the null hypothesis is true, and it is used in hypothesis testing to assess whether an observed effect is statistically significant. Analysts do this by comparing the p-value to a significance threshold such as 0.05. For example, a warehouse tests whether a new picking method reduces average picking time, a low p-value suggests the improvement is unlikely to be due to chance, supporting adoption of the new method.

Fisher's Exact Test
Fisher's Exact Test assesses the relationship between two categorical variables, especially when sample sizes are small, and is commonly used in quality control and clinical studies. Practitioners do this by creating a contingency table and calculating the exact probability of the observed distribution. For example, a factory compares defect versus no-defect counts between two small production lines, Fisher's Exact Test determines whether one line genuinely has a higher defect rate or if the difference might be due to chance.

1.10 Exploration & Visualization

Data Exploration
Data exploration is the initial process of summarizing, visualizing, and investigating raw data to understand its structure, quality, and key patterns. It is used at the start of every analytics project to identify issues before modeling or decision-making. Analysts do this by calculating quick summaries, plotting distributions, checking for missing values, and scanning for unusual spikes or inconsistencies. For example, before creating a demand forecast, an analyst loads three years of order data and notices several weeks with zero demand due to a system outage. By spotting these anomalies during exploration, the analyst corrects the data and prevents the forecasting model from interpreting the outage as a genuine drop in customer demand.

Histogram
A histogram shows how often a numeric variable falls into different bins. It helps with analytics by understanding the shape, spread, and focus of the data before choosing statistical methods or creating models. Analysts group data into intervals and check whether the distribution is normal, skewed, multimodal, or has unusual spikes. For example, a transportation analyst creates a histogram of delivery times for thousands of shipments and quickly notices a long right tail, indicating frequent delays at a specific port. This insight leads to a closer look at that route before the company renegotiates carrier contracts.

Scatter Plot
A scatter plot shows the relationship between two numeric variables by plotting each observation as a point. It helps identify correlations, clusters, and nonlinear patterns that affect modeling choices. Analysts typically place one variable on each axis and look for trends, curves, or random distributions. For example, a logistics analyst plots shipping distance against transportation cost and notices that costs rise sharply after 800 km, revealing a pricing threshold to consider for forecasting freight expenses or choosing carriers.

Heatmap
A heatmap displays data using color in a grid, emphasizing intensity, density, or patterns across two factors such as time, location, or product categories. Analysts use it by assigning metrics to color scales to quickly identify hotspots or anomalies. For instance, a warehouse manager creates a heatmap showing pick frequency by zone and hour, the visualization reveals that Zone C becomes very crowded every afternoon, prompting a re-slotting effort that moves fast-moving items to reduce travel time and improve efficiency.

Box Plot
A box plot summarizes a distribution by showing the median, quartiles, and potential outliers. It is used to compare variability and identify extreme values across groups. Analysts create box plots for categories such as suppliers, regions, or product lines to spot which groups show unstable performance. For example, a procurement analyst compares lead-time variability across five suppliers and notes that Supplier D has a much wider interquartile range and more outliers, indicating reliability issues that may warrant renegotiation or adding a backup supplier.

Line Chart
A line chart shows how a metric changes over time and is used for trend analysis, performance monitoring, and forecasting. Analysts do this by plotting time on the x-axis and the metric on the y-axis to spot seasonality, cycles, or structural breaks. For example, an inventory analyst reviews a line chart of monthly stockout incidents over three years and notices a recurring spike every November. This pattern indicates a seasonal demand surge not reflected in current safety stock policies, prompting an adjustment before the next peak season.

2. Descriptive Analytics

2.1 Summary Statistics

Mean (Arithmetic Mean)
The mean, also called the arithmetic mean, is the sum of all values divided by the number of observations. It is used in business to measure typical performance across stores, products, employees, or time periods. Analysts calculate it by adding all values and dividing by the total count to establish a benchmark for comparison. For example, a retailer finds that the average daily sales per store across 200 locations is $18,500. Stores consistently below this benchmark are flagged for further analysis to determine whether staffing, inventory, or local competition is causing underperformance.

Median
The median is the middle value in a sorted dataset and is used when analysts need a measure of central tendency that is resistant to extreme outliers. Analysts apply it by sorting the values and selecting the midpoint, which provides a more stable indicator when the data is skewed. For example, a city government analyzes household income across neighborhoods and uses the median rather than the mean because a few ultra-high earners would distort the average, the median helps planners allocate social programs more accurately.

Mode
The mode is the value that appears most often in a dataset and is used in operations and inventory planning to identify common patterns or dominant behaviors. Analysts find it by counting how often each value occurs and selecting the one with the highest count. For example, a warehouse reviews order quantities for a popular SKU and discovers that the mode is "2 units," meaning most customers purchase two at a time. This insight helps the warehouse optimize carton sizes and picking strategies to reduce packing time and material waste.

Geometric Mean
The geometric mean is the nth root of the product of n values and is used to analyze growth rates, index values, and multiplicative processes. Analysts use it by multiplying all values and then taking the appropriate root, which helps smooth out volatility in percentage changes. For example, a marketing team assesses monthly website traffic growth over

the course of a year, with highly variable increases and decreases. The geometric mean provides a more accurate measure of typical growth than the arithmetic mean, helping the team set realistic performance targets.

Harmonic Mean
The harmonic mean is the reciprocal of the average of reciprocals and is used when averaging rates such as speeds, processing times, or cost per unit. Analysts apply it by converting each value to its reciprocal, averaging the reciprocals, and then taking the reciprocal of the average. For example, a logistics analyst calculates the average speed of a delivery truck that travels half the distance at 40 km/h and the other half at 80 km/h, the harmonic mean properly accounts for the slower segment and provides a more accurate estimate of total travel time than the arithmetic mean.

2.2 Measures of Dispersion

Variance
Variance measures the average squared deviation from the mean and is used in manufacturing, forecasting, and quality control to evaluate process stability and risk. The population Analysts determine it by calculating deviations from the mean, squaring them, and then averaging the results. For example, a bottling plant monitors the variance of fill volumes across thousands of bottles, an increasing variance signals rising instability in the filling machine, prompting maintenance before defective products reach customers.

Standard Deviation
Standard deviation is the square root of variance and indicates the average deviation from the mean in the same units as the data. It is used to monitor consistency and identify unusual variation. Analysts do this by calculating the square root of variance and comparing it to control limits or historical norms. For example, a cereal factory targets 500g boxes, but daily samples range from 470g to 530g. The high standard deviation indicates an unstable filling process and suggests the need for accuracy to prevent customer complaints and regulatory issues.

Mean Absolute Deviation (MAD)
MAD measures the typical dispersion of data by averaging the absolute deviations from the mean. It involves taking the absolute difference of each data point from the mean and then calculating the average of these differences. Since MAD does not square deviations, it is less affected by

outliers compared to variance or standard deviation. This makes MAD a practical and easy-to-understand statistic for describing the usual spread of a dataset in a clear, interpretable unit.

2.3 Relationship Analysis

Correlation

Correlation measures the strength and direction of a linear relationship between two numeric variables and is used in marketing, finance, and operations to identify associations that can guide further analysis. Analysts do this by calculating the correlation coefficient and interpreting whether the relationship is positive, negative, or negligible. For example, a marketing analyst examines the correlation between weekly advertising spend and sales and finds a strong positive relationship. This does not prove causation. It does suggest that advertising levels are worth including as a candidate feature in future predictive models.

2.4 Exploratory Data Analysis (EDA)

Distribution Analysis

Distribution analysis examines the shape, center, and spread of a variable and is used to determine whether the data meet the assumptions of statistical models or require transformation. Analysts use it to plot histograms, density curves, or box plots and assess skewness, modality, and variability. For example, a planner reviewing weekly demand data finds a bimodal distribution caused by alternating promotional and non-promotional weeks, this insight prompts them to build separate forecasting models for each condition.

Outlier Detection

Outlier detection finds values that are unusually high or low and don't follow typical patterns. It is used in fraud detection, quality control, and spotting unusual behavior. Analysts use statistical thresholds, visualization, or machine learning to identify these suspicious points. For example, a finance team notices a sudden increase in refund transactions from one store, this outlier prompts an investigation that reveals a cashier is processing fraudulent returns.

Data Profiling

Data profiling assesses data completeness, uniqueness, consistency, and validity, and it is used during system migrations, data integration, and quality improvement initiatives. Analysts apply it by scanning datasets for missing values, duplicates, inconsistent formats, and invalid entries. For example, before integrating customer master data into a new CRM system, a data engineer profiles the dataset and discovers thousands of duplicate customer IDs and inconsistent phone number formats, prompting a cleanup effort to prevent downstream reporting errors.

2.5 Performance Visualization

Gain Chart

A gain chart shows how well a model or strategy identifies high-value targets compared with random selection, and it is used in marketing, credit scoring, and churn prevention. Analysts rank customers by predicted likelihood and plot cumulative gains. For example, a marketing team evaluates a conversion model and finds that targeting the top 20% of customers identified by the model produces 60% of total expected conversions, this insight helps them allocate campaign budgets more effectively.

Lift Chart

A lift chart compares a model's performance to a baseline, usually a random choice, to measure how much better it performs than chance. Analysts calculate lift values across deciles or percentiles of ranked predictions. For example, a retention team uses a lift chart to evaluate a churn model and finds a lift of 3 in the top decile, meaning the model is three times better than random at identifying customers likely to churn, this helps the team focus outreach on the highest-risk segment.

3. Inferential Analytics

3.1 Hypothesis Testing

Hypothesis Testing Concepts
Hypothesis testing is a systematic method for determining whether an observed effect is statistically significant or could have occurred by chance. Organizations use it to test changes before implementing them broadly. It works by comparing sample results to what would be expected if there were no real difference. For example, a warehouse tests whether a new picking process reduces average picking time by collecting data from workers using the new method and comparing it to the old one. If the improvement is large compared to natural variation, analysts conclude that the new process genuinely improves performance.

Confidence Intervals
A confidence interval is a range of values constructed from sample data such that, if the same procedure were repeated many times, a specified percentage of the resulting intervals (such as 95%) would contain the true population parameter. It quantifies the uncertainty in an estimate rather than stating the probability that any single interval contains the true value. For example, if a supplier's average lead time is estimated at 10 days with a 95% confidence interval of 9–11 days, planners use the upper bound when setting safety stock to guard against delays.

Type I Error (False Positive)
A Type I error occurs when analysts believe an effect exists when it does not, especially when evaluating process changes, where acting on a false improvement can be costly. It is managed by setting a significance level that limits the risk of approving a change in error. For instance, a company might think a new routing algorithm reduces delivery times based on a small test, but the observed improvement was due to random fluctuations, implementing it can waste money and disrupt operations because there is no real impact.

Type II Error (False Negative)
A Type II error happens when analysts fail to identify a real effect. It is used to test whether improvements truly work, even when they seem insignificant due to small sample sizes. It involves ensuring an adequate sample size and sufficient statistical power. For example, a manufacturer tests a new machine setting that reduces defects, but because the sample

size is small, the test is not statistically significant, causing the company to miss a real quality improvement opportunity.

A/B Testing

A/B testing is a controlled experiment that compares two versions (A = current state, B = new version) to determine which performs better. It is used in operations, marketing, and product design to validate changes before scaling. The process involves randomly assigning users or orders to each version and measuring a key outcome. For example, an e-commerce company tests two checkout flows by assigning half of its customers to Version A and half to Version B, if Version B yields a statistically significant increase in completed orders, the company confidently adopts it across all markets.

3.2 Statistical Tests

ANOVA (Analysis of Variance)

ANOVA compares the means of three or more groups to determine whether at least one differs significantly and is used when organizations test multiple options simultaneously. It works by analyzing variation within groups compared to variation between groups. For example, a warehouse tests three layout designs by measuring the average picking time for each, ANOVA helps determine whether the layout design affects performance or if the differences are due to chance.

MANOVA (Multivariate Analysis of Variance)

MANOVA compares multiple dependent variables across groups and is used when performance cannot be captured by a single metric. It analyzes whether groups differ on a combined set of outcomes. For example, when evaluating three employee training programs, managers assess both picking speed and error rate together, MANOVA determines whether the type of training influences overall performance rather than just one aspect.

Student t-Tests

A Student's t-test compares the mean of one sample to a known value or the means of two groups. It is used to evaluate before-and-after changes or to compare two options. The test assesses whether the difference in means is large relative to the variability. For example, a warehouse measures the average order processing time before and after a system upgrade. A paired t-test determines whether the observed reduction is statistically significant.

Chi-Square Test
The chi-square test assesses whether two categorical variables are associated, and it is used to analyze patterns in categorical data. It works by comparing observed frequencies to expected frequencies. For example, a quality engineer examines whether defect occurrence (defective vs. non-defective) is related to shift (day vs. night). The chi-square test assesses whether defects are disproportionately occurring during a specific shift.

Non-Parametric Tests
Nonparametric tests do not assume a specific distribution and are used when data are skewed, ordinal, or violate normality assumptions. They work by ranking data instead of using raw values. For example, when comparing customer satisfaction ratings (1–5 stars) between two carriers, a Mann–Whitney U test is more suitable than a t-test because the data is ordinal and not normally distributed.

3.3 Regression Foundations

Regression Concepts
Regression models the relationship between a dependent variable and one or more independent variables, and it is used to measure how different factors influence an outcome. It does this by fitting a line or curve that best predicts the target variable. For example, a warehouse model shows how order volume, number of SKUs, and staffing levels affect daily picking time, regression analysis quantifies each factor's contribution and helps managers forecast labor needs for future demand.

Causation vs. Correlation
Correlation measures association, while causation means one variable directly influences another. This distinction is important when interpreting relationships in business data. Causation is established through experiments or controlled studies. For example, marketing spend and sales may be highly correlated, but without proper experimental design, analysts cannot conclude that increasing spend will always boost sales, both may be affected by seasonality or promotions.

4. Predictive Analytics

4.1 Supervised Learning

Linear Regression

Linear regression predicts a numerical value by fitting a straight line to the relationship between inputs and outputs. It is utilized by organizations to forecast continuous outcomes, such as demand or processing time. The model is trained on historical data to understand how each variable influences the target. For instance, a warehouse forecasts the upcoming week's order volume using factors such as day of the week, promotions, and prior sales, helping managers plan staffing and inventory replenishment.

Logistic Regression

Logistic regression estimates the probability of a binary outcome, such as late/on-time or churn/stay and is used when organizations need to classify events and take preventive measures. It functions by modeling how input variables influence the likelihood of an event. For example, a logistics team predicts whether a shipment will be late based on factors such as distance, carrier, weather, and warehouse congestion, allowing the team to identify high-risk shipments and intervene proactively.

Decision Trees

A decision tree predicts outcomes by splitting data into branches using simple if-then rules, making it useful for organizations that need interpretable models that explain why a prediction was made. It works by recursively dividing data based on the most informative variables. For example, a distribution center analyzes delayed orders and, using a decision tree, finds that "carrier = X AND distance > 500 km" has the highest probability of delay, helping to guide targeted improvements.

Random Forest

A random forest combines many decision trees trained on different samples to produce more accurate and stable predictions, and it is used when organizations need robust models that handle complex interactions. It is applied by aggregating predictions from multiple trees. For example, a manufacturer predicts product defects using hundreds of trees trained on temperature, pressure, operator, and machine settings, capturing subtle patterns that a single tree would miss.

Support Vector Machines (SVM)
SVMs find the optimal boundary that separates classes, even in complex or high-dimensional spaces, and are used when organizations need precise classification in scenarios with overlapping classes. It works by transforming data into a higher-dimensional space to identify a separating hyperplane. For example, a quality team classifies parts as defective or non-defective based on sensor readings, thereby improving detection accuracy.

K-Nearest Neighbors (KNN)
KNN predicts outcomes based on the most similar past cases and is useful for organizations that want simple, intuitive models relying on historical patterns. It works by finding the closest data points to a new observation. For example, a maintenance team predicts which spare parts are needed for a new machine failure by comparing it to the most similar past breakdowns.

Naïve Bayes
Naïve Bayes is a probabilistic classifier that applies Bayes' theorem under the assumption that features are conditionally independent given the class label. It is commonly used in text classification and email routing. The classifier operates by computing the probability of each class contingent upon the words or features present. For instance, a customer service center trains a Naïve Bayes classifier on thousands of labeled emails to identify which words are associated with categories such as "delivery delay," "billing issue," or "product defect," enabling the automatic routing of new emails to the appropriate team.

Gradient Boosting / XGBoost
Gradient boosting builds trees sequentially, with each new tree correcting the errors of previous trees, and is used when organizations require high-accuracy predictions in complex environments. It optimizes a loss function through iterative improvements. For example, a retailer predicts customer churn using dozens of behavioral features, such as purchase frequency and complaint history, and uses XGBoost to capture nonlinear interactions.

Neural Networks (ANN, Deep Learning)
Neural networks learn complex nonlinear relationships through interconnected layers of nodes. Organizations use them when working with large datasets or unstructured data such as text, images, and audio.

Training proceeds by passing data through multiple layers, each extracting progressively more abstract features. For instance, a retailer uses a deep learning model to forecast weekly sales, incorporating factors such as promotions, holidays, weather, and competitor pricing.

Gradient Descent
Gradient descent is an iterative optimization technique that adjusts variables in the direction of steepest decrease to minimize a function. It is used in machine learning, pricing optimization, and forecasting. The process involves calculating the gradient of the loss function with respect to each parameter and updating parameters by moving a small step (the learning rate) in the direction that reduces the loss. This repeats until the loss converges to a minimum. The learning rate controls the step size: too large causes divergence, too small causes very slow convergence. For example, a marketing team uses gradient descent to train a regression model that predicts customer conversions, the algorithm repeatedly adjusts coefficients until the prediction error is minimized.

Stochastic Gradient Descent (SGD)
Stochastic gradient descent updates model parameters using a single observation or a small batch at a time, making it suitable for large-scale machine learning when full-dataset updates are too slow. It works by randomly sampling data points and performing quick, incremental updates. For example, an e-commerce company uses SGD to train a recommendation model on millions of customer interactions. The algorithm updates its weights continuously as new data arrives, enabling real-time personalization.

4.2 Unsupervised Learning

K-Means Clustering
K-means groups data into clusters based on similarity, and it is used when organizations need to segment customers, products, or suppliers. It works by assigning each observation to the nearest cluster center. For example, a retailer segments customers into groups such as "bulk buyers," "seasonal buyers," and "frequent small-order buyers," enabling targeted marketing.

Hierarchical Clustering
Hierarchical clustering creates a tree of clusters that shows how groups merge or split, helping organizations understand natural groupings at

different levels. It works by progressively combining or dividing clusters. For example, a procurement team groups suppliers based on lead time, defect rate, and cost, revealing which suppliers are strategic or risky.

Principal Component Analysis (PCA)
PCA reduces many correlated variables into a smaller set of uncorrelated components and is used when organizations need to simplify high-dimensional data. It works by transforming variables into principal components that explain most of the variance. For example, a factory with 40 machine sensors uses PCA to reduce them to a few key components for easier monitoring.

Association Rule Mining
Association rule mining identifies items that frequently occur together and is used in retail, e-commerce, and recommendation systems. It works by analyzing transaction patterns. For example, a supermarket notices that customers who buy "printer + paper" frequently also buy "ink," which helps guide promotions and store layout.

4.3 Reinforcement Learning

Reinforcement Learning
Reinforcement learning trains an agent to make sequential decisions by maximizing cumulative reward over time. The agent learns by exploring possible actions, receiving reward signals for outcomes, and updating its policy to favor actions that lead to higher long-term returns. It is used in robotics, routing, and dynamic optimization. It is implemented by allowing the agent to explore actions and learn from feedback. For example, a warehouse robot learns the fastest picking route by trying different paths and receiving rewards for shorter completion times.

4.4 Model Evaluation & Validation

Confusion Matrix
A confusion matrix summarizes the performance of a classification model by tallying true positives (TP), false positives (FP), true negatives (TN), and false negatives (FN). It is used to evaluate classification models and derive key performance metrics. Precision = TP / (TP + FP). Recall (Sensitivity) = TP / (TP + FN). Specificity = TN / (TN + FP). F1 Score = 2 × (Precision × Recall) / (Precision + Recall). It compares predicted labels to actual outcomes. For example, a late-shipment classifier may correctly

identify 80% of late shipments but also incorrectly flag many on-time shipments, as the confusion matrix reveals.

Precision

Precision measures the proportion of predicted positives that are truly positive, calculated as TP / (TP + FP). It is used when false alarms are costly, such as in fraud detection, where flagging legitimate transactions as fraudulent imposes direct costs on customers and operations. For example, in fraud detection, high precision ensures that most flagged transactions are genuinely suspicious.

Recall (Sensitivity)

Recall measures the proportion of actual positives that the model correctly identifies, calculated as TP / (TP + FN). It is used when missing a positive case is costly, such as in defect detection, where an undetected defective unit reaches the customer. For example, in defect detection, high recall ensures that most defective units are caught before shipping.

Specificity

Specificity measures the proportion of actual negatives correctly identified as negative, calculated as TN / (TN + FP). It is used when false positives carry high cost or harm. For example, in equipment failure prediction, high specificity ensures that healthy machines are not incorrectly flagged for maintenance.

ROC Curve

The ROC curve illustrates the trade-off between the True Positive Rate (Recall) and the False Positive Rate across all possible classification thresholds. It helps select the optimal operating threshold for a model. The Area Under the Curve (AUC) summarizes the curve as a single number between 0 and 1. An AUC of 1.0 indicates perfect discrimination. An AUC of 0.5 indicates performance no better than random selection. It is constructed by plotting performance metrics at various thresholds. For example, a churn model might perform best at a threshold that balances identifying at-risk customers and avoiding overburdening the retention team.

R-Squared

R-squared measures the proportion of variation in the target variable explained by a regression model and is used to evaluate models that predict continuous outcomes. It is applied by comparing model predictions to actual values. For example, a sales forecasting model with an R^2 of 0.80 explains 80% of the variation in sales.

MAE (Mean Absolute Error)
In forecast evaluation, what practitioners sometimes call "MAD" is actually **Mean Absolute Error (MAE)** – the average absolute difference between actual and forecasted values. Unlike MAD (defined in Section 2.2 as dispersion around the sample mean), MAE measures prediction accuracy against observed outcomes. To avoid ambiguity, use MAE for model assessment and reserve MAD strictly for describing data spread. When comparing models, MAE is preferred over MSE when outliers are a concern, as it shares MAD's robustness while being correctly applied to forecast errors.

MSE (Mean Squared Error)
MSE is the average of squared prediction errors and is used when large errors are especially costly. It is calculated by squaring each error and then averaging them. For example, in high-value inventory planning, MSE penalizes large forecast errors more heavily.

RMSE (Root Mean Squared Error)
RMSE is the square root of MSE and is expressed in the same units as the target. It is used when organizations want a measure that emphasizes large errors. It is calculated by taking the square root of MSE. For example, an RMSE of 1.8 days in lead-time forecasting indicates the model's typical error is about two days.

MAPE (Mean Absolute Percentage Error)
MAPE calculates the average absolute percentage difference between predicted and actual values and is used to compare forecast accuracy across products with different scales. It is determined by averaging the absolute percentage errors. MAPE cannot be used when actual values are zero or near zero because division by zero is undefined. For example, an MAPE of 8% indicates the forecast is off by 8% on average.

Forecast Bias
Forecast bias indicates whether predictions systematically overestimate or underestimate actual outcomes. It is used to identify directional errors by comparing the average forecast error to zero. For example, if a demand model consistently underpredicts holiday sales, analysts recognize that the model is missing seasonal effects.

4.5 Model Diagnostics

Heteroscedasticity

Heteroscedasticity occurs when the variance of regression errors varies across levels of an independent variable, violating the assumption of constant variance. It is used to evaluate regression models and ensure that coefficients and significance tests are reliable. It is identified through residual plots or statistical tests. For example, when modeling delivery time as a function of distance, short trips may have low variability, whereas long trips vary widely. Analysts often apply log transformations or use heteroscedasticity-consistent standard errors to stabilize the variance.

Multicollinearity

Multicollinearity arises when independent variables are highly correlated, leading to unstable coefficients and unreliable interpretations. It is a diagnostic tool in regression analysis, commonly assessed through the variance inflation factor (VIF). For instance, including both "discount percentage" and "final price" in a pricing model introduces redundancy, therefore, removing or combining these variables improves model stability.

Residual Analysis

Residual analysis checks for model errors, such as nonlinearity, outliers, or missing variables, and helps verify whether a model's assumptions are correct. It is done by plotting residuals against predictions. For example, if a forecasting model consistently underpredicts during promotions, residual patterns indicate the problem and prompt analysts to add promotion features.

Overfitting / Underfitting

Overfitting happens when a model memorizes noise in the training data rather than the underlying pattern. Underfitting occurs when a model is too simple to capture the real relationships in the data. Both are evaluated by comparing training and test performance. For example, a model that performs very well on training data but poorly on new data is overfitting and may need regularization or simplification.

Data Leakage

Data leakage occurs when information about the future or the target variable is present in the training data, leading to unrealistically high performance. It is used during model validation. This is done by carefully reviewing features. For example, including "account closed date" in a churn model leaks the answer, making the model ineffective in production.

4.6 Feature Engineering

Feature Selection

Feature selection identifies the most relevant variables and removes noise, improving both model performance and interpretability. It involves selecting the variables that contribute most to the prediction. For example, when predicting delivery delays, analysts keep features such as distance, carrier, and weather, while removing irrelevant ones such as customer age.

Feature Creation

Feature creation involves developing new variables from existing data to identify important patterns. It is used when raw data does not fully reflect the underlying behavior. This process includes engineering meaningful metrics. For example, creating "days since last purchase" or "average order value" helps improve churn prediction accuracy.

Handling Class Imbalance

Managing class imbalance involves techniques used when one class in a dataset is much less common than the other. This situation often occurs in predictive modeling, where the minority class may represent the event of interest, such as delayed shipments, fraud cases, equipment breakdowns, or customer churn. Such management is achieved by adjusting the training data or the model itself to enable the detection of rare events rather than always predicting the majority class. For example, if only 2% of shipments in a logistics dataset are delayed, a simple model might always predict "on-time" for all shipments, achieving 98% accuracy but remaining ineffective. To address this, analysts may oversample late shipments, under-sample on-time shipments, or use class-weighted algorithms to help the model focus on rare late-shipment cases and learn the patterns that cause delays.

5. Prescriptive Analytics

5.1 Decision Analysis

Decision Trees (as Decision Tools)

A decision tree is a visual diagram that maps decisions, uncertainties, and potential outcomes. It is used in business to evaluate different actions when future conditions are uncertain. The process involves defining decision points, assigning probabilities to uncertain events, and calculating the expected payoff for each branch to find the most beneficial choice. For example, a retailer deciding whether to launch a new product creates a decision tree with branches for "launch now," "delay launch," and "cancel," each associated with probabilities of high, medium, or low demand. The tree shows that launching now yields the highest expected profit when marketing costs and demand uncertainty are accounted for, helping leadership choose the best option.

Decision Matrices

A decision matrix is a grid tool that compares multiple alternatives based on weighted criteria and is used in procurement, vendor selection, and strategic planning when decisions involve several competing factors. It works by listing alternatives, setting evaluation criteria, assigning importance weights, scoring each option, and calculating weighted totals to identify the best choice. For example, a procurement team evaluating three logistics providers creates a decision matrix with criteria such as cost, delivery reliability, capacity, and technology integration, after assigning higher weights to reliability and capacity, Provider B scores the highest overall, leading the company to choose it despite it not being the cheapest option.

Expected Value

Expected value is the probability-weighted average of all possible outcomes, used in risk-based decision-making when uncertainty affects financial or operational outcomes. It is calculated by multiplying each outcome by its probability and summing the results to compare options objectively. For example, a supply chain manager deciding whether to ship by air or ocean computes the expected cost for each option, considering the probabilities of delays, penalties, and expedited fees. Expected value analysis shows that ocean shipping is generally cheaper despite occasional delays, helping the manager choose the most cost-effective option.

Influence Diagrams

An influence diagram is a compact graphical model that illustrates the relationships among decisions, uncertainties, and outcomes. It is used in strategic planning and risk analysis to clarify how variables interact before creating a full decision model. This is done by mapping decision, chance, and value nodes to show dependencies and information flow. For example, a hospital designing a new staffing model uses an influence diagram to demonstrate how patient volume, staff availability, and regulatory requirements impact wait times and operating costs. This high-level overview helps leadership understand the system's structure before developing a detailed optimization model.

5.2 Multi-Criteria Decision Making (MCDM)

Analytic Hierarchy Process (AHP)

AHP is a systematic method for ranking options by breaking down decisions into a hierarchy of criteria and performing pairwise comparisons. It is used in areas like capital planning, vendor selection, and strategic prioritization. The process involves comparing criteria two at a time, calculating priority weights, and scoring alternatives based on those weights. For example, a city transportation department may use AHP to decide between expanding bus routes, building bike lanes, or adding parking structures. Pairwise comparisons can reveal that safety and congestion reduction are most important, guiding investment toward the most aligned option, such as expanding bike lanes.

Multi-Criteria Decision Analysis (MCDA)

MCDA is a framework for comparing options across multiple conflicting criteria, especially when decisions can't be reduced to a single metric such as cost. It involves defining criteria, normalizing scores, assigning weights, and ranking options to find the best overall choice. For example, an energy company evaluating renewable projects uses MCDA to compare solar, wind, and hydro options across factors such as cost, environmental impact, reliability, and regulatory incentives. The analysis indicates that wind offers the best balance for the region, helping guide investment decisions.

Multiple Objective Decision Analysis (MODA)

MODA evaluates decisions involving multiple objectives that must be optimized simultaneously. It is used in supply chain design, engineering, and policy planning, where trade-offs need to be measured clearly. It works by defining objectives, creating utility functions, and finding solutions that balance conflicting priorities. For example, a distribution network redesign uses MODA to reduce transportation costs while increasing service levels. The model identifies a setup with slightly higher costs but much better delivery performance, which leadership then chooses as the best compromise.

Value-Focused Thinking

Value-Focused Thinking emphasizes identifying core values and goals before creating options. It is used in strategic planning and policymaking to ensure that decisions support long-term aims. The process involves pinpointing fundamental values, turning them into measurable objectives, and developing alternatives that maximize those objectives. For example, a healthcare organization might prioritize patient safety, accessibility, and cost efficiency, using value-focused thinking, analysts develop a new clinic scheduling system that reduces wait times, ensures safety, and stays within budget.

5.3 Optimization & Mathematical Programming

Linear Programming

Linear programming is a mathematical technique used to optimize an objective function within linear constraints. It finds applications in logistics, production planning, workforce scheduling, and financial allocation. The process involves defining decision variables, formulating a linear objective (such as minimizing costs or maximizing profits), and setting constraints that reflect real-world limitations. For instance, a manufacturer may use linear programming to determine the optimal production mix of three products given labor hours, machine capacity, and material availability. The model then identifies the combination that maximizes profit while adhering to all resource limits.

Integer Programming

Integer programming is an optimization technique where some or all decision variables must take integer values. It is used in facility location, routing, staffing, and capital budgeting, where fractional decisions are not feasible. The method involves defining variables with integer restrictions and solving the model using branch-and-bound or similar algorithms. For example, a retailer uses integer programming to decide which distribution centers to open from a list of potential sites, the model selects the combination that minimizes total transportation and operating costs while meeting service-level requirements.

Mixed Integer Programming (MIP)
Mixed-integer programming combines continuous and integer variables in a single optimization model and is used for complex planning problems that involve both discrete choices and continuous quantities. It models decisions such as "open or close a facility" alongside continuous variables, such as shipment amounts. For example, a global supply chain uses MIP to decide which warehouses to operate and how much inventory to ship on each route, the model finds a network configuration that minimizes total cost by balancing fixed facility costs with variable transportation costs.

Nonlinear Optimization
Nonlinear optimization addresses problems where the objective function or constraints are nonlinear and is used in engineering design, pricing optimization, and energy management. It works by modeling nonlinear relationships such as diminishing returns, capacity curves, or nonlinear cost structures. For example, a utility company uses nonlinear optimization to find the optimal power generation mix across plants with nonlinear fuel-efficiency curves, the model determines generation levels that minimize total cost while satisfying demand and emissions constraints.

Dynamic Programming
Dynamic programming solves complex problems by breaking them into overlapping subproblems and storing intermediate results. It is used in inventory planning, pricing optimization, and resource allocation. The method involves defining states, decisions, and transition rules to efficiently compute optimal solutions. For example, an airline uses dynamic programming to set ticket prices over time, the model determines the optimal price each day to maximize revenue while accounting for remaining seats and expected demand.

Multi-Objective Optimization
Multi-objective optimization addresses problems with two or more conflicting goals, and it is used in supply chain design, portfolio optimization, and engineering trade-offs. It works by creating a Pareto frontier that displays the best possible trade-offs between objectives. For example, a logistics team uses multi-objective optimization to reduce

transportation costs while increasing delivery speed, the Pareto frontier it generates helps leaders select the best balance that meets customer expectations and budget constraints.

Robust Optimization
Robust optimization develops solutions that perform reliably under uncertainty and is used in supply chain planning, workforce scheduling, and financial risk management. It works by modeling uncertain parameters as ranges rather than fixed points and by finding solutions that remain feasible across all scenarios. For example, a retailer uses robust optimization to determine inventory levels that stay effective despite fluctuating supplier lead times, the model generates stock levels that prevent stockouts even when delays happen.

Sensitivity Analysis
Sensitivity analysis examines how variations in model inputs influence the optimal solution, helping to understand risk, prioritize data accuracy, and support managerial decisions. It involves adjusting parameters such as costs, capacities, or demand and observing how the optimal decision changes. For instance, a production planner conducts a sensitivity analysis of labor costs in a scheduling model and finds that a slight increase in overtime rates shifts production to a different plant, this insight helps leadership develop contingency plans.

Shadow Prices
Shadow prices indicate the rate of change in the optimal objective function value resulting from a one-unit increase in the right-hand side of a binding constraint, valid within the allowable range of that constraint. A shadow price of zero indicates the constraint is not binding. Shadow prices are used in capacity planning, resource allocation, and budgeting to identify bottleneck resources and quantify the value of relaxing constraints. For example, a factory's optimization model shows a high shadow price on machine hours, meaning that adding one more hour of machine capacity would greatly increase profit. This insight supports investing in additional equipment.

Duality
Duality is a mathematical concept that connects every optimization problem (the primal) to its dual, and it helps interpret constraints, assess resource value, and verify model solutions. It is used by analyzing dual variables to understand the economic significance of constraints. For

example, a transportation model's dual solution shows which shipping routes are binding constraints and which have extra capacity, helping managers identify where to invest for the greatest benefit.

5.4 Classic Optimization Problems

Knapsack Problem

The knapsack problem finds the best combination of items to maximize value while staying within a capacity limit. It is used in logistics, budgeting, and resource allocation, where efficient use of limited capacity is essential. The process involves assigning each item a value and a weight, then selecting the combination that maximizes total value subject to the constraints. For example, a delivery company loading a small van uses the knapsack model to decide which packages to load first when space is limited, by prioritizing packages with the highest revenue per cubic foot, the company maximizes profit per trip while staying within the vehicle's capacity.

Traveling Salesman Problem (TSP)

The traveling salesman problem finds the shortest possible route that visits a set of locations once and returns to the starting point. It is used in transportation, field service, and delivery routing. The problem is modeled by representing each location as a node and the distances between them as edges, then identifying the route with the minimum total distance. For example, a technician responsible for servicing 15 ATMs in a city uses a TSP model to determine the most efficient route, this optimized route reduces total travel time by 25%, allowing the technician to complete all service calls within a single shift.

Vehicle Routing Problem (VRP)

The vehicle routing problem extends the TSP to include multiple vehicles, capacity limits, and delivery constraints, and it is used in fleet management, last-mile delivery, and distribution planning. It involves assigning customers to vehicles and sequencing stops to minimize total distance or time while respecting capacity and time windows. For example, a grocery delivery service uses VRP to assign 200 daily orders to 12 vans, the optimized routes reduce fuel costs and ensure all customers receive deliveries within their promised two-hour window.

Minimum Spanning Tree (MST)

A minimum spanning tree connects all nodes in a network using the least total edge cost. It is used in network design, telecommunications, and utility infrastructure planning. It works by choosing connections that link all points without forming cycles, and at the lowest overall cost. For example, an internet provider designing a new fiber-optic network employs MST to find the cheapest way to connect all neighborhoods, the resulting layout minimizes installation costs while ensuring full coverage.

Assignment Problem

The assignment problem involves matching tasks to agents to minimize overall cost or maximize efficiency. It is used in workforce scheduling, machine assignment, and project staffing. The process involves creating a cost matrix and selecting the assignment that yields the lowest total cost. For example, a call center assigns agents to shifts using an assignment model that pairs agents with the right skills to the busiest time slots, reducing average wait times and improving customer satisfaction.

Scheduling Models

Scheduling models determine the optimal timing and order of tasks to minimize delays, costs, and resource conflicts. They are used in manufacturing, healthcare, and project management. These models work by analyzing tasks, durations, dependencies, and resource limits to create an optimal schedule. For instance, a factory uses scheduling models to plan production jobs on shared machines, this optimized schedule helps minimize machine idle time and ensures urgent orders are finished before their deadlines.

Inventory Models

Inventory models determine optimal order quantities and reorder points to balance holding costs, ordering costs, and stockout risk. They are used in retail, manufacturing, and distribution to model demand, lead times, and cost parameters and to calculate economic order quantities or safety stock levels. For example, a pharmacy uses an inventory model to determine how much of each medication to order each week, the model ensures that high-demand drugs stay in stock while minimizing expired inventory and storage costs.

5.5 Heuristics & Metaheuristics

Greedy Algorithms

A greedy algorithm makes the best local choice at each step, hoping to find the overall best solution, and it is used in routing, scheduling, and resource allocation when quick, straightforward solutions are needed. It works by choosing the best immediate option without reconsidering earlier choices. For example, a warehouse uses a greedy algorithm to assign pickers to the nearest available order, while not always the best overall, this method greatly reduces picker travel time during peak hours.

Genetic Algorithms

Genetic algorithms are search techniques inspired by natural selection, used for complex optimization problems that traditional methods find difficult. They generate candidate solutions, evaluate their fitness, and improve them through selection, crossover, and mutation. For example, an airline applies a genetic algorithm to optimize crew schedules across thousands of flights, the algorithm generates schedules that reduce overtime costs while meeting regulatory rest requirements.

Simulated Annealing

Simulated annealing is a metaheuristic that searches for solutions by sometimes accepting worse options to avoid getting stuck in local optima. It is used in layout design, routing, and scheduling. The method works by gradually lowering the chance of accepting worse solutions as the algorithm "cools down." For example, a manufacturing plant employs simulated annealing to design the layout of machines on the shop floor, the resulting layout reduces worker travel distances and minimizes production bottlenecks.

Tabu Search

Tabu search is a metaheuristic that guides local search by maintaining a list of forbidden moves to prevent cycling, and it is used in routing, scheduling, and network design. It works by exploring neighboring solutions while avoiding recently visited configurations. For example, a logistics company uses tabu search to optimize delivery routes across multiple cities, the algorithm avoids repeating inefficient routes and finds a configuration that cuts total mileage by 12%.

5.6 Simulation-Driven Decisions

Simulation Optimization

Simulation optimization combines simulation models with optimization techniques to find the best decision under uncertainty. It is used in manufacturing, logistics, and service operations where systems are too complex for traditional mathematical optimization. This approach involves simulating thousands of scenarios, adjusting decision variables, and selecting the configuration that performs best under uncertainty. For example, a distribution center uses simulation optimization to determine optimal staffing levels and picking strategies during peak season. After running numerous simulated demand patterns, the model identifies a staffing plan that minimizes overtime while maintaining a 98% on-time fulfillment rate.

Monte Carlo Simulation

Monte Carlo simulation assesses decisions by generating thousands of random scenarios based on probability distributions and is used in finance, supply chain planning, and risk analysis to measure uncertainty. It works by defining uncertain inputs, running numerous simulations, and examining the distribution of outcomes. For example, a retailer predicting holiday sales uses a Monte Carlo simulation to model demand uncertainty, the simulation shows a 20% chance of stockouts for a high-demand toy, prompting the planner to increase safety stock before the season starts.

Discrete Event Simulation

Discrete event simulation models systems in which state changes occur at discrete points in simulated time, triggered by specific events such as arrivals, completions, or failures. The simulation clock advances directly to the next scheduled event rather than progressing in fixed time increments. It is used in warehouses, hospitals, call centers, and manufacturing lines to study process flow and identify bottlenecks. It works by modeling events like arrivals, service times, and queue lengths to assess system performance. For example, a hospital emergency department uses discrete-event simulation to test different staffing schedules, the simulation shows that adding one triage nurse during evening hours reduces patient wait times by 35%, helping inform staffing decisions.

Continuous Simulation

Continuous simulation models systems that change over time and are used in chemical processing, energy systems, and environmental modeling. It is applied by defining differential equations that represent the system's behavior and simulating how the variables evolve. For example, a water treatment plant uses continuous simulation to model chemical concentration levels throughout the purification process, the simulation helps operators adjust flow rates to maintain safe output levels under varying input conditions.

Agent-Based Modeling

Agent-based modeling mimics the actions of individual agents and their interactions. It is used in fields like epidemiology, market behavior, and supply chain resilience. The process involves setting rules for each agent and observing how group behavior develops. For instance, a retailer might use agent-based modeling to simulate how customers move inside a store. The model shows that moving promotional displays can lessen congestion near the entrance and boost sales by improving traffic flow.

5.7 System Dynamics & Queuing for Decision Optimization

Queuing Theory

Queuing theory examines waiting lines to improve service capacity and is used in call centers, hospitals, retail checkout lines, and transportation hubs. It involves modeling arrival and service rates, as well as queue structures, to estimate wait times and resource needs. For example, a bank uses queuing theory to determine how many tellers to staff during lunch hours, the model shows that adding one more teller reduces average wait time from 12 minutes to 4 minutes, boosting customer satisfaction and reducing abandonment.

Little's Law

Little's Law states that the average number of items in a system equals the arrival rate multiplied by the average time in the system. It is used in manufacturing, logistics, and service operations to identify bottlenecks. It is applied by measuring throughput and cycle time to estimate work-in-progress levels. For example, a factory producing 200 units per hour with an average cycle time of 3 hours applies Little's Law to determine that 600 units are in process at any time. When WIP exceeds this level, managers recognize that a bottleneck is forming and investigate the affected workstation.

Cycle Time
Cycle time measures how long it takes for a unit to move through a process from start to finish and is used in manufacturing, order fulfillment, and service delivery to assess process efficiency. It is determined by tracking timestamps at each stage and spotting delays or bottlenecks. For example, an e-commerce warehouse tracks cycle time from order receipt to shipment and finds that packing accounts for 40% of the total time. This insight prompts reorganizing packing stations to reduce handling time and boost throughput.

Throughput
Throughput is the rate at which a system generates output and is a crucial metric in production planning, logistics, and service operations for evaluating capacity and efficiency. It is determined by counting the number of units completed within a specific time frame and assessing how process modifications affect output levels. For instance, a bottling facility can enhance throughput by reducing machine changeover times. After adopting standardized changeover procedures, the facility increases output by 15% per hour without requiring additional equipment.

Utilization
Utilization measures the percentage of time a resource is actively working and is used in capacity planning, workforce management, and equipment scheduling. It is calculated by dividing active time by total available time to identify under- or overused resources. For example, a call center finds that agents are utilized at 92% during peak hours, leading to long wait times, managers hire two additional part-time agents, reducing utilization to 80% and improving service levels without overstaffing.

Stock & Flow Models
Stock and flow models depict systems as accumulations (stocks) and movement rates (flows). They are used in supply chains, inventory systems, and environmental modeling to analyze how systems behave over time. These models work by showing how inflows and outflows impact stock levels. For example, a retailer might use a stock-and-flow model to predict inventory levels under different reorder policies, the model shows that increasing reorder frequency can reduce stockouts without significantly increasing holding costs.

System Dynamics
System dynamics models complex systems through feedback loops, delays, and nonlinear relationships, and it is used in strategic planning, policy design, and long-term forecasting. It is applied by mapping causal relationships and simulating how changes spread through the system. For example, a city government uses system dynamics to model housing demand, construction rates, and population growth. The simulation shows that permitting delays cause long-term shortages, prompting reforms to speed up approval processes.

6. Specialized Analytics Domains

6.1 Bayesian Analytics

Bayesian Theory

Bayesian theory provides a mathematical framework for updating beliefs as new evidence emerges and is used in risk analysis, fraud detection, medical diagnostics, and machine learning. It starts with a prior probability, uses likelihood functions to incorporate new data, and computes a posterior probability that reflects an updated understanding. For example, a bank monitoring suspicious transactions applies Bayesian theory to update the likelihood that an account is involved in fraud, when a customer suddenly makes multiple high-risk international transfers, the posterior probability increases enough to trigger an automated fraud review.

Conditional Probability

Conditional probability measures how likely an event is to happen given that another event has already occurred. It is used in forecasting, risk modeling, and customer analytics. It works by calculating the chance of an event under specific conditions rather than on its own. For example, an insurance company examines the conditional probability that a driver will file a claim given that they have had two previous accidents. The higher conditional probability leads the company to adjust premiums and classify the driver as high risk.

Bayesian Networks

A Bayesian network is a graphical model that represents probabilistic relationships among variables and is used in diagnostics, root cause analysis, and decision support systems. It works by defining nodes for variables, representing conditional dependencies, and computing posterior probabilities when new evidence arrives. For example, a telecom company employs a Bayesian network to diagnose network outages, when sensors detect abnormal latency in one area, the network updates probabilities across related nodes and identifies a failing router as the most probable cause.

Evidence Nodes

Evidence nodes represent observed data within a Bayesian network and are used to update the probabilities of related variables. They work by setting the value of an evidence node and recalculating posterior probabilities throughout the network. For example, in a medical diagnostic system, entering a patient's symptom, such as "persistent cough," as an evidence node updates the likelihood of conditions like pneumonia or bronchitis, helping clinicians prioritize further tests.

Hypothesis Nodes

Hypothesis nodes represent possible explanations or outcomes in a Bayesian network and are used to compare scenarios based on available evidence. They are implemented by connecting hypothesis nodes to evidence nodes and updating their probabilities as new information becomes available. For example, a cybersecurity team uses hypothesis nodes to determine whether unusual login activity indicates a compromised account. As evidence accumulates, the probability of the "account compromised" hypothesis increases, prompting immediate security measures.

Indicator Nodes

Indicator nodes serve as intermediate variables that clarify the links between evidence and hypotheses, aiding in modeling intricate systems with multiple dependencies. They are connected to observable data and underlying causes to function effectively. For instance, in a supply chain risk model, "supplier delay risk" is an indicator node influenced by weather forecasts and port congestion, deteriorating weather conditions cause the indicator to update, increasing the likelihood of shipment delays.

Conditional Probability Tables (CPTs)

Conditional probability tables (CPTs) specify the probabilities of each outcome for a node given the states of its parent nodes, quantifying relationships within Bayesian networks. They are used by assigning probabilities based on expert judgment, historical data, or statistical estimates. For example, a manufacturing-quality model uses CPTs to assess how machine temperature and operator experience affect defect likelihood, as temperature rises and the operator is inexperienced, the CPT indicates a significantly higher risk.

Sensitivity to Findings

Sensitivity to findings indicates how changes in evidence influence the probabilities of outcomes in a Bayesian network. It helps identify which variables most affect decisions by adjusting evidence values and observing shifts in posterior probabilities. For instance, a credit risk model tests sensitivity by varying income verification results, the analysis shows that verified income has a greater impact on the likelihood of loan approval than variations in credit score. This information helps lenders prioritize income verification in their process.

Markov Chains

Markov chains are models that describe systems transitioning between states, where the probability of moving to the next state depends only on the current state, not on the history of previous states. This property is called the Markov property (memorylessness). Markov chains are used in customer analytics and operations to forecast movement through defined stages over time. The process involves defining possible states, estimating transition probabilities from historical data, and using these to predict future distributions or long-term stable states. For instance, a subscription service may monitor how customers shift monthly among "Active," "At-Risk," and "Churned." If the data indicate that 10% of Active customers become At-Risk and 5% churn each month, the Markov chain can forecast the number of Active customers over time and identify when interventions are necessary to prevent revenue decline.

6.2 Customer & Marketing Analytics

Churn Analysis

Churn analysis identifies customers likely to discontinue a product or service, and is commonly used in subscription-based industries, telecom, banking, and SaaS platforms to minimize customer attrition. It examines behavioral trends, usage habits, complaints, and demographic details to forecast churn risk. For instance, a telecom provider may notice that customers who experience three consecutive dropped calls and reduced data usage are at high risk of leaving, and then proactively offers tailored retention incentives to prevent switching.

Customer Lifetime Value (CLV)

Customer lifetime value (CLV) is the present value of the net revenue or margin a customer is expected to generate over the entire course of their relationship with a business. It is used in marketing, pricing, and customer segmentation to identify and prioritize high-value customers. The calculation involves modeling purchase frequency, retention probability, and average order value to predict long-term contribution. For example, an e-commerce retailer finds that loyalty program customers generate three times as much revenue over two years. This insight prompts the company to invest more in loyalty program enrollment efforts.

6.3 Time Series & Forecasting

Trend

A trend indicates the long-term direction of a time series and is used in sales forecasting, financial planning, and capacity management to gauge overall movement. Analysts examine historical data to identify whether the pattern is upward, downward, or stable. For instance, a retailer notices a consistent increase in online sales over three years, this trend justifies expanding warehouse automation to manage growing order volume.

Seasonality

Seasonality refers to recurring patterns in a time series that repeat at fixed, known intervals, such as daily, weekly, monthly, or annual cycles. It differs from cyclical patterns, which recur over variable multi-year periods driven by economic or business factors. Seasonality is used in demand forecasting, staffing, and inventory management. For instance, a grocery store notices a clear weekly pattern in fresh produce sales, with peaks on weekends. This information helps managers plan staff schedules and stock up on inventory before busy days.

Cycles

Cycles are long-term fluctuations in time-series data driven by economic or business factors, used for financial planning and strategic forecasting. They involve analyzing multi-year patterns that do not recur at fixed intervals, distinguishing them from seasonal patterns. For instance, an automotive company detects a four-year sales cycle tied to economic conditions, understanding this cycle allows management to proactively adjust production capacity before a downturn.

Noise

Noise denotes random, unpredictable variations in time series data and helps evaluate data quality and model reliability. It is extracted by filtering out noise from significant patterns using techniques like smoothing or decomposition. For instance, a call center examines daily call volumes and detects high noise levels caused by unpredictable customer behavior, understanding this noise enables analysts to avoid overreacting to short-term fluctuations when planning staffing needs.

ARIMA
ARIMA (AutoRegressive Integrated Moving Average) is a statistical model used for forecasting that identifies autocorrelation and trends in time series data. It finds application in finance, retail, and operations planning. The model parameters (p, d, q) are chosen based on autocorrelation analysis and then fitted to historical data. For instance, a utility company employs ARIMA to forecast monthly electricity demand, the model accurately predicts seasonal peaks, allowing the company to plan maintenance during times of lower demand.

Exponential Smoothing
Exponential smoothing predicts future values by assigning progressively smaller weights to older data and is commonly used in inventory management, sales forecasting, and service demand estimation. It involves choosing smoothing parameters that balance responsiveness and stability. For instance, a fashion retailer employs exponential smoothing to forecast weekly sales of fast-moving clothing, this approach quickly adjusts to shifting trends, enabling planners to prevent stockouts during sudden spikes in demand.

Seasonal Decomposition
Seasonal decomposition divides a time series into trend, seasonal, and residual components, helping identify underlying patterns before choosing forecasting models. This process employs either additive or multiplicative methods to separate each component. For instance, an airline analyzing monthly passenger data finds pronounced summer seasonality alongside a long-term growth trend, which then informs fleet planning and route expansion strategies.

Forecasting Models
Forecasting models predict future values using historical data and support activities such as budgeting, staffing, inventory management, and strategic planning. They involve selecting suitable models, including ARIMA, exponential smoothing, or machine learning, and validating them with past data. For example, a restaurant chain may use forecasting models to estimate weekly foot traffic at each location. Accurate forecasts help managers schedule staff efficiently, reducing labor costs while maintaining service quality.

6.4 Artificial Intelligence & Expert Systems

Artificial Intelligence (AI)

Artificial intelligence involves systems that perform tasks requiring human-like reasoning, learning, or decision-making. It is employed in areas such as automation, personalization, fraud detection, and predictive modeling. This is achieved by training algorithms on historical data to identify patterns and generate predictions or recommendations. For instance, a bank uses AI to monitor transaction patterns and spot fraud in real time, when unusual spending is detected, the system automatically flags the account for further review.

Expert Systems

Expert systems are rule-based AI systems that imitate human experts' decision-making and are commonly used in diagnostics, troubleshooting, and compliance checks. They work by encoding expert knowledge into rules and employing inference engines to assess new cases. For instance, a manufacturing firm uses an expert system to diagnose machine failures. When operators enter symptoms, the system applies its rules to determine the most probable cause and suggest corrective measures.

Fuzzy Logic

Fuzzy logic handles reasoning with vague or uncertain data and is used in control systems, risk analysis, and customer scoring, where binary logic is too inflexible. It operates using fuzzy sets and rules, allowing partial membership rather than strict yes/no decisions. For instance, an HVAC system uses fuzzy logic to fine-tune temperature settings based on inputs such as “slightly warm” or “very cold,” resulting in smoother, more energy-efficient climate control than conventional on/off systems.

Appendix

Chapter 1: Practice Questions Answers

A1: C. The "5 Whys" is a root cause analysis tool. Its purpose is to iteratively ask 'why' to move beyond symptoms, such as 'the machine stopped,' and uncover the fundamental process or system failure, such as 'the preventative maintenance schedule was not followed.' This enables corrective action to prevent recurrence.

A2: B. A problem statement should describe the issue neutrally. Introducing a solution ("we need a chatbot") can limit exploration and lead to solving the wrong problem. A good statement describes the undesirable current state and desired state, allowing for multiple potential solution paths.

A3: C. The 'Achievable' criterion forces realism. It asks: Do we have the data, skills, time, and technology to reach this goal? An objective to "predict stock prices with 99% accuracy" is unlikely to be achievable, whereas "improve demand forecast accuracy by 5%" might be.

A4: B. The 'A' (Accountable) is the single person with ultimate yes/no authority and accountability for the task's completion. Having more than one 'A' creates confusion, diffuses responsibility, and is a classic project management error.

A5: B. SIPOC (Suppliers, Inputs, Process, Outputs, Customers) is a high-level process mapping tool. Its value in framing is creating a one-page, shared visual that defines the boundaries of the process under study, ensuring everyone agrees on where the problem starts and ends.

A6: B. Solutioneering jumps to an answer. The critical phase of problem framing is to understand the problem deeply. Prescribing a solution (like "build a dashboard") prematurely can blind the team to better, cheaper, or simpler ways to address the underlying need (such as improved process design or training).

A7: B. TCO is a holistic complete financial assessment. It includes upfront capital and one-time costs, as well as all recurring operational, maintenance, support, and training expenses over the solution's useful life. Underestimating TCO is a common cause of projects becoming financially unsustainable.

A8: B. The critical path is the longest duration path through the network of dependent tasks. Tasks on this path have zero slack. A delay in any one of them directly delays the project end date. Identifying the critical path is central to schedule management.

A9: C. The Charter is the project's foundational document and social contract. Formal sign-off by the sponsor and key stakeholders gives the project manager the authority to execute and serves as a reference point for resolving disputes about scope and objectives later.

A10: B. The Maximin (or Wald) criterion is for the risk-averse decision-maker. It evaluates each alternative by its worst possible outcome and selects the alternative with the best (maximum) of these worst-case (minimum) outcomes, avoiding catastrophic loss.

A11: C. AHP is designed for complex multi-criteria decisions. It uses pairwise comparisons to derive priority weights for different objectives (e.g., cost, quality, and speed) based on decision-makers' subjective judgments, and then scores alternatives against these weighted objectives.

A12: B. This requirement describes a specific behavior or function of the system, *what* it must do. Functional requirements define capabilities, actions, and responses.

A13: A. This requirement specifies a quality attribute, *how well* the system must perform a function (in this case, loading speed). Non-functional requirements include performance, security, usability, and reliability.

A14: B. High-power, low-interest stakeholders (like a CFO or senior executive) need to be kept satisfied. They require enough information to maintain their support and avoid surprises, but do not want deep involvement in daily details.

A15: C. Minimax Regret minimizes the maximum potential regret. Regret is the difference between the payoff received from the chosen alternative and the best possible payoff for the actual state of nature that occurs. It is a criterion for someone who hates "missing out."

A16: C. Intangible benefits are real and valuable but difficult to measure precisely in monetary terms. Improved brand perception, employee morale, strategic alignment, and a stronger culture of better decision-making are classic examples. They should be listed and qualitatively discussed in a business case.

A17: B. A Charter with explicit "Out-of-Scope" sections is the primary contractual tool to manage expectations. When new requests arise, the project manager can refer to the signed charter to determine whether the request is a change that requires formal review, additional funding, or a timeline adjustment.

A18: A. In DMAIC, the **Define** phase is about scoping the problem and the project. Creating a SIPOC is a key activity for defining the process boundaries before measurement and analysis begin.

A19: B. Value-Focused Thinking argues that decision processes often start by comparing given alternatives. A superior approach is to first define what you truly value (your objectives), which often leads to the creation of new and better alternatives that wouldn't have been considered otherwise.

A20: C. While technical risks (data, model performance) are important and often highlighted, post-mortem analyses of failed projects consistently show that people factors, including lack of sponsorship, user resistance, poor communication, and inadequate change management, are the most frequent and significant causes of failure.

Chapter 2: Practice Questions Answers

A1: B. The core objective of this translation is to create a focused, actionable question that guides the technical work. The other options are not the primary purpose.

A2: D. This statement starts with an analytical verb ("Identify"), specifies the target ("product features...correlated with renewal rates"), and the data source ("usage log data"). It is specific and actionable. A is vague, B presupposes a solution, and C is a business goal rather than an analytics problem.

A3: C. The output, dependent, or target variable is what you are modeling. Inputs (A, B, D) are the factors used to predict or explain the output.

A4: B. At the framing stage, you are forming hypotheses to guide analysis. You need clear, testable statements. Proving causation (A) often comes later. Complexity (C) and linearity (D) are not required.

A5: C. Predictive analytics relies entirely on the premise that patterns learned from the past will persist to make future predictions.

A6: B. Representativeness is a statistical property that must be checked by comparing distributions. Size (A) does not guarantee representativeness. Opinions (C) and model performance (D) are not direct tests of this assumption.

A7: B. Real-world constraints like labor agreements are critical business environment limitations that directly shape the feasible solution space. The other options are irrelevant constraints.

A8: C. Precision measures the proportion of positive identifications that were actually correct, calculated as TP / (TP + FP). Minimizing false positives is the goal of high precision.

A9: C. A held-out test set provides the only unbiased estimate of how the model will perform on new, unseen data, the true measure of its utility.

A10: B. The baseline is the "before" measurement. Improvement (lift, ROI) can only be calculated by comparing the "after" result to this baseline.

A11: B. People, process, and adoption risks consistently rank as more significant than purely technical risks in analytics project post-mortems.

A12: B. Bias in data leads to bias in model predictions, which can cause discriminatory or unfair treatment, the primary ethical and practical danger.

A13: B. Clearly defined scope boundaries prevent scope creep and ensure each team (analytics vs. engineering) understands their deliverables, leading to better collaboration.

A14: B. A change in a core business metric (churn rate) directly demonstrates business value. The other options are important technical metrics, but are steps removed from ultimate business impact.
A15: B. Percentage lift is calculated as (New Rate - Old Rate) / Old Rate * 100% = (12-10)/10 * 100% = 20%.

A16: B. Model drift occurs when the real-world data changes. Scheduled retraining with recent data is the standard mitigation to keep the model aligned with current conditions.
A17: D. Prescriptive analytics is concerned with recommending optimal actions, which is signaled by the verb "Optimize."

A18: B. The goal of formal alignment and sign-off is to establish a shared agreement on deliverables (the charter) that serves as a reference point for managing expectations and preventing disputes later.

A19: B. Salary is a factor that likely influences an employee's decision to leave, making it a potential input variable in a turnover prediction model.

A20: C. This is a data-based assumption that can be tested by comparing the income distributions of the two groups using statistical methods. A, B, and D are assumptions that are difficult or impossible to verify objectively before deployment.

Chapter 3: Practice Questions Answers

A1: C. The source is high value but low feasibility (costly, difficult to integrate). In the 2x2 matrix, this is a Strategic Investment: plan and budget for it deliberately. Critical sources combine high value with high feasibility and are acquired first. Option A fits low value and low feasibility. Option B fits low value and high feasibility.

A2: B. A Data Lake is optimized for flexible storage of raw, varied data for exploration. Daily standardized reporting on clean, structured data is the classic use case for a Data Warehouse. Using a lake adds governance and processing complexity without providing a benefit. Options A, C, and D are not the primary risks, cost might be lower, it can store structured data, and ML performance is a strength, not a risk.

A3: B. Enforcing data quality standards and governance policies. Rationale: The Data Steward is an operational role responsible for the hands-on management of data quality and policy adherence. Option A is the role of a Data Owner or Chief Data Officer. Options C and D are typically the responsibility of the financial and engineering teams, respectively.

A4: A. An unrepresentative sample is a flaw in the data collection process (systemic), not a random fluctuation. Collecting more data the same way will not fix this bias. Option B (statistical uncertainty) decreases with more data. Options C and D describe other problems, but not the core issue of a biased sample frame.

A5: C. A composite feature is explicitly created by combining two or more existing features through a mathematical or logical operation. Options A (transformed feature) and B (normalized feature) are types of transformations applied to single features. Option D refers to converting categorical variables.

A6: C. Completeness measures the proportion of stored data against the potential for "100% complete." Null values represent missing data and directly affect completeness. Accuracy (A) measures correctness against a truth source. Validity (B) checks against defined rules. Uniqueness (D) measures the number of duplicate records.

A7: C. For comparing distributions (central tendency and spread) across several groups, side-by-side box plots are the most efficient and standardized visual. They show the median, quartiles, and outliers. Pie charts (A) are for parts of a whole. A stacked bar (B) is for part-to-whole comparisons across groups. A single histogram (D) would show only one combined distribution.

A8: C. Randomization spreads the effect of uncontrolled, time-related variables (e.g., tool wear, operator fatigue) across all factor levels, preventing them from biasing the results for any one factor setting. It does not affect speed (A), run count (B), or distribution shape (D).

A9: C. The Box-Cox transformation is a parameterized family of power transformations designed to find the optimal transformation (log, square root, etc.) that achieves normality. Min-Max Scaling (A) and Z-score (B) change scale but not shape. One-Hot Encoding (D) is for categorical data.

A10: B. This is the defining legal and technical distinction. Anonymized data is no longer considered personal data. Pseudonymized data is still personal data because re-identification is possible. The other options misstate the purposes and regulatory implications.

A11: B. An INNER JOIN returns only the records where there is a match in both tables, effectively filtering the Customers table to only those who have a purchase. A LEFT JOIN (A) would keep all customers. A RIGHT JOIN (C) would keep all purchases. A FULL OUTER JOIN (D) would keep all records from both tables.

A12: B. Veracity is about trustworthiness. Profiling reveals quality issues (completeness, validity), while provenance provides the origin and processing history, both of which are critical for assessing trust. Cost and volume (A) relate to feasibility, not veracity. Loading it (C) is premature. Stratifying (D) is a sampling technique.

A13: B. The categories have a clear order (Never to Always), but the intervals between them are not quantifiably equal. Nominal (A) has no order. Interval (C) and Ratio (D) require numeric scales with meaningful distances.

A14: B. The Transform stage is where the core data preparation work happens to ensure quality and consistency. Option A describes the goal of the Extract and Load stages. Option C is part of the extract planning. Option D is an access control function, separate from ETL.

A15: C. K-means uses distance metrics. Features on vastly different scales will bias the algorithm toward the feature with the larger magnitude. Scaling puts them on a comparable scale. It does not handle missing values (A), create composites (B), or directly fix skewness (D).

A16: C. Stratified sampling divides the population into homogeneous strata and samples from each to ensure all subgroups are represented according to their proportion in the population. Option A describes Cluster sampling. Option B describes Simple Random sampling. Option D is a benefit of Cluster sampling.

A17: B. Correlation does not imply causation. A third variable (e.g., marketing spend) could cause both. Or increased sales could lead to more website visits (reverse causality). A large sample size (C) does not fix this logical fallacy. Scatter plots (D) can indeed show correlation.

A18: A. "Schema-on-Read" means the structure is applied when the data is queried, not when it is stored. This provides the flexibility to store raw data in any format. Data Warehouses and relational databases use a rigid "Schema-on-Write" approach.

A19: B. Winsorizing reduces the impact of outliers by limiting extreme values, not removing them (which would be trimming, option A). It is not a normalization technique (C) or an imputation method for missing values (D).

A20: B. This is a responsible and common refinement detailed in Lesson 3.9. It aligns the project with data reality. Option A risks building an invalid model. Option C is premature without exploring refinements. Option D is unethical if not documented and transparent.

Chapter 4: Practice Questions Answers

A1: C. Unsupervised learning, specifically clustering, is designed to find hidden patterns or groups in data without pre-existing labels. Supervised learning (A) requires labeled outcomes. Reinforcement Learning (B) is for sequential decision-making. Prescriptive optimization (D) is for recommending actions, not discovery.

A2: B. The p-value is defined as the probability of obtaining a test statistic as extreme as, or more extreme than, the one observed, assuming the null hypothesis (often "no effect") is true. A p-value of 0.04 means there's a 4% chance of seeing this data if the null were true.

A3: C. The median is the middle value and is robust to extreme values (outliers), like billionaire incomes. The mean (A) would be pulled upward by the outliers, giving a distorted view of "typical" income.

A4: C. Linear regression coefficients provide a direct, interpretable measure of the expected change in the target variable (price) for a one-unit change in a predictor, holding others constant. This meets the requirement for clear interpretability of feature impact.

A5: B. In a service system such as a call center, the "average customer wait time" is a primary component of the total cycle time (the time from call arrival to resolution). The analysis focuses on how adding staff reduces this time.

A6: C. The shadow price is the rate of improvement in the optimal objective value per unit increase in the right-hand side of a constraint, within its allowable range. It is the value of an extra unit of the constrained resource.

A7: C. Holt-Winters exponential smoothing is explicitly designed to handle time series with both trend and seasonality. The seasonal period parameter (s) should be set to the cycle frequency (3 for quarterly).

A8: B. The core purpose of Monte Carlo simulation is to propagate input uncertainties (modeled as probability distributions) through a computational model to produce a distribution of possible outputs, thus quantifying risk.

A9: C. Expected Monetary Value (EMV) assumes risk neutrality. For a risk-averse decision-maker, the diminishing marginal value of money must be accounted for by using a concave utility function. Maximizing expected utility, not EMV, is the rational criterion.

A10: C. This is a classic application of Bayes' Theorem. With very low prevalence (prior = 0.0001), even a highly accurate test yields a posterior probability that remains quite low. Calculation: P(D|+) = [Sensitivity * Prior] / [(Sensitivity*Prior) + ((1-Specificity)*(1-Prior))] = (0.99*0.0001) / (0.99*0.0001 + 0.01*0.9999) ≈ 0.0098 or ~1%. Approximately 1% is the only accurate assessment.

A11: C. One-way Analysis of Variance (ANOVA) is the appropriate test for comparing the means of three or more independent groups when the data is normally distributed, and variances are assumed equal (or similar). It controls the overall Type I error rate better than performing multiple t-tests.

A12: C. The harmonic mean is the correct average for rates when the denominators (time in this case) are the unit of comparison across equal distances. Average speed = total distance / total time.

A13: C. In DES, an "event" is a discrete instant in time that triggers a change in the system state (e.g., an entity arrives, a service ends, a resource fails). Patient arrival is a quintessential event.

A14: B. PCA is an unsupervised dimensionality reduction technique. It transforms the original variables into new, uncorrelated principal components, ordered by the variance they explain, enabling a lower-dimensional representation.

A15: B. The linear relationships point to a linear model. The requirement that some products be made in whole units introduces integer constraints on those decision variables, making it a (Mixed-)Integer Programming problem.

A16: A. Little's Law states $L = \lambda W$. Solving for W: $W = L / \lambda = 15$ customers / (3 customers/hour) = 5 hours.

A17: B. Regularization adds a penalty term to the model's loss function based on the magnitude of coefficients. This shrinks coefficients, reducing model complexity and variance and helping prevent overfitting to the training data.

A18: B. This is the definition of Pareto efficiency or non-dominance. The Pareto frontier consists of all Pareto-efficient solutions, representing the best possible trade-offs.

A19: C. The "fanning out" pattern of residuals is a clear sign of heteroscedasticity, a violation of the homoscedasticity assumption in linear regression. The error variance is not constant.

A20: B. The Chi-square test relies on an approximation to the Chi-square distribution, which becomes poor when expected counts are low. Fisher's Exact Test calculates an exact p-value and is the recommended alternative for small samples, particularly in 2x2 tables.

Chapter 5: Practice Questions Answers

A1: C. Prescriptive models focus on recommending actions, which require defining what can be decided (variables), what to optimize (objective), and the limits (constraints). A is for descriptive, B for predictive, and D for descriptive clustering.

A2: D. Using future information (next month's credit score) to predict a future event (default) is data leakage, as this information would not be available at prediction time in a real scenario.

A3: C. Recall (Sensitivity) measures the ability to correctly identify all positive cases. In a medical context where missing a disease is costly, maximizing recall is critical to minimize false negatives.

A4: B. Using only data from "survivors" (current employees) ignores those who failed or left, leading to a biased understanding of the traits of "top performers."

A5: B. The F1 Score is the harmonic mean of Precision and Recall, providing a single metric that balances both.

A6: B. K-Fold Cross-Validation involves dividing the data into k folds and using each fold once as the validation set, providing a reliable estimate of performance.

A7: C. RMSE squares errors before averaging, thus giving a disproportionately higher weight to larger errors compared to MAE.

A8: B. Executives need to understand strategic alignment, value, and high-level risk, not technical details, daily operations, or full statistical reports.

A9: C. An infeasible formulation occurs when constraints are contradictory, leaving no possible solution that satisfies all of them simultaneously.

A10: C. Backward elimination starts with all features and removes the least significant iteratively. Forward selection starts with none and adds.

A11: C. The ROC curve plots the True Positive Rate (Sensitivity) on the Y-axis against the False Positive Rate (1 - Specificity) on the X-axis.

A12: D. BIC includes a penalty term of k*log(n), where n is the sample size, meaning it penalizes complexity more heavily than AIC as n grows, often preferring simpler models.

A13: C. The first step in calibration is root cause analysis. The feedback suggests a systematic gap related to a specific condition (social media), which may indicate missing data or features.

A14: B. A sequence of models in which the output of one serves as the input to the next defines an analytical pipeline. An ensemble combines models for the same task.

A15: C. A lift chart shows the ratio of the model's positive identification rate in a segment compared to the overall average (random) rate.

A16: C. High bias, or underfitting, occurs when a model is too simple, leading to poor performance because it cannot capture underlying patterns.

A17: B. The Assumptions Log is a critical part of the documentation that clarifies the model's validity boundaries, ensuring users understand when the model applies.

A18: B. MAPE's primary advantage is its ability to express error as a percentage, which is easily understood by business stakeholders. It has disadvantages with zeros and skew but is valued for interpretability.

A19: B. Error propagation is a major risk in integrated systems, where inaccuracies from upstream components are fed into and amplified by downstream components.

A20: B. R-squared is specifically defined as the proportion of the variance in the dependent variable that is predictable from the independent variables.

Chapter 6: Practice Questions Answers

A1: C. In CRISP-DM, the Deployment phase explicitly includes planning for maintenance, monitoring, final reporting, and handoff. A describes the Modeling phase. B describes the Data Preparation phase. D describes the Business Understanding phase.

A2: C. The "Measure" phase in DMAIC is dedicated to collecting data to establish a baseline and measure the current state or the impact of a change. A is part of the "Improve" phase. B is the "Analyze" phase. D is part of the "Control" phase.

A3: B. SIPOC is a high-level process mapping tool used to gain a shared understanding of process scope, which is foundational for aligning stakeholders on where and how a solution will integrate. A is too detailed for SIPOC. C relates to model documentation. D is a different artifact.

A4: C. UAT is a business validation activity conducted by end users to confirm that the solution meets their operational needs. A and B are technical/QA testing activities. D is a developer activity.

A5: C. Random assignment is a fundamental requirement for a valid A/B test to ensure groups are comparable and control for confounding variables. A introduces selection bias. B is not a controlled test, it's a replacement. D describes "peeking," which is a flawed practice.

A6: B. This information is essential for reproducibility, knowledge transfer, and future maintenance. A and D are irrelevant personnel/financial details. C is speculative and not a factual record of the developed model.

A7: C. Operational requirements cover runtime concerns like uptime, support, and maintenance procedures. A is a model performance requirement. B is a usability/design requirement. D is a business case element.

A8: B. A silent failure does not cause an obvious crash but leads to a gradual decline in performance, often due to data pipeline problems. A, C, and D are all overt failures that would likely trigger immediate alerts.

A9: C. The Control phase in DMAIC focuses on sustaining gains through ongoing monitoring, which aligns directly with post-deployment monitoring. A and D occur earlier in the process. B is a reporting activity that may occur at various stages.

A10: B. Repeatedly checking results and stopping when a target is hit violates the statistical assumptions of the test, increasing the chance of a false positive. A and C are potential side effects but not the primary statistical risk. D is not guaranteed.

A11: D. SIPOC is meant to be a high-level overview, a common mistake is adding too much detail to the Process column. A and B are standard, correct practices for creating a SIPOC. C can be correct if the IT department supplies data inputs.

A12: B. UAT is about validating business fit ("building the right thing"), whereas QA is about technical verification ("building it right"). A describes QA. C and D are specific types of technical testing.

A13: B. Versioning creates a historical record and enables recovery, which is critical for operational stability. A is a separate concept (parallel training). C is not automatic, retraining may improve accuracy. D is false.

A14: C. The Executive Summary is designed for busy decision-makers and must answer their key questions upfront. A, B, and D contain details that belong in subsequent sections of the report.

A15: B. Data drift in inputs is a leading indicator that often precedes a degradation in model performance (a lagging indicator). A, C, and D are business outcomes that change slowly and would only show a problem long after it began.

A16: B. The Deployment Charter formalizes stakeholder agreements and serves as a reference for the deployment team. A is a marketing activity. C is a training activity. D is a runbook or implementation plan.

A17: B. The ethical compliance review specifically assesses societal and legal impact. A assesses technical performance. C assesses design. D assesses financial viability.

A18: C. This ensures the pilot captures temporal variations (e.g., weekly patterns, end-of-month effects) that could affect performance. A might increase risk but doesn't address duration. B avoids real-world conditions. D is about management, not duration.

A19: B. Hypercare is a temporary, intense support period immediately after launch to ensure stability. A describes a permanent organizational change, not a temporary protocol. C and D are activities for a later time.

A20: B. This directly connects a technical outcome (automation) to a tangible business impact (cost savings), which is the goal of business impact analysis. A is a technical metric. C is an implementation detail. D is a model characteristic.

Chapter 7: Practice Questions Answers

A1: A. The scenario describes a solution that is technically sound (high uptime, adoption) but fails to meet its core mission of improving a business KPI. This is the classic pitfall of tracking vanity or technical metrics while losing sight of the primary business outcome. User satisfaction (B) is positive here. Alert thresholds (C) and system latency (D) are technical concerns, not the root cause of the business KPI stagnation.

A2: C. The question explicitly states that the input feature distribution has shifted, but the underlying relationship between inputs and output (failure) remains valid. This is the definition of Data Drift (or Covariate Shift). Performance Drift (B) is the observed symptom (declining precision), but the root cause is Data Drift. Concept Drift (A) would involve a change in the relationship itself.

A3: B. Performing a controlled rollback is a complex, hands-on operational task. The most effective training for such procedural knowledge involves interactive practice in a safe, simulated environment. A webinar (A) or a lecture (D) is too passive. A one-page FAQ (C) is insufficient for a complex recovery procedure.

A4: B. The improvement in retention is correlated with the tool's deployment, but a major confounding variable (competitor exit) exists. To validate the business case, one must disentangle the tool's effect from other factors using attribution analysis (e.g., comparing similar customer segments, analyzing trends). Recalculating TCO (C) is important but comes after impact is established. Declaring success (A) is premature. Retraining (D) is unrelated to business case validation.

A5: C. This addresses a key exam trap and real-world pitfall in fairness. Simply removing a protected attribute, such as race, or its direct proxy (zip code), does not eliminate bias if other features (e.g., occupation, shopping history, educational institution) are correlated with the protected attribute and retain the discriminatory pattern. The model can learn to use these other proxies.

A6: B. The core purpose of drift detection is proactive monitoring. It is an early warning system that allows teams to investigate and remediate (e.g., retrain) *before* model degradation impacts business outcomes. It does not auto-retrain (A), replace dashboards (C), or calculate ROI (D).

A7: C. Training a new model using only the most recent N periods of data (in this case, the previous four weeks) is the definition of a windowed or sliding window retraining strategy. Full retraining (A) uses all historical data. Incremental learning (B) updates continuously as individual data points arrive. Ensemble retraining (D) combines multiple models.

A8: C. Tools like SHAP and LIME are specifically designed to provide post-hoc explanations for individual model predictions, enhancing the interpretability and understandability of the model's logic. This is a direct contribution to the Transparency pillar of FAT. Fairness (A) concerns equitable outcomes, and Accountability (B) concerns responsibility.

A9: B. This is the precise definition of a runbook. It is operational documentation for technical staff. Strategic alignment (A) is for executives. A model version archive (C) is part of model version control. Compliance certificates (D) are part of a governance dossier.

A10: B. The "human element" refers to the people who use and are affected by the solution. Key metrics to monitor here are adoption (are they using it?) and satisfaction (do they find it valuable?). Technical metrics such as API times (A), data distributions (C), and holdout accuracy (D) are non-human-system metrics.

A11: B. The meaning of the input (the phrase) has changed in relation to the target (sentiment). The fundamental mapping from the text feature to the positive/negative label has evolved. This is a change in $P(Y|X)$, as defined by Concept Drift. The input data distribution (the words) may not have changed, ruling out Data Drift (A). Performance Drift (C) is the symptom, not the cause.

A12: D. This is the fundamental distinction. Scheduled retraining is time-based (e.g., quarterly). Triggered retraining is event-driven, responding to alerts from performance monitoring, drift detection, or known business events. Options A, B, and C incorrectly assign these properties.

A13: B. This is the textbook definition of a negative feedback loop in analytics. A classic example is a predictive policing model that targets a neighborhood, leading to more police reports from that area, which the model then uses as further "evidence" to target it more. Other options describe different failure modes.

A14: A. Historical bias is bias that is embedded in the historical records used for training. If past hiring, lending, or policing decisions were discriminatory, a model trained on that data will learn and perpetuate those patterns. Faulty sensors (B) cause measurement error. Unrepresentative test sets (C) cause evaluation bias. Hardware differences (D) relate to deployment.

A15: C. TCO is a comprehensive measure that captures the full cost of owning and operating an asset over its life. This includes not just initial development (A or B) but also cloud costs, support labor, maintenance, and allocated overhead. Omitting indirect costs is a common pitfall.

A16: B. A model card is a documentation artifact that provides key information about a model's purpose, performance, training data, and limitations. It is a technical document primarily intended for those who maintain, evaluate, and are accountable for the model. Executives (A) need a value dashboard. End-users (C) need a user guide. Auditors (D) need a governance dossier.

A17: C. Leading indicators are predictive in nature. For example, a drop in click-through rate might signal a future decline in revenue, or a shift in input data distribution might signal a future drop in model accuracy. They allow for proactive intervention. Options A and D are lagging indicators of business outcomes. Option B describes a lagging technical indicator.

A18: C. Relying solely on a calendar schedule ignores the reality that models can degrade at any time due to unforeseen events, data drift, or concept drift. A performance drop in month two would not be addressed until month three, causing potentially significant business harm. Computational efficiency (A) and manual intervention (B) are secondary concerns. Version control (D) is still possible.

A19: B. Accountability is about answerability and governance. It ensures there are defined owners responsible for the system's development, deployment, monitoring, and addressing any harms it causes. Explainability is part of Transparency (A). Equal performance is part of Fairness (C). Open-source code (D) is unrelated to accountability.

A20: C. Documentation debt, like technical debt, represents the future cost of not maintaining proper documentation. The primary operational risks are an inability to troubleshoot effectively, slower onboarding of new staff, a higher risk of errors during maintenance, and the loss of critical knowledge if key personnel leave. It is a risk/cost issue, not primarily about storage (A), software fees (B), or internet speed (D).

CAP Glossary

A

Term	Definition	Domain
5S	A workplace organization metho d using Sort, Set in Order, Shine, Standardize, Sustain	Business Problem Framing
5 Whys	A technique that repeatedly asks "Why?" to uncover root causes	Business Problem Framing
80/20 Rule (Pareto Principle)	The idea that a small number of causes account for most results	Business Problem Framing
Accuracy	The degree to which predictions match actual outcomes	Model Lifecycle Management
Activity-Based Costing (ABC)	A costing method assigning expe nses based on resource usage	Business Problem Framing
Agent-Based Modeling	A simulation method modeling interaction of autonomous agents	Methodology
Algorithm	A step-by-step procedure for solving a problem	Model Building
Amortization	Spreading a cost or loan repayment over time	Business Problem Framing
Analytical Benefits	The measurable value an analysis is expected to produce, such as improved decisions, cost savings or revenue gains	Analytics Problem Framing
Analytics	The systematic use of data, statistics, and computation to generate insights	Analytics Problem Framing
Analytics Professional	An individual skilled in analyzing and interpreting data	Model Lifecycle Management
ANOVA	A method for comparing means across groups	Model Building
ANCOVA	A technique combining ANOVA and regression	Model Building
Artificial Intelligence	The simulation of human intelligence by machines	Methodology
Artificial Neural Networks	Computing models inspired by biological neurons	Model Building

Term	Definition	Domain
Assemble-to-Order	A production strategy assembling products after receiving orders	Deployment
Automation	Using technology to perform tasks with minimal human input	Deployment
Average	A general term for measures of central tendency	Data

B

Term	Definition	Domain
Batch Production	Producing goods in groups or batches	Deployment
Benchmark Data	Reference data used to compare performance	Data
Benchmark Problems	Standardized problems for evaluating methods	Model Lifecycle Management
Bias	Systematic deviation from the true value	Model Lifecycle Management
Big Data	Extremely large datasets requiring advanced processing techniques	Data
Box-and-Whisker Plot	A graphical display showing distribution spread and quartiles	Data
Branch-and-Bound	An algorithm for solving integer programming problems	Methodology
Business Analytics	The use of data and analysis to support business decisions	Analytics Problem Framing
Business Benefits	The value or advantages gained from a project or decision	Business Problem Framing
Business Case	A justification for a project based on expected outcomes and costs	Business Problem Framing
Business Intelligence	Technology-driven processes for analyzing business data	Analytics Problem Framing
Business Process Modeling	A method for representing and analyzing organizational processes	Business Problem Framing
Business Process Owners	Individuals responsible for managing specific processes	Business Problem Framing

Term	Definition	Domain
Business Validation	Assessing whether a model aligns with business needs	Deployment
Bystanders	People indirectly affected by a project's outcomes	Business Problem Framing

C

Term	Definition	Domain
CHAID	A decision-tree technique using chi-square tests	Model Building
Chief Analytics Officer	An executive overseeing analytics strategy	Model Lifecycle Management
Classification	Assigning data to predefined categories	Model Building
Classification Problem	A predictive problem with categorical outcomes	Model Building
Clustering	Grouping objects based on similarity	Model Building
Combinatorial Optimization	Optimization over discrete solution spaces	Methodology
Confidence Interval	A range constructed from sample data such that, across many repetitions of the same procedure, a specified percentage of intervals would contain the true population parameter	Data
Confidence Level	The proportion of confidence intervals, constructed using the same procedure across many repeated samples, that would contain the true population parameter	Data
Confusion Matrix	A table comparing predicted and actual classifications	Model Lifecycle Management
Conjoint Analysis	A technique for determining how consumers value attributes	Methodology
Constraint	A restriction in an optimization model	Model Building
Constraint Programming	A method for solving problems by enforcing constraints	Methodology

Term	Definition	Domain
Continuous Production	Manufacturing products continuously without interruption	Deployment
Correlation	A measure of association between two variables	Data
Cost of Capital	The required return needed to finance a business or investment	Business Problem Framing
Cube	A multidimensional data structure used in analytics	Data
Cumulative Density Function	A function showing the probability a variable is ≤ a given value	Data
Customers	End users or recipients of a product or service	Business Problem Framing
Cutting Stock Problem	An optimization problem minimizing waste in cutting materials	Methodology

D

Term	Definition	Domain
Data	Factual information used for analysis or decision-making	Data
Data Context	The environment and conditions surrounding data	Data
Data Custodians	Personnel responsible for storing and protecting data	Data
Data Mining	Discovering patterns in large datasets	Data
Data Owner	The entity responsible for data accuracy and security	Data
Data Stewards	Individuals enforcing data governance policies	Data
Data Warehouse	A system for storing and managing large volumes of data	Data
Database	An organized collection of structured data	Data
Decision Tree	A tree-structured model for decision-making	Model Building

Term	Definition	Domain
Decision Variables	Variables that determine outcomes in optimization	Model Building
Design of Experi ments	A structured method for studying variable effects	Methodology
Descriptive Analytics	Methods for summarizing historical data	Analytics Problem Framing
Diagnostic Analytics	Techniques for identifying causes behind outcomes	Analytics Problem Framing
Discrete Event Simulation	A simulation method modeling systems as event sequences	Methodology
Dynamic Programming	Solving problems by breaking them into subproblems	Methodology

E

Term	Definition	Domain
Effective Domain	The subset of values where a model or process operates validly	Data
Efficiency	Achieving maximum output with minimal wasted effort or resources	Business Problem Framing
Engagement	The level of involvement and participation of individuals in activities	Business Problem Framing
Enterprise Resource Planning	Integrated management of core business processes	Deployment
ETL (Extract, Transform, Load)	A process for integrating data from multiple sources	Data
Experimental Design	The planning of experiments to study variable effects	Methodology
Expert Systems	Computer systems using expert rules for decision-making	Methodology

F

Term	Definition	Domain
Factor Analysis	A method identifying underlying variable relationships	Model Building

Term	Definition	Domain
Forecasting	Predicting future values based on historical data	Model Building
Fuzzy Logic	A reasoning method handling imprecise or uncertain information	Methodology

G

Term	Definition	Domain
Game Theory	A framework for analyzing strategic interactions	Methodology
Genetic Algorithms	Search heuristics inspired by natural selection	Methodology
Global Optimal	The best solution across the entire solution space	Model Building
Goodness of Fit	A measure of how well a model matches data	Model Lifecycle Management
Graphical User Interface	A visual interface for interacting with software	Deployment
Greedy Heuristics	Methods making locally optimal choices at each step	Methodology

H

Term	Definition	Domain
Heuristic	A simplified problem-solving ap proach using practical rules	Methodology
Histogram	A bar chart showing the distribut ion of numerical data	Data
Holdout Data	Data reserved for final model tes ting	Model Lifecycle Management
Hyperparameter	Configuration settings chosen before model training	Model Building
Hypothesis Testing	A method for making inferences about populations	Model Building

I

Term	Definition	Domain
Impact Analysis	Evaluating the effects of changes or decisions	Deployment

Term	Definition	Domain
Influence Diagrams	Visual representations of relationships among decisions and outcomes	Analytics Problem Framing
Integer Program	An optimization model with integer decision variables	Methodology
Integrity	The accuracy and consistency of data throughout its lifecycle	Model Lifecycle Management

K

Term	Definition	Domain
KDD (Knowledge Discovery in Databases)	The process of extracting useful knowledge from data	Data

L

Term	Definition	Domain
Lead Time	The time between initiating and completing a process	Deployment
Lean Production	A production approach focused o n reducing waste and improving flow	Business Problem Framing
Lift Curve	A graph showing classification m odel performance	Model Lifecycle Management
Linear Program	An optimization model with l inear objective and constraints	Methodology
Lineage	The record of data origins and t ransformations	Data
Little's Law	A queueing relationship linking average items, arrival rate, and wait time	Methodology
Local Optimal	The best solution within a limited region	Model Building
Logistic Regression	A model predicting binary outcomes	Model Building

M

Term	Definition	Domain
Machine Learning	Algorithms that learn patterns from data	Methodology

Term	Definition	Domain
MANOVA	A test comparing multiple dependent variables across groups	Model Building
Mean	The sum of all values divided by the number of observations. A weighted measure of central tendency	Data
Mean Squared Error	The average squared prediction e rror	Model Lifecycle Management
Mean Time Between Failures	The average time between syste m failures	Model Lifecycle Management
Median	The middle value in an ordered d ataset	Data
Merge/Join	Combining datasets based on shared keys	Data
Metaheuristics	High-level strategies guiding heuristic search	Methodology
Method	A detailed plan for implementing a solution	Methodology
Methodology	A structured strategy for addressing a problem	Methodology
Mode (Variable Data)	The most frequently occurring value in a dataset	Data
Monte Carlo Simulation	A technique using random sampling to approximate outcomes	Methodology

N

Term	Definition	Domain
Navigating	Identifying and following pathw ays to address challenges or objectives	Business Problem Framing
Negotiating	Reaching agreements between parties with differing interests	Business Problem Framing
Net Present Value (NPV)	The present value of future cash flows discounted at a specified rate	Business Problem Framing

Term	Definition	Domain
Network Optimization	Optimization applied to network flow or routing	Methodology
Next Best Offer	A model recommending the optimal offer for a customer	Model Building
Normalization (Database)	Structuring data to reduce redundancy	Data
Normalized Data	Data adjusted to a consistent scale or structure	Data

O

Term	Definition	Domain
Objective Function	A mathematical expression defining an optimization goal	Model Building
OLAP	Technology enabling fast multidimensional data analysis	Data
OLAP Cube	A multidimensional data structure for analytical queries	Data
Operations Management	Managing production and business operations	Deployment
Operations Research	The discipline of applying analytical methods to decisions	Methodology
Opportunity Cost	The value of the best alternative forgone when a choice is made	Business Problem Framing

P

Term	Definition	Domain
Parameters	Numerical factors defining model behavior	Model Building
Pareto Concept	The principle that a minority of causes drive the majority of outcomes	Business Problem Framing
Pattern Recognition	Identifying patterns in data	Model Building
Payback	The time required to recover an investment	Business Problem Framing
Principal Component Analysis (PCA)	A technique reducing data dimensionality	Model Building
Pie Chart	A circular chart showing	Data

Term	Definition	Domain
	proportions of a whole	
Predictive Analytics	Techniques for forecasting future outcomes	Analytics Problem Framing
Prescriptive Analytics	Techniques recommending optimal actions	Analytics Problem Framing
Precision	The proportion of predicted positives that are correct	Model Lifecycle Management
Pricing	Determining the value at which a product or service will be sold	Business Problem Framing
Primary Measures of Success	Key metrics used to evaluate project outcomes	Business Problem Framing
Primary Stakeholder	The individual or group most affected by a project	Business Problem Framing
Probability Density Function	A function describing likelihoods for continuous variables	Data
Problem Assessment Framing	The process of defining and understanding a problem	Business Problem Framing
Project Management	Organizing resources to achieve project goals	Deployment
Proprietary Data	Data owned and controlled by an organization	Data

Q

Term	Definition	Domain
Queuing Theory	The mathematical study of waiting lines	Methodology

R

Term	Definition	Domain
Random	Occurring by chance without predictable pattern	Data
Range	The difference between maximum and minimum values	Data
RFM (Recency, Frequency, Monetary	A technique for segmenting customers based on purchasing behavior	Analytics Problem Framing

Term	Definition	Domain
Value)		
Recoding	Transforming data values for clarity or consistency	Data
Regression	Methods modeling relationships between variables	Model Building
Regression Anal ysis	A technique modeling dependent-independent variable relationships	Model Building
Regression Problem	A predictive problem with continuous outcomes	Model Building
Response Surface Methodology	A method for optimizing processes influenced by several variables	Methodology
Revenue Management	Optimizing pricing and capacity to maximize revenue	Business Problem Framing
Risk	The potential for loss or adverse outcomes	Business Problem Framing
Robust Optimization	An optimization approach that finds solutions remaining feasible and near optimal across a range of uncertain input values, rather than optimizing for a single fixed scenario	Methodology

S

Term	Definition	Domain
Scenario Analysis	Evaluating possible future events by considering alternative outcomes	Business Problem Framing
Scatter Plot	A graph showing the relationship between two continuous variables	Data
Scheduling	Planning the timing of tasks and resources	Deployment
Sensitivity Analysis	Assessing how input changes affect outputs	Model Lifecycle Management
Simulated Annealing	A search technique inspired by metal annealing	Methodology
Six Sigma	A quality methodology focused on reducing defects	Model Lifecycle Management

Term	Definition	Domain
Skewness	A measure of distribution asymmetry	Data
Societal Benefits	Positive impacts on society resulting from a project	Business Problem Framing
Spreadsheet Analysis	Using spreadsheet tools for data analysis	Data
Stakeholders	Individuals or groups with an interest in project outcomes	Business Problem Framing
Standard Deviation	A measure of variability around the mean	Data
Stated Drivers	Explicitly identified factors influencing decisions or strategies	Business Problem Framing
Statistics	The study of data collection, analysis, and interpretation	Data
Structure of the Data	The arrangement and organization of data elements	Data
Supply Chain Management	Managing the flow of goods and services	Deployment
System Dynamics	A modeling approach for comple x systems over time	Methodology

T

Term	Definition	Domain
Technique	A defined set of steps for completing a task	Methodology
Testing Data	Data used to evaluate model performance	Model Building
Tolerance	Acceptable deviation in measurements or conditions	Model Lifecycle Management
Traceability	The ability to track data origins and changes	Data
Training Data	Data used to train a model	Model Building
Traveling Salesman Problem	A routing problem seeking the shortest path visiting all locations	Methodology

U

Term	**Definition**	**Domain**
Uncertainty	The lack of complete knowledge about outcomes or data	Business Problem Framing
Univariate	Analysis of a single variable	Model Lifecycle Management
Unsupervised Models	Models identifying patterns without labeled outputs	Model Building

V

Term	**Definition**	**Domain**
Validation Data	Data used to tune or validate a model	Model Lifecycle Management
Variation Reduction	Methods for reducing process variability	Model Lifecycle Management
Variance	The average squared deviation from the mean	Data
Vehicle Routing Problem	An optimization problem determining efficient vehicle routes	Methodology
Verification	Ensuring a model is correctly mplemented	i Model Lifecycle Management

W

Term	**Definition**	**Domain**
Web Analytics	The measurement and analysis of web usage data	Analytics Problem Framing

Y

Term	**Definition**	**Domain**
Yield	The output or results produced rel ative to input	Business Problem Framing

References

Aarts, E., & Lenstra, J. K. (Eds.). (2003). *Local search in combinatorial optimization*. Princeton University Press.

Agresti, A. (2018). *Statistical methods for the social sciences* (5th ed.). Pearson.

Akaike, H. (1974). A new look at the statistical model identification. *IEEE Transactions on Automatic Control, 19*(6), 716–723.

Allen, R. G. D. (1938). *Mathematical analysis for economists*. Macmillan.

Amershi, S., Begel, A., Bird, C., DeLine, R., Gall, H., Kamar, E., Nagappan, N., Nushi, B., & Zimmermann, T. (2019). Software engineering for machine learning: A case study. In Proceedings of the 41st International Conference on Software Engineering: Software Engineering in Practice (ICSE-SEIP)* (pp. 291–300). IEEE Press.

Anderson, D. R., Sweeney, D. J., & Williams, T. A. (2019). *Statistics for business and economics* (14th ed.). Cengage Learning.

Banks, J., Carson, J. S., Nelson, B. L., & Nicol, D. M. (2010). *Discrete event system simulation* (5th ed.). Pearson.

Barocas, S., Hardt, M., & Narayanan, A. (2019). *Fairness and machine learning: Limitations and opportunities*. fairmlbook.org.

Bass, L., Clements, P., & Kazman, R. (2012). *Software architecture in practice* (3rd ed.). Addison-Wesley Professional.

Belsley, D. A., Kuh, E., & Welsch, R. E. (1980). *Regression diagnostics: Identifying influential data and sources of collinearity*. Wiley & Sons.

Bender, E. M., & Friedman, B. (2018). Data statements for natural language processing: Toward mitigating system bias and enabling better science. *Transactions of the Association for Computational Linguistics, 6*, 587–604.

Bertsekas, D. P. (2016). *Nonlinear programming* (3rd ed.). Athena Scientific.

Bertsekas, D. P., & Tsitsiklis, J. N. (2008). *Introduction to probability* (2nd ed.). Athena Scientific.

Box, G. E. P., & Draper, N. R. (2007). *Response surfaces, mixtures, and ridge analyses* (2nd ed.). Wiley & Sons.

Box, G. E. P., Jenkins, G. M., Reinsel, G. C., & Ljung, G. M. (2016). *Time series analysis: Forecasting and control* (5th ed.). Wiley & Sons.

Breiman, L. (2001). Random forests. *Machine Learning, 45*(1), 5–32.

Chapman, P., Clinton, J., Kerber, R., Khabaza, T., Reinartz, T., Shearer, C., & Wirth, R. (2000). *CRISP-DM 1.0: Step-by-step data mining guide. SPSS Inc.

Clemen, R. T., & Reilly, T. (2014). *Making hard decisions with decision tools* (3rd ed.). Cengage Learning.

Cormen, T. H., Leiserson, C. E., Rivest, R. L., & Stein, C. (2022). *Introduction to algorithms* (4th ed.). MIT Press.

DAMA International. (2017). *DAMA-DMBOK: Data management body of knowledge* (2nd ed.). Technics Publications.

Dantzig, G. B. (1963). *Linear programming and extensions*. Princeton University Press.

Dasu, T., & Johnson, T. (2003). *Exploratory data mining and data cleaning.* John Wiley & Sons.
Davenport, T. H., & Harris, J. G. (2007). *Competing on analytics: The new science of winning*. Harvard Business Review Press.
Dietterich, T. G. (2002). Machine learning for sequential data: A review. In T. Caelli (Ed.), *Structural, syntactic, and statistical pattern recognition* (pp. 15–30). Springer.
Doran, G. T. (1981). There's a S.M.A.R.T. way to write management's goals and objectives. *Management Review, 70*(11), 35–36.
Forrester, J. W. (1961). *Industrial dynamics.* MIT Press.
Freeman, R. E. (1984). *Strategic management: A stakeholder approach.* Pitman.
Gelman, A., Carlin, J. B., Stern, H. S., Dunson, D. B., Vehtari, A., & Rubin, D. B. (2013). *Bayesian data analysis* (3rd ed.). CRC Press.
Giarratano, J., & Riley, G. (2005). *Expert systems: Principles and programming* (4th ed.). Course Technology.
Goldberg, D. E. (1989). *Genetic algorithms in search, optimization, and machine learning*. Addison Wesley.
Goodfellow, I., Bengio, Y., & Courville, A. (2016). *Deep learning*. MIT Press.
Harry, M., & Schroeder, R. (2000). *Six sigma: The breakthrough management strategy revolutionizing the world's top corporations.*
Friedman, J., Hastie, T., & Tibshirani, R. (2009). *The elements of statistical learning: Data mining, inference, and prediction* (2nd ed.). Springer.
Hillier, F. S., & Lieberman, G. J. (2021). *Introduction to operations research* (11th ed.). McGraw Hill.
Holland, J. H. (1975). *Adaptation in natural and artificial systems.* University of Michigan Press.
Hultman, K., & Hultman, J. (2014). *The ethical executive: Becoming aware of the root causes of unethical behavior.* University of South Carolina Press.
Hyndman, R. J., & Athanasopoulos, G. (2021). *Forecasting: Principles and practice* (3rd ed.).
James, G., Witten, D., Hastie, T., & Tibshirani, R. (2021). *An introduction to statistical learning with applications in R* (2nd ed.). Springer.
Juran, J. M., & Godfrey, A. B. (1999). *Juran's quality handbook* (5th ed.). McGraw Hill.
Keeney, R. L. (1992). *Value-focused thinking: A path to creative decision making*. Harvard University Press.
Kelleher, J. D., & Tierney, B. (2018). *Data science: A hands-on approach.* MIT Press.
Kerzner, H., & Kerzner, H. R. (2017). *Project management: A systems approach to planning, scheduling, and controlling* (12th ed.). John Wiley & Sons.
Kim, W. C., & Mauborgne, R. (2005). *Blue ocean strategy: How to create uncontested market space and make the competition irrelevant.* Harvard Business Review Press.
Kimball, R., & Ross, M. (2013). *The data warehouse toolkit: The definitive guide to dimensional modeling* (3rd ed.). John Wiley & Sons.

Kleppmann, M. (2017). *Designing data-intensive applications: The big ideas behind reliable, scalable, and maintainable systems.* O'Reilly Media.
Koller, D., & Friedman, N. (2009). *Probabilistic graphical models: Principles and techniques.* MIT Press.
Kotler, P., & Keller, K. L. (2016). *Marketing management* (15th ed.). Pearson.
Law, A. M. (2014). *Simulation modeling and analysis* (5th ed.). McGraw Hill.
Leek, J. T., & Peng, R. D. (2015). What is the question? *Science, 347*(6228), 1314–1315.
Little, J. D. C. (1961). A proof for the queuing formula L = λW. *Operations Research, 9*(3), 383–387.
Loshin, D. (2013). *Enterprise knowledge management: The data quality approach.* Morgan Kaufmann.
Makridakis, S., Wheelwright, S. C., & Hyndman, R. J. (1998). *Forecasting: Methods and applications*(3rd ed.). Wiley & Sons.
Malcolm, D. G., Roseboom, J. H., Clark, C. E., & Fazar, W. (1959). Application of a technique for research and development program evaluation. *Operations Research, 7*(5), 646–669.
McGilvray, D. (2021). *Executing data quality projects: Ten steps to quality data and trusted information* (2nd ed.). Morgan Kaufmann.
Metcalf, J., & Crawford, K. (2016). Where are human subjects in big data research? The emerging ethics divide. *Big Data & Society, 3*(1), 1–14.
Miller, T. W. (2015). *Modeling techniques in predictive analytics.* Pearson.
Montgomery, D. C. (2019). *Introduction to statistical quality control* (8th ed.). Wiley & Sons.
Nemhauser, G. L., & Wolsey, L. A. (1999). *Integer and combinatorial optimization.* Wiley & Sons.
Newell, A., & Simon, H. A. (1972). *Human problem solving.* Prentice Hall.
Ohno, T. (1988). *Toyota production system: Beyond large-scale production.* Productivity Press.
O'Neil, C. (2016). *Weapons of math destruction: How big data increases inequality and threatens democracy.* Crown Publishing Group.
Pearl, J. (2009). *Causality: Models, reasoning, and inference* (2nd ed.). Cambridge University Press.
Project Management Institute. (2021). *A guide to the project management body of knowledge (PMBOK® guide)* (7th ed.). Project Management Institute.
Provost, F., & Fawcett, T. (2013). *Data science for business: What you need to know about data mining and data-analytic thinking.* O'Reilly Media.
Russell, S. J., & Norvig, P. (2021). *Artificial intelligence: A modern approach* (4th ed.). Pearson.
Saaty, T. L. (1980). *The analytic hierarchy process.* McGraw Hill.
Sculley, D., Holt, G., Golovin, D., Davydov, E., Phillips, T., Ebner, D., Chaudhary, V., Young, M., Crespo, J.-F., & Dennison, D. (2015). Hidden technical debt in machine learning systems. In C. Cortes, N. D. Lawrence, D. D. Lee, M. Sugiyama, & R. Garnett (Eds.), *Advances in Neural Information Processing Systems 28* (pp. 2503–2511). Curran Associates, Inc.

Shmueli, G., Bruce, P. C., Gedeck, P., & Patel, N. R. (2020). *Data mining for business analytics: Concepts, techniques, and applications in Python* (2nd ed.). Wiley & Sons.

Sterman, J. D. (2000). *Business dynamics: Systems thinking and modeling for a complex world.* McGraw Hill.

Winston, W. L. (2022). *Operations research: Applications and algorithms* (5th ed.). Cengage Learning.

Zadeh, L. A. (1965). Fuzzy sets. *Information and Control, 8*(3), 338–353.

Zhu, X., & Goldberg, A. B. (2009). *Introduction to semi-supervised learning.* Morgan & Claypool.

Index

About the Author

Dr. Ibrahim Said spent twenty years with an international organization working across different regions of the world, from a New York headquarters to field operations in Africa, in environments where data was never academic. Decisions rested on it, under pressure, with real consequences for real people.

That career built extensive experience across technology, data management, risk and change, and one conviction: difficult ideas deserve simple explanations. This book began as his own study companion and was refined until every concept earned its place.

He holds a Doctorate in Business Administration and professional certifications spanning analytics, data management, risk, project management, and change, among others, and he has published peer-reviewed papers in international journals. Today he leads ELTILA, a Toronto consultancy helping organizations govern data and artificial intelligence with evidence.

He lives in Hamilton, Ontario, Canada. Find him at eltila.com.

www.ingramcontent.com/pod-product-compliance
Lightning Source LLC
LaVergne TN
LVHW010712061126
851857LV00014B/1146

* 9 7 8 1 0 6 7 7 9 9 5 1 9 *